AFRICAN-AMERICAN ORGANIZED CRIME

DATE DUE

OC 13 97		
OC 10 9		
OC 1 99		
AP 24 '00		
JE 8 00		
NO 1 00		
MR 19 0		
JE 1 0		

DEMCO 38-296

AFRICAN-AMERICAN ORGANIZED CRIME
A SOCIAL HISTORY

RUFUS SCHATZBERG
ROBERT J. KELLY

RUTGERS UNIVERSITY PRESS
NEW BRUNSWICK, NEW JERSEY

First published in cloth by Garland Publishing, Inc., 1996

First published in paperback by Rutgers University Press,
New Brunswick, New Jersey, 1997

Library of Congress Cataloging-in-Publication Data

Schatzberg, Rufus, 1917–
    African American organized crime : a social history / Rufus
Schatzberg, Robert J. Kelly.
        p.   cm.
    Previously published: New York : Garland, 1996.
    Includes bibliographical references and index.
    ISBN 0-8135-2445-8 (alk. paper)
    1. Organized crime—United States—History—20th century. 2. Afro-
American criminals—History—20th century. 3. Afro-Americans—
Social conditions. I. Kelly, Robert J. II. Title.
    [HV6446.S38   1997]
    364.1'06'08996073—dc21   96-49061
                                                                CIP

Manufactured in the United States of America

CONTENTS

LIST OF TABLES

List of Figures

PREFACE

This study is an essay in social history. To declare that one is writing social history is really to say nothing until the terms have been defined. History of this sort explores the behaviors of African Americans in specific types of activity within their communities and in the larger society. It also claims to show something distinctive about the characteristics of African-American criminal phenomena that have been ignored in the general literature on crime in America. One of our major claims is that organized crime in African-American communities did not emerge spontaneously, nor was it merely an outcome of a confluence of compellingly irresistible events but a calculated response to conditions and circumstances surrounding the lives of those confined in ghettos, slums, and racial enclaves. In many respects, the kinds of organized crime prevalent—especially in the pre–World War II period—may be understood primarily as informal or illegal strategies to meet basic communal and individual needs. Certainly the constrictions of racism play a major role in shaping African-American responses and reactions to the deprivations and humiliations fostered by segregation, discrimination, and widespread prejudice.

It is the haunting image of Ralph Ellison's metaphorical characterization of the African American as "invisible" that seems apt as a general description of the larger white society's indifference toward African-American communities. Invisibility is harsh and cruel, but accurate nonetheless. Its ramifications and implications are examined throughout this book.

As will be seen, there was more to the relationship between whites and non-whites than mere collective insouciance. African Americans were the victims of exploitation of all sorts: preyed upon by venal politicians, mistreated by commercial entrepreneurs, brutalized by police and white criminals, and victimized by each other. Their community life continues to be an ongoing nightmare, but at the same time, most people live in neighborhoods built upon the sturdy institutions of church, school, and communal life that serve as a bulwark against the depredations of crime and despair.

This book is only a panel in a larger story, and not just because it is limited to crime. It is in part an effort at moral history, which is greater than criminological history, but which illuminates the latter.

A few words on method are in order. In the chapters devoted to the internal migration and demographics of African-American settlement patterns in the late nineteenth and early twentieth centuries, we trace some of the underlying causes that produced a unique expression of criminal behavior by examining the contexts and collective attitudes that shaped the structures of everyday life. We hope it is sufficient to say here that we find incomprehensible the fashion among some policy specialists to divorce the study of criminal behavior from its social sources. Taking crime out of its natural settings distorts its meanings and mystifies our capacities to understand and finally to control it.

It may seem surprising that a study focused on organized crime spends some time, particularly in the opening chapters on events, circumstances, and personalities, in the pre–World War II social setting. It is not just a pious deference or allegiance to the notion of "history" and what it implies; there are special reasons for bringing the vivid past of this century alive. The idea is not that the demands of modern life are no different from those of almost a century ago. On the contrary, it seems that the demands of modern life on African Americans are unprecedented, and many criminological ideas embodied in most contemporary theory on organized crime cannot satisfactorily conceptualize them, and this means ultimately that criminal justice policy is inadequately equipped to cope with the alarming violence and mayhem in many communities. But some extension of earlier thinking and description about the conditions and causes of crime developed by African-American thinkers and social scientists, when modified, might be able to inform modern approaches and policies. Our research suggests that artists, writers, and journalists, among others, are astute observers whose work repays close reading along these lines. Thus, our work draws on over a half century of writing and research on aspects of African-American urban life, and on the observations and analyses of others. Ours then is a privileged access to the thinking of African-American scholars, some long ignored, regrettably, whose views in many instances possess startling relevance today.

Finally, this book is based on the conviction that to understand modern manifestations of African-American organized crime, its roots must be investigated and its evolution reconstructed, for the processes that influence contemporary criminal organization would seem to be the result of a combination of the old and new. Nevertheless, the modern conditions that African Americans confront also suggest that there are profound breaks between the traditional African-American criminal entrepreneur in the ghettos and communities at the turn of the century and those in today's inner cities. Still, the fluid and flexible structure of African-American vice industries enabled them to metamorphose and thereby survive the many threats they encountered.

Acknowledgments

We wish to thank Phyllis Korper, senior editor, and Adrienne Makowski, production editor, from Garland Publishing and Marilyn D. McShane and Frank P. Williams III, general editors for the series Current Issues in Criminal Justice, who have given us many reasons to be thankful. They carefully, not to say aggressively, read the entire manuscript, proving, if nothing else, that such a thing is possible. Their detailed advice called attention to many difficulties that required revision. We are grateful to them and to many of our colleagues for advice and encouragement.

Since the chapters have been written and rewritten during months of preparation in which our own research and experiences and masses of information were examined, the themes may appear recurrent rather than consecutive steps in an argument. Repetitions are inevitable and we hope more illuminating than irritating. Our experience with commentators and readers has not convinced us that repetition is needless. Inconsistencies are less forgivable, and we trust fewer.

AFRICAN-AMERICAN
ORGANIZED CRIME

1 INTRODUCTION

There is not yet any great capital in America, but there are already very large towns. In 1830 the population of Philadelphia was 160,000 and of New York, 202,000. The lowest classes in these vast cities are a rabble more dangerous even than that of European towns. The very lowest are the freed Negroes condemned by law and opinion to a hereditary state of degradation and wretchedness. Then, there is a crowd of Europeans driven by misfortune or misbehavior to the shores of the New World: such men carry our worst vices to the United States without any of those interests which might counteract their influence. Living in the land without being citizens, they are ready to profit from all the passions that agitate it; thus quite recently there have been serious riots in Philadelphia and New York. Such disorders are unknown in the rest of the country, which does not get excited because the populations of the towns do not at present exercise any authority or influence over the country people. Nevertheless, I regard the size of some American cities and especially the nature of their inhabitants as a real danger threatening the future of the democratic republics of the New World, and I should not hesitate to predict that through them they will perish, unless their government succeeds in creating an armed force which, while remaining subject to the wishes of the national majority, is independent of the peoples of the towns and capable of suppressing their excesses.

Alexis de Tocqueville (1848)
Democracy in America[1]

Why study African-American organized crime?[2] The glib answer is we do so for much the same reason that we study organized crime in general. African-American organized crime, like its manifestations in other communities and among other minorities, interacts with its environment and plays a vital part in shaping social outcomes. Not coming to terms with it, not understanding it, means that many of the important events occurring in African-American communities across the nation must remain incomprehensible.

In the early decades of the twentieth century, groups of individuals engaged in "crime" (as defined by the larger society), constituted one of the modes around which social networks of a relatively independent *civil society* developed. The power of these groups was largely a function of external social forces that insulated African-American communities and deprived them of access to crucial resources. African-American organized crime emerged as it did among other oppressed minorities because it was able to meet general social needs. Precisely because of this, those individuals satisfying social, economic and psychological needs survived and thrived.

Tocqueville's dire prediction relating poverty, oppression, and mayhem with catastrophic consequences for cities has not quite materialized in the manner in which he envisioned it. It is of interest that he pointed out two distinctive categories of city dwellers whose social and economic situation were likely to precipitate violence and destruction: European immigrants and freed African Americans relegated to pariah social status. To be sure, urban areas were dangerous places with much violence and crime. At the same time, they were not as disorganized, chaotic, and demoralized as many observers, including Tocqueville, believed. Ghettos and slums did not lack a social order of their own; they were different and even bizarre perhaps, but were nonetheless guided by normative rules that imposed some degree of stability and coherence across the social spaces making up neighborhoods of the poor.[3]

Crime is a technical legal concept that describes behaviors that violate laws and statutes. As we shall see, the term is often used not merely descriptively to portray violence and lawlessness but also suggests ways of surviving invented by individuals and groups whose access to legitimate means of opportunity are deliberately blocked. Consequently, the study of social organization and mobility among minorities stigmatized by color, religion, ethnicity or a legacy of oppression has been frustrated by labeling many of their survival strategies as criminal activity. Putting aside this conceptual compression between the legalistically descriptive and morally evaluative, our purpose in this book is to examine how an oppressed minority group—African Americans—created, developed, and modified some techniques that enabled them to sustain themselves in environments that were and still are hostile. Our focus is on organized crime, on deviant methods and illegal tactics that come into play in the lives of some individuals. Of course, the vast majority of African Americans have managed somehow to remain law-abiding in a society that too often has taunted them into lawlessness. But the community infrastructure, the church, school, extended family, and kinship groups constituted a complex social system that created a viable social life for most in spite of a legacy of oppression. Even though these institutions are constantly challenged and threatened by economic conditions in the archipelago of ghettos spread out like a spider's web across America, they still retain their strength in working-class and middle-class strata that contain the bulk of the African-American population.

URBAN DECAY, JOB LOSS, RACISM, AND CRIME

In view of the profound problems facing many African Americans today, it may seem ludicrous to discuss organized crime. Yet, it has been and remains a palpable reality. The historical consequences of this phenomenon have been mixed: Organized crime in the generic sense of the term has provided employment and positive tangible goods to large segments of ghettoized African Americans, and in the last decades it has increasingly become a predatory force within the community, sapping its strength and draining off much of its talent, wealth, and energy.

Law enforcement officials, politicians, and community activists across the nation recognize that crime in all its forms is a major scourge. Official statistics clearly show the paralyzing grip of crime and how the institutions and the lifestyles of people caught up in it are profoundly affected. Increasingly, schools, businesses, and social life in general seem to be held hostage to predatory criminal activities, especially in poor neighborhoods.

The social costs of crime are not difficult to measure, especially in the inner-city minority communities. Over the last two decades, a new and socially destructive class structure has emerged in the ghetto.[4] As Wilson sees it, the main culprit is economic deindustrialization whose dynamics have left a dispirited and hopeless underclass in its wake. With massive factory relocations of major industrial enterprises, African-American urban areas have lost entry-level jobs, and blue-collar occupations that absorbed skilled and semiskilled workers in the auto, garment, plastic, and steel industries in competition with foreign manufactures have virtually collapsed. To survive economically and to enjoy the material success associated with the "American Dream," ghetto residents in a position to do so have abandoned their communities, leaving behind an economically helpless, immobilized underclass. It is from this group of undereducated, unskilled, and deprived individuals that a disproportionate number of criminals have emerged who directly victimize neighborhoods through crime and indirectly victimize them by creating or intensifying multiple social and economic ills that define the fate of today's ghetto dwellers.

The underclass problem is complex. In communities overwhelmed with problems, people are being mugged, raped, murdered, and businesses are under siege. Most residents who are law-abiding live in constant fear for their children, who are regularly threatened by street gangs and drug dealers. These depressed living-environment experiences and other indirect consequences of crime victimize the community as a whole and dampen a neighborhood's economic stability and development. And there is a loss of a sizable fraction of the communities' male population to jails or prisons and the dangerous influence drug dealers exercise on the young. The crime in the community causes and perpetrates other ills. Schools are unable to function effectively for the most part because of the violence generated by predatory criminals who hang around and produce a disorderly atmosphere that permeates the entire social milieu.

The concentrations of crime and criminals in ghetto neighborhoods are nothing new, and the idea that urban decay constitutes a "breeding ground" for predatory street crime has been part of the dominant scholarly perspective for some time. But what of the crime itself? Is it simply opportunistic and episodic, or is the criminal behavior that is widespread in ghetto communities afflicted with high rates of violent behavior more organized, more structured? Poverty, broken homes, joblessness, single-parent families, and other factors have been identified as the "underlying causes" of crime. These conditions cause crime, the argument goes; as they worsen—as the ghetto community becomes an underclass community—crime worsens. But since the 1970s, the conventional perspective on crime causation has been challenged by analyses that suggest that the relationships among poverty, unemployment, and criminality are more ambiguous than supposed. Furthermore, the extent and impact of organized criminal activity in African-American communities have never been taken seriously as a factor affecting the pervasiveness and violence of crime.[5] These are issues we shall address in this book.

In 1986, the President's Commission on Organized Crime gave scant attention to African-American organized criminality, referring only fleetingly to radical political prison groups such as the Black Guerrilla Army that existed in California's prison system more than twenty years ago, is presumably active today, and possibly linked to the Black Liberation Army that carried out armed robberies and the murder of police persons.[6] This is indeed puzzling because the hearings conducted by the President's Commission in 1985 sought testimony from representatives of federal and local law enforcement agencies that have been significantly involved in combating heroin trafficking, and heard from private citizens who provided grim firsthand information on their participation as leaders or couriers in heroin trafficking networks in African-American communities run by African Americans. The testimony presented at the hearings suggested a level of organization that was fairly sophisticated and highly structured.[7]

The problem of ignoring African-American organized crime is not unique to the President's Commission on Organized Crime. During a symposium on organized crime control, the FBI Assistant Director of Investigation referred to "non-traditional" organized-crime groups, as "the outlaw motorcycle gangs, Mexican and Colombian narcotics cartels and Oriental organized crime gangs" with no mention of African-American criminal groups.[8] Despite vigorous prosecutions against the Mafia throughout the United States and mounting evidence that organized crime is not limited to La Cosa Nostra and its crime families, "Italian geography" [9] still seems to dominate official and public thinking. The Commission's final report, *The Impact* (1986),[10] did note that Asian and Central and South American groups play significant roles in drug trafficking and minor extortion rackets in their ethnic communities. For some time the position of government agencies has been that organized crime is not limited to La Cosa Nostra but is an integral part of the social system. Still, the fixation with Mafia—a legacy perhaps from the Kefauver days and the emphasis placed on it by many official and academic studies—persists.[11]

Scholarly treatments of organized crime have also ignored the role of African-American organized crime before World War II; one such example in a widely used text observes that

Heroin provided the vehicle by which black criminal operators were able to enter the ranks of organized crime. Resistance from already established Mafia entrepreneurs proved futile, and emerging black criminal organizations revealed a willingness to use violence on a scale that neutralized otherwise formidable opposition.[12]

Abadinsky overlooked a body of literature that convincingly shows the existence of African-American organized criminality before World War II, in numbers gambling networks in Harlem, Detroit, Chicago, and other locations.[13]

Local law enforcement organizations have argued that African Americans were not disposed to creating an organized criminal enterprise. As late as 1989, the New Jersey Commission of Investigation reported:

Law enforcement has long been reluctant to accept the existence of

7

Afro-lineal organized crime, based primarily on an opinion that such ethnic groups were incapable of structuring syndicates of any consequence.[14]

THE DEMISE OF LA COSA NOSTRA

The recent trials and convictions of major organized crime figures signal not only the decline and fall of the country's most powerful mobsters, but also the apparent erosion of Mafia influence and power on the whole. Once seemingly invincible, America's La Cosa Nostra is beset by problems. The murder and racketeering trials of John Gotti, boss of the Gambino crime family, the most powerful Mafia organization in the United States, served as a showcase for the weaknesses sapping the strength of La Cosa Nostra.

The crux of the government's case—Gotti's role in the murder of Paul Castellano, his boss and rival—was one of many lethal feuds that have wracked the Italian-American underworld in recent years. Then, the decision of Gotti's number-two man, Salvatore Gravano, to testify against his boss showed the extent to which the criminal subculture of Mafia, and its once sacred code of silence, had dangerously lapsed. Most telling of all were the FBI tapes used by the government in the trial. That the government could penetrate the headquarters of the Gambino family, the Ravenite Social Club in Little Italy, demonstrated how vulnerable the Mafia had become.

As La Cosa Nostra appears to fade as the dominant force in crime, a new underworld is taking shape, or, rather, is being acknowledged. Today, many different "Mafias" are at work in America—Colombian cocaine cartels; Chinese Triad/Tongs; Jamaican Posses; Dominican gangs; Haitian, Pakistani, Russian, Israeli, and Nigerian syndicates.

Like the Italian peasants who arrived at the turn of the century, the new groups are made up mostly of recent immigrants. And, like the Mafia, they depend on ethnic ties to give their criminal enterprises coherence. But in other respects the new crime syndicates differ markedly from La Cosa Nostra—in their indiscriminate violence, frequent turf wars, and concentration on drugs as their principal and sometimes sole source of illicit income.

Mafia violence, although brutal, had always been tempered by Old World conceptions of honor and propriety. If a mafioso had to be eliminated, the execution was usually carried out professionally, without injury to innocent parties, if possible. Above all, wives and children of victims were strictly off-limits. By contrast, the new Mafia does not flinch at murdering a rival's entire family.

Most of the new nontraditional criminal groups rely heavily on drugs as their primary source of income. In comparison, the La Cosa Nostra families support a diversified portfolio of illegal activities to perpetuate their criminal networks. This includes labor racketeering, the infiltration of legitimate businesses, loansharking, extortion, pornography, sports gambling, and massive systematic thefts from airports and ship cargoes to supplement intricate networks of fencing outlets. Narcotics undeniably has been a profitable project for La Cosa Nostra groups, but it is only one of many illegal activities and is neither predominant nor exclusive to their operations.

In general, the staggering increases in the number of drug users during the past three decades have given rise to an international criminal network of unprecedented scope and sophistication. The Colombian cocaine cartels manage a five thousand mile pipeline involving thousands of people, including cultivators, chemists, quality-control experts, pilots, couriers, security forces, distributors, accountants, bankers, and lawyers. Heroin is smuggled into Western Europe and the United States by an equally complex network involving opium growers in southwestern Asia, Iranian smugglers, Balkan smugglers, and chemists, all under the supervision of the Turkish and Sicilian Mafia. In Asia, Chinese traffickers working out of Hong Kong move heroin from Burma and Laos through Thailand and southern China across the Pacific to Australia, the Philippines, Canada, and the United States. It is the size, profitability, and international linkages in the drug trade that define some African-American organized criminals in the United States today. This has not always been so.

A variety of home-grown African-American criminal groups exist throughout the United States alongside the El Rukns of the Chicago area, Crips and Bloods of Los Angeles, and the Jamaican Posses that operate throughout the country. Criminal organizations in New York, Los Angeles, Detroit, Chicago, Philadelphia, Baltimore, and Washington, D.C. are mainly in the drug business. Unlike La Cosa Nostra, Jewish, Irish, or WASP criminal syndicates, African-American criminal groups are locked out of many activities, including labor racketeering and loansharking; drugs, however, know no racial barriers. Still, until the Vietnam War Era, African-American criminal groups had to rely on Mafia families for heroin.

Two major benchmarks have defined contemporary African-American organized crime, and each was a socially and politically tumultuous period that has had profound initial impact on African-American community life in the United States and has rippled through the social fabric of the nation as a whole. The Vietnam War exposed many African-American soldiers to the heroin markets of the Asian Golden Triangle—the Shan States of Indochina, where opium is cultivated in the remote hills and other regions. First, partly as a result of the overseas experience, African-American crime groups were able eventually to circumvent their Mafia patrons and buy direct from Asian suppliers. Second, the enormous influx of cocaine from Latin America gave rise to the crack trade that dramatically transformed ghetto street gangs into drug-trafficking organizations. Crack/cocaine has spawned competing criminal groups in the African-American communities to such an extent that many areas are nothing more than war zones in which lethal turf wars and drive-by shootings take many gang members and innocent bystanders' lives.

The current identifications with heroin and crack notwithstanding, African-American organized crime has a longer and deeper social history than the explosion of drugs across the country. Before World War II, it thrived in the segregated ghettos of America's large cities. African-American settlements in the urban areas of the Northeast and Midwest that came into being at the turn of the century filled up with a mix of artisans, ex-slaves, southern migrants, and an educated bourgeoisie of service-professionals and entrepreneurs. The communities were segregated and exploited but they were also partly self-sufficient. The lack of social services, of financial institutions' commercial investment and development, and the ubiquitous political powerlessness of the segregated ghettos gave rise to informal, "parallel institutions," many of which operated in the gray areas between legitimacy and criminal behavior.

Policy was one such socially accepted form of gambling that had a semblance of legitimacy within the African-American community but carried the stigma of being a crime in the larger society. Unlike traditional organized crime in the white community, where career criminals and street hoodlums dominated the vice industries, rackets, policy, and other illegal services, the African-American communities were managed by individuals who represented a cross-section of the population. In the pre–World War II period, white career criminals were the predominant forces in policy, loansharking, prostitution, and illegal alcohol distribution. After the war, as drugs gained an unshakable grip on the communities, the nature of criminal activity produced a collective victimization. Predatory criminals sapped the vitality of the community; crime became more violent and more impersonal. The communal lack of political influence fostered law enforcement indifference and corruption that made living conditions even worse because of the prevalence of criminogenic commodities in the communities. The social costs are evident in the high rates of homicide, drug abuse, interpersonal violence, and indescribable squalor that characterize so many contemporary African-American ghettos.

This book offers some reflections on African-American organized crime and what the prospects for its growth or control are likely to be. It examines three different periods of African-American history: (1) early policy numbers gambling that surfaced in New York City between 1920 and 1940, (2) the African-American criminal groups of the 1940–1970 period that operated in the ghettos, and (3) the status of African-American gang activities from the 1970s to the present, which are now firmly embedded in their neighborhoods and have expanded nationally.

In the latter part of the nineteenth and the early twentieth century, politicians protected local, white criminal gangs against police enforcement. For this, they were able to use the gangs in electoral politics to ensure favorable returns. Gang members would vote repeatedly or intimidate others to support the favored candidates. Throughout this early period of white gang development, African Americans were not visible in the structure of any significant organized criminal process. Indeed, African-American criminals who entered the twentieth century had no documented history of a leadership role or any significant active affiliation with any organized crime group. The political structure would not support them and without that crucial support, criminals could not develop or maintain organic bonds with their clientele.

In the first two decades of the twentieth century—when Caribbeans migrated in large numbers and native-born African Americans moved into Northeastern and Northcentral cities—operation of illegal gambling, illegal alcohol drinking establishments, and other illegal vice activities evolved. Although there continue to be lively debates about the degree to which contemporary African-American criminal organizations were independently run, the extent of their threat in the years ahead, and their involvement in organized crime, has been greatest in the traditional vices of gambling, drugs, prostitution, and to a lesser extent, loansharking, theft/fencing, and labor racketeering.

Parenthetically, it should be noted that when referring to African-American organized criminal groups, the term *African American* refers to a broad grouping that includes criminal groups or alliances of African Americans, Jamaicans, West Indians, Nigerians, Haitians, and others.[15] Police and federal government agency reports suggest that the two principal types of recruitment utilized in organizing African-American criminal networks are rooted in social and cultural connections. There is first a domestic kinship network, generally headed by a dominant male, and including close relatives. Second, associational networks have been identified that appear to be based on friendships developed in street gangs, prison, or among neighborhood peer groups that emerge as a criminal force in a community. Confirmatory evidence of the different types of African-American crime networks may be located in the accounts of African-American numbers racket operators in the 1920s. These did not develop from street gangs or prison acquaintances.[16] The associational type of gang organization that surfaced in the decades after World War II coalesces principally around narcotics trafficking. At the moment, African-American organized crime groups prey almost exclusively on African Americans and this occurs mostly in segregated neighborhoods, particularly within the inner cities.[17]

The book examines the processes that produced the forms of crime in each period that were, in retrospect, relatively benign compared to the modern patterns of drug-induced, violent predatory crime that is transforming communities into wastelands of despair and pain. This book begins with an account of organized crime in general and then traces the great post–Civil War migrations that flowed into the major Northeastern and Northcentral cities. These newly formed African-American communities organized themselves and coped as best they could with rampant racism. Crime itself emerged in these circumstances for many as a viable substitute for legitimate social mobility and economic opportunities. Organized crime in the United States is not a recent phenomenon; its presence was felt early on in American history. As will be seen, Tocqueville's fears for America, in which lawless and landless groups roamed, never quite materialized in the manner he envisioned. Outlaw passions and energies were ingeniously but precariously harnessed to the political system.

NOTES

1. Alexis de Tocqueville, *Democracy in America,* ed. by J. P. Mayer, trans. by George Lawrence (New York: Doubleday Anchor Book, 1969), 287.

2. The term *Afro-lineal organized crime* refers to a broad category that includes criminal core groups or syndicates of African Americans, Jamaicans, West Indians, Nigerians, Haitians and other persons of African ancestry.

3. Gerald Suttles, *The Social Order of the Slum* (Chicago: University of Chicago Press, 1968); William F. Whyte, *Street Corner Society* (Chicago: University of Chicago Press, 1973).

4. William J. Wilson, "The Ghetto Underclass: Social Service Perspectives." *Annals of the American Academy of Political and Social Science* 501 (Jan. 1989): 8–25.

5. Part of the popular wisdom is that communities in which organized criminals live and work are fairly safe habitats. Street crime is law and the community is stable. It may be supposed the *street justice* prevails in these neighborhoods and that predatory hoodlums fear retaliation by criminal organizations. Such a view is superficial for several reasons. First, it is ahistorical. In Italian-American communities today, street crime is indeed comparatively low. Second, during the period of mass immigration, when Italian neighborhoods were flooded by newcomers without skills, jobs or literacy, crime was rampant and quite violent. It is only after massive social mobility and cultural assimilation into the middle and working class that Italian ghettos

quieted down. With economic stability crime diminished to controllable levels, notwithstanding La Cosa Nostra's presence.

6. President's Commission on Organized Crime, *The Impact: Organized Crime Today* (Washington, DC: U.S. Government Printing Office, April 1986), 79.

7. President's Commission on Organized Crime, *Organized Crime and Heroin Trafficking* (Washington, DC: U.S. Government Printing Office, Record of Hearing V, Miami, FL, Feb. 20–27, 1985), 194–245. According to the testimony of Leroy "Nicky" Barnes a "Council" of narcotics traffickers was formed in Harlem in the 1970s. Its prime purpose was to pool their capital for more lucrative wholesale buys. The Council also provided other services to its members. It made available other economic instruments that could be collectively shared: money launderers, attorneys, loans, and pharmaceutical supplies. While each Council member retained control over his own organization, each had access to automobiles for transporting drugs and cash, numerous milling houses for processing and packaging, safe drops for street dealers, and more enforcement muscle otherwise unavailable in the absence of syndication.

8. Oliver B. Revell, "The Many Faces of Organized Crime." Paper presented on *Major Issues in Organized Crime Control: Symposium Proceedings* (Langley, VA: The National Institute of Justice, September 25–26, 1986).

9. The term is Jimmy Breslin's. It refers, as James Dubro points out in his *Mob Rule: Inside the Canadian Mafia*, to the practice of gathering information with no discernible purpose other than the information itself. According to Breslin:

> This is practiced by the FBI, and many police intelligence units and newspapers and magazines. "Italian geography" is the keeping of information on gangsters: the price they pay for clothes, the restaurants in which they eat, the news of all relatives out to the fifth cousins, their home address and their visible daily movements. All this information is neatly filed and continually added to. This data is never used for anything, still the process goes on until the death of the individual concerned. But Italian geography keeps many people busy and collecting salaries, and is considered a commendable occupation.

See, Jimmy Breslin, *The Gang That Couldn't Shoot Straight* (New York: Viking Press, 1968), 171. Another devastating critique of a preoccupation with the Mafia may be found in Frederick Martens, "Media Magic, Mafia Mania." *Federal Probation*, (June, 1985): 60–68.

10. President's Commission on Organized Crime, *The Impact: Organized Crime Today*, 81–118.

11. "Mafia" is not a secret society in the ordinary sense of the phrase. Unlike the Masons, the Knights of Columbus, or the Knights of Pythias, it has no president, no general initiation (there is some question as to induction rituals), dues, election or bylaws, except unwritten ones. Its cohesiveness is guaranteed by family relationships that go back over generations and an uncodified ideology captured in the phrase "*honore e famiglia.*" Joseph L. Albini, *The American Mafia: Genesis of a Legend* (New York: Appleton-Century-Crofts, 1971); F.A.J. Ianni, "The Mafia and the Web of Kinship." *The Public Interest* 22 (1971): 1–22.

12. Howard Abadinsky, *Organized Crime*, 2d ed. (Chicago: Nelson-Hall, 1985), 255.

13. Rufus Schatzberg, *Black Organized Crime In Harlem: 1920–1930* (New York: Garland Publishing, 1993); Saunder J. Redding "Playing the Numbers," *The North American Review* 238, no. 6 (Dec. 1934): 533–542; Gustav G. Carlson, "Number Gambling: A Study of a Culture Complex," Ph.D. diss., Ann Arbor, University of Michigan, 1940.

14. New Jersey Commission of Investigation, *21st Annual Report* (State of New Jersey, 1989), 32.

15. Ibid. The term *West Indian organized crime* refers to those individuals in-

volved in criminal groups originating in the Bahamas, the British or U.S. Virgin Islands, Trinidad, the Greater Antilles, the Lesser Antilles, Belize, Barbados, Grenada, and the Cayman Islands.

16. Schatzberg, *Black Organized Crime In Harlem.*

17. The Bureau of Justice Statistics, and the National Crime Survey report that African Americans suffer relatively more violent crime than other Americans and that crimes against them caused greater injury than similar crimes committed against persons of other races. U.S. Department of Justice, Office of Justice Programs, Bureau of Justice Statistics, *Black Victims* (Washington, DC: U.S. Government Printing Office, April, 1990).

2 ORGANIZED CRIME IN AMERICA

DEFINING ORGANIZED CRIME

Organized crime is not just another species of crime. Admittedly, its characteristics are difficult to describe with precision; it varies considerably over time in the milieu in which it occurs, and often it expands in communities because its growth is engendered by publics who are (theoretically at least) its victims.

There are many definitions of organized crime. State jurisdictions around the country and social scientists have spelled it out with results ranging from the ludicrous (where two or more individuals constitute organized criminality) to the impossibly intricate. The problems underlying the confusion have to do with descriptions and legalistic definitions of organized crime—the latter being an attempt to provide a set of legal penalties and remedies to attack it, whereas the former, the descriptive, is an effort to demonstrate its distinctive features.

Organized crime actually consists of numerous, familiar statutory offenses such that their occurrence under legally prescribed circumstances and conditions constitutes categorizations as organized criminal conduct; Racketeer Influences and Corrupt Organizations (RICO), the federal law, is a good example of this. The language of RICO contains references to generic crimes such as murder, arson, extortion, loansharking, the Hobbs Act (prostitution) and gambling. There are also two statutory provisions that are specifically directed at career organized criminals: "a pattern of racketeering activities" in furtherance of "criminal enterprises." Together, these define an organized crime conspiracy and set the grounds for prosecutions. The enterprise refers to "any individual, partnership, corporation, association or other legal entity, and any union or group of individual associated in fact."[1] The United States Supreme Court has ruled that the term *enterprise* comprises both legitimate businesses and wholly criminal organization and associations.[2]

In general, most investigations of organized crime are driven by the structure of federal RICO and state versions of it.[3] The implementation of RICO and the cumulative experience gained with it have enabled law enforcement agencies to develop sophisticated investigations and prosecutions against organized crime figures. Over the past decade, the application of RICO in civil and white-collar crime cases has significantly broadened and empowered the law. Recently, the Supreme Court ruled that antiabortion demonstrators who act in a violent manner during protests may be prosecuted under RICO. The potency of the law is in its structure of penalties which are described later.

The question of organized crime is not as clear as might be supposed by the fact of a legal apparatus that succeeds in convicting organized criminals. There is no general agreement among scholars as to what exactly constitutes the phenomenon. Definitions that seek to describe its structure, composition, hierarchy, and membership focus not on its actions but rather on the structure of criminal and racketeering enterprises.

Curiously, this debate has raged for more than a half-century and never have African-American aspects figured into its definition and analyses.[4] In spite of this, to properly understand African-American organized crime it is necessary to describe how the phenomenon in general is conceived, and how scholars and law enforcement experts approach it and seek to develop policies of control and containment. A fairly standard mode of analysis among scholars and academics is to ask about the attributes of groups that make them "organized crime." Most scholars have identified several features, including corruption, violence, continuity, structure, discipline, multiple enterprise, bonding rituals, participation in legitimate enterprise, and durability, that function as elements in a general operational definition.

In his capacity as counsel to the McClelland Committee, which investigated organized criminal penetration of labor unions, and later as a chief counsel to the President's Task Force on Organized Crime in 1967, G. Robert Blakey observed that *organized crime* like *crime* itself is a political term.[5] The term is applied to those entities that permit criminal conspiracies about which there is agreement that it is appropriate to use particularly severe instruments (either investigative or punitive) because of the peculiar dangers they present to society. Utilizing descriptions and criteria for labeling criminal conspiracies as particularly threatening to the social order, the danger that groups or gangs pose involves systematic coercion and corruption as a tool neutralizing the police. Thus, groups of individuals involved in systematic law-breaking using violence and credible threats thereof constitute organized criminal enterprises. It is a matter of judgement as to which defining features are characteristic of particular groups, how deep their conspiracies go, the extent to which they are durable over time, and how much internal discipline and organization they possess. All of these together make up working definitions of organized crime.[6]

The main point is that the criminality of persons in organized crime differs from that committed by conventional criminals because of organization, which allows them to commit crimes of a different variety (labor racketeering) and/or conventional crimes on a larger scale than less organized colleagues.

For purposes of economy we can define *organized crime* as continuing criminal conspiracy that seeks profit from illicit activities in great public demand. Its continued existence is based on the use of violence, threats, and the corruption of law enforcement and public officials.

Among all the organized criminal groups in the United States, none has attracted as much attention as the Cosa Nostra or the American Mafia. By dominating the underworld for more than a half-century, it has shown a remarkable resilience and flexibility in meeting both law enforcement challenges and the encroachments of criminal competitors. To a great extent, the "crime families," as La Cosa Nostra is sometimes called, have become synonymous with organized crime.

THE RISE AND FALL OF THE AMERICAN MAFIA

The predominance of La Cosa Nostra over the past fifty years, and the social reality in which it was nurtured and grew to the levels of power and prestige it achieved not only in America but worldwide, are worth examining because they illustrate the plight   and some of their reactions to the social, economic, and pol   they encountered. More important for our purposes, its histo   comparative background for a consideration of African-Amer   organized criminality.

The word *mafia* describes a phenomenon far more complex than headlines about a vaunted, secret criminal association. Mafia[7] is more than a criminal organization; it is also a set of behaviors and methods for achieving certain ends and goals not possible under normal legitimate circumstances. It is, above all, private power employed and exercised in social conflicts by individuals who do not hesitate to use illegal violence to get their way.

For many centuries in Sicily, where mafia originates, the people faced oppression and domination by one conqueror after another, and in response to this they banded together in brotherhoods dedicated to honor, loyalty, and mutual protection. How, then, have we come to identify the Mafia with extortion and violence? A look at the Mafia's evolution and development and its links with the United States during the time of the latter's growth and economic expansion offers some fascinating clues as to the genesis of organized crime.

In the complicated history of Italy, the unification process begun in the mid-nineteenth century (the Risorgimento) never fully embraced Sicily, Calabria, and the other regions of southern Italy that were, as a result, shamelessly exploited by powerful landowners, bureaucrats, and other official bodies. The culture of mafia developed under these twin conditions of neglect and oppression. Whereas, for instance, the police could not guarantee someone immunity against burglary or kidnapping, or recover stolen property, the mafiosi could. Where the slow, expensive process of the legal system could not ensure justice, they, the "men of respect," administered their own—rough and crude perhaps, but quick and effective. Work too was their gift for support and silence.

In the long run of Sicily's tormented history of colonization, occupation, and oppression, it was the power of the social position of the mafioso which preserved him. Yet his code of silence (*omertà*) and mystique are more than just an elaborate screen; they represent the ritual and discipline of organization. The man of respect, the boss, is always referred to as "Don" (which derives from the Latin *dominus, lord*). The boss (referred to more commonly as *capo*) has a special status. This is because he often risks his life for a price, favor or concession, and because, at least theoretically, his life is always threatened, the mafioso's prestige and power are considerable.

Dominance is the mafioso's objective. At the same time, he also provided some institutional stability, some informal law and order, in an environment where one's pride, career, home, and family could be easily crushed by others. Thus, in exchange for protection and the advantages of association with him, one could hope to survive. The legal category of crime was hypocritical in a world in which wealth and power determined one's fate, and the mafioso's amoral disdain for such distinctions was not held against him—at least not until mafia reshaped itself into a purely criminal way of life in which everyone was subjected to its intimidation and violence.

Mafia degenerated into a predatory, parasitic criminal enterprise as its numerous social, political, and economic functions declined. Its two main characteristics, violence and corruption, remained intact and sustained its transformation from a rural version of informal government to urban crime families. Interdependent connections with formal, legal authority characterized the Mafia's ties with the legitimate sector such that the legitimate and illegitimate relied on each other to thrive.[8] In America, those same interwoven dependencies define the successful criminal enterprise—it cannot survive though violence alone, nor can it grow and diversify without the compliance and conspiratorial support of legitimate businesses, law enforcement agencies, and markets that the public openly and deliberately or indirectly supports. In Sicily and southern Italy, mafia and local government were often indistinguishable.

Like power brokers elsewhere, mafiosi wielded their influence in two spheres, and their actual control in either depended upon their success in dealing with the other. Far from replacing the state, or constituting a state within a state, as has so often been believed, mafiosi depended on the state, as their local and regional power existed only by virtue of their access to larger domains of the state. (The concepts of "political middlemen" and "power brokers" are particularly useful in understanding this symbiosis.) The very articulation of mafiosi with public authorities and national politicians rendered any state-based action or reform against them abortive.

The central characteristic of mafia is the private use of unlicensed violence as a means of control in the public arena. The frameworks of social life amounted to a three-class system of landless poor laborers, a landed absent gentry, and between these two distant social groupings, leaseholders and estate overseers, who freely employed strong-arm men to keep unruly tenants and workers in line. This system of stratification and exploitation created a sociological paradox: It produced a mafia in a cruel and cautious fashion. The set of social arrangements called mafia is ordinarily understood as the antithesis of strong and orderly government; yet that same mafia could not exist without great concentrations of power in states. Mafioso cannot threaten and manipulate ordinary people without having some claim on the protection of more wealthy, influential persons who, at the same time, cannot enjoy their autonomy of action and power without the backing of mafia *cosche*.[9]

Nevertheless, the reciprocal ties between legitimate, corrupted power and mafiosi would dwindle should the former collapse. In their function at the local level, the *cosche* parallel government and intertwine with it; and like government whose functionaries, officials, agents, and illegitimate clients rely on coercion that is, ultimately, concentrated and effective as a means of keeping the population submissive, mafiosi too depend on a fragile, delicate interplay with government, such that the latter never intervenes directly in the local scene but must be close enough to repress uprisings encouraged by mafia rivals such as trade unions, worker cooperatives, and reformists. The murder, thefts, and mutilations used to sustain control—to make, in short, the "men of honor" respected—are only the most lurid manifestations of its evil.

Finally, it helps to remember that mafiosi are not bandits or simple street thugs. Bandits operate on their own, without patrons or protection from the legitimate centers of political and economic power; those who kill and plunder for gain are bandits. Bandits (or common street criminals) differ from mafiosi in at least two important respects: (1) they do most of their work through the use of force; in contrast, mafiosi only employ force when someone steps out of line; (2) bandits do not belong to long, reliable and protective patron–client chains. To the extent that they are successful, bandits tend to be drawn into mafia. As they build up their power domains, bandits threaten mafia; mafiosi must then co-opt or destroy them. Mafia is thus more similar to conventional government and more dependent on it than is banditry. In this regard, one might conceive of a continuum running from anarchy to banditry to mafia to routine government.[10]

Mafia is in no sense a residue of the lawless past. It is an outgrowth of a process in which national systems of power expanded; the state spread out across Sicily, but without absorbing or obliterating local power, and the emergent connections between the two were few, weak, and accessible to monopoly control. For a long period, the remote central government in Rome competed with Palermo, Sicily's historic administrative capital, and was obliged to work through its rivals, the landowners, politicians, and mafiosi they had helped to create. In this arrangement, they resembled the Chinese Manchu governments of the late nineteenth and early twentieth centuries, which had little choice but to deal with gentry and warlords. Another example would be the Central American governments that reached the people through *caciques*.[11] If mafia is considered as a single, monolithic association, with, in its contemporary versions in both Italy and North America, a stable organizational structure like that of a commercial enterprise, one runs the risk of a dangerous illusion because mafia is quintessentially the set of criminal collusions and deeply rooted alliances with close ties to the political system.

With the great transatlantic migration from Europe at the end of the nineteenth century, many mafiosi arrived in the United States and located themselves in the midst of the immigrant enclaves. Almost all commentators on the phenomenon suggest that more than wealth and power, the ability to manipulate events and individuals was the primary motive of the "men of honor" during their halcyon days of influence and control.[12]

Transformed by its experiences in the United States, the Mafia re-emerges at the pinnacle of criminal power after World War II. During the 1920s and 1930s, other gangs rose to prominence and incorporated mafiosi into their lucrative alcohol syndicates.

Why African Americans did not develop "mafia-type" criminal organization in the oppressive conditions they experienced is a real question. We shall return to this issue later, but here it suffices to say that most writers on the subject of race relations in the United States agree that an African-American "underworld" of vice indeed existed. What has not been an issue among scholars is why African-American organized crime has not been a matter for serious inquiry among law enforcement officials and in the academic research community. Any investigation has to consider the question of race and racism and how these figure into the lack of scholarly interest.

Many theories of organized criminal origins and genesis have been developed from data sources limited to white ethnic communities and groups that must raise questions as to the scientific validity and utility of the theories adduced from the empirical data. Perhaps the most widely known (and most facile) theoretical perspective is Daniel Bell's "queer ladder of social mobility."[13] Bell's analyses are a restatement, applied to the United States, of Pirenne's theory of social mobility in capitalist societies.[14] Briefly, the argument describes a process of social sequences in which enterprising individuals from poor backgrounds are able to ascend to the capitalist class by engaging in marginal and illicit activities—criminal activities, actually. And when sufficient capital has been generated, shrewd investments in legitimate economic activities—land, commodities, and so on—serve to confer social acceptability and respectability. According to Bell, because of the frustration of unfair social conditions, many immigrants seized on crime as a way out and up from poverty. Once established, each group would forsake crime for an honest, legitimate living. By 1963, Bell concluded that most of the old rackets had become legitimate, replaced by the upperworld's preferred forms of white-collar crime or purely legal economic activities. Bell's interesting interpretations of ethnic social mobility trends—whether legal or illegal—are a social–structural exploration of how organized criminality becomes viable for those who perceive the social institutions aligned against them when opportunities to get ahead legitimately through a combination of hard work, sacrifice, and merit are constricted or blocked because of one's ethnicity, religion, or social status. The alternative is to seek out noninstitutional means, to embrace crime as a way of amassing wealth and resources that constitute the ingredients of social mobility and status. Theoretically, the argument could plausibly apply to African Americans whose collective destitution is clearly traceable to institutional barriers arbitrarily erected by a racist society. But Bell's sources of data are the experiences of white immigrant groups. This empirical exclusion is not deliberate, it must be said: Little evidence beyond anecdotal accounts of African-American organized criminality was available, nor was it clear in the period covered by Bell's analyses that African-American crime could be described as a major force in the American underworld. It probably could not. The kind of crime widespread in the ghettos was characteristically internal to them, with no broader impact than the local neighborhoods and urban areas where African Americans lived and worked.

Undoubtedly, those who chose crime as a way of life rather than the legitimate struggle against the enormous obstacles of poverty, poor education, limited job opportunities, and racism were the rebels, innovators, and others. But whether these conditions produced a criminal underworld that we associate with La Cosa Nostra, that not only conducted wide-scale vice activities but also reached beyond the confines of the ethnic slum and enclave and penetrated into legitimate businesses, developing racketeering enterprises and colluding with politicians and police, is another matter altogether. The racial ghettos were surely exploited by racketeers, although we cannot be sure to what degree these gangsters grafted on to their activities members of an African-American underworld or subordinated them because the latter lacked the power to resist or to develop their own crime organizations that could defend themselves.

Of special interest in considering the status of African Americans in the underworld as it redefined and mobilized itself during the era of Prohibition and the Great Depression are the ways in which criminal syndicates and ethnic gangs formed, merged, and developed to meet the insatiable public demands for illicit alcohol.

PROHIBITION AND BUCCANEER CAPITALISM

As Kenneth Allsop points out, "the gangster of the Prohibition era was almost invariably second-generation American; he was almost invariably a Sicilian, an Irishman or a Jew."[15] It was mainly from the sons of the late nineteenth-century immigrants that the underworld drew its most apt recruits for Prohibition.

At first there were street gangs with parochial interest, ruling a few streets, getting along modestly on the proceeds of extortion, petty theft, and robbery. The tempo of criminal life quickened after World War I, when demobilized soldiers faced unemployment, economic depression, and growing social protest as the trade unions agitated and flexed their organizational muscles.

Into this potentially explosive situation in the 1920s, the United States government introduced the prohibition of liquor—an experiment that was to prove socially disastrous. The gangs that existed within the immigrant ethnic communities found themselves with the ingredients of an illegal industry, bootlegging, in which criminals positioned themselves to satisfy a public demand for alcoholic beverages. The public was not inclined to obey a puritan injunction to abstain and welcomed opportunities to indulge in illicit drinking. All over the United States, but particularly in Chicago and the Northeast, where geographical and social conditions favored illegal liquor operations, the gangs fastened onto this new source of revenue and used it to establish themselves. Prohibition cast an aura of semilegitimacy over the gangs and was instrumental in unifying, consolidating, and rationalizing the underworld.

Before the 1930s, at the turn of the century, when the European immigrants arrived in massive numbers, specific ethnic groups dominated the migrant population, filling up the cities on the East Coast of the United States. The "push-and-pull" factors that drove African Americans out of the war-ruined and race-blighted South into the Northeast and Midwest frightened the European masses who had felt the palpable threats of social, political, and economic upheavals in their homelands.

The potato famines that swept across Ireland in the 1830s and 1840s brought tens of thousands (eventually more than two million) Irish immigrants to the streets and tenements of New York, Boston, Philadelphia, Baltimore, and other cities.[16] Facing systematic discrimination and overt prejudice, the Irish formed self-defense gangs, and while many would find work and success, others would carve out criminal careers in the streets.[17]

Although criminal in their everyday activities, the Irish street gangs served as recruiting grounds for many who would rise in machine politics through Tammany Hall in New York or its equivalent in other cities, or in organized crime groups. Often, status in all of these constituted the pathway into legitimate upperworld acceptability in politics and commerce. In street gang activity, reputations and alliances linking the underworld and upperworld were forged.

In New York City, the sordid history of Tammany Hall exemplifies the style and character of ethnic politics and crime. Through all of this tumultuous history, the African-American population sat silently by, excluded from the struggle for rights and representation in the economic and political life of the city. In New York City in 1864, it was a convenient scapegoat and victim when riots erupted among mainly Irish immigrants protesting the draft acts that Lincoln authorized to fill the depleted ranks of the bloodied Union armies.

Immigrant politics and crime came together early quite naturally in New York. The "American Dream" became little more than a nightmare for many new arrivals. They quickly perceived, it was impossible not to, the hypocrisy between the idea of a land of opportunity and freedom and its grim reality. Crammed into the teeming ghettos in uninhabitable slums, bewildered by the strange customs—and for Southern and Continental European immigrants, strange language—the European poor joined the ranks of the indigenous American poor. Alienated from their homelands and from their new country, many immigrants retreated psychologically into despair and the perfunctory security of ghetto life.

However, some, especially the young, instinctively adjusted and if violence and corruption permeated all strata in society, then, they too would employ it in their own interest.

Organized crime in America is an imported vice, so to speak. No doubt, it would have existed had the first waves of migration in the late nineteenth century not brought to the United States many of the underworld elements of Europe, but it would have been a lesser type of crime, neither so ferocious nor so well organized as it became.

In order to ensure a secure work environment, the criminal gangs that gravitated to illegal alcohol production and distribution had to adopt some basic business principles. To control the criminal enterprise, three steps had to be taken: (1) the aid and connivance of politicians and police had to be assured; (2) the source of supply of, first, beer and then liquor, had to be secured; and (3) unity had to be brought to the multiplicity of gangs at loose throughout the country. Violence, co-optation, and gang mergers transformed the small gangs into criminal syndicates—sleek, streamlined business enterprises utilizing the most sophisticated commercial techniques to develop and expand the liquor markets. Sources of supply were developed domestically and internationally. In this, the criminal entrepreneurs showed a talent for attracting legitimate people with the required skill to keep supply plentiful. Neutralizing law enforcement through corruption was fairly easy. Through bribery and political clout, the alcohol syndicates were able in many cases to harness local and federal agents to work for them.

The Prohibition period was a benchmark for the American underworld in yet another way. Their spread beyond the impoverished ghettos, their accumulated wealth, exposure to large-scale business, and the tolerance and acceptability of the public who demanded their services and products, enabled the more enterprising gangsters to move into other sectors of the legitimate upperworld economy where the knowledge they acquired in alcohol industries was put to use in other business projects. No longer were gangsters mere street predators or parasites; they had cultivated symbiotic relationships with legitimate society and began to function as indispensable components in numerous upperworld institutions.

The general growth of criminal enterprises triggered by Prohibition did not sweep up all criminal groups in its wake. African Americans were sealed off in their communities. They did not play significant roles in the larger picture and were, in effect, suppressed by white criminals who preyed upon the ghettos.

THE PASSIONS FOR POWER: OVERLORDS AND WARLORDS IN THE URBAN CRIME SCENE

When Dutch Schultz muscled in on the Harlem policy rackets in 1931, the Depression was in some ways a better business climate than that of the 1920s for organized criminals. The racketeers were the dispensers of dreams and escape—in the form of alcohol, gambling, drugs, and sex—and by the 1930s, their considerable wealth and influence had been amassed while the effects of unemployment and economic decline left the rest of the country prostrate and dispirited.

The door of opportunity had been opened for many young street-gang members, and when they eventually assumed control, they brought to leadership roles American values and attitudes. Prohibition was an economic windfall for criminals and a social phenomenon with revolutionary cultural implications. Ethnic gangsters, those who had been born and raised in Europe, were suspicious of the multiethnic syndicates consolidating around the alcohol rackets. Out of fear, many resisted working with Irish, Italians, Jews, Germans, and Poles. Thus, within the ethnic enclaves, internal dissension festered and culminated in gang wars. Two types of gang conflict spilled into the streets during Prohibition: struggles among ethnic gangs competing for territorial control of liquor, and a bloody war of attrition within the ethnic enclaves themselves, among the traditional gang bosses and young, Americanized Turks who were impatient with the ancient prejudices that stymied business. The outcome of these conflicts would define the future course of organized crime in unexpected ways.

Success in the ruthlessly competitive bootlegging business required an unimaginable array of technologies and assets that the traditionalist, who operated in the familiar neighborhoods of their communities that provided comparatively modest illegal income, could neither fathom nor approve. A bootlegging operation meant ships, stills, breweries, landing and shipping sites, trucks, drivers, guards, warehouses and bars, clubs, restaurants, and other means of distribution. In addition to a network of bribers and payoffs, lawyers, accountants, and bankers had to be hired to maintain accounts. Such an enterprise required a broad cosmopolitan orientation that many of the "Mustache Petes" (a nickname defining a traditionalist) simply lacked.

Huge profits produced a temporary detente, a truce that could not last as rivalries and fears persisted. The younger men, Arnold Rothstein,

Meyer Lansky, Lucky Luciano, Frank Costello, and Johnny Torrio of Chicago, saw the necessity of cooperation and not just in cities like New York, Chicago or Philadelphia; the linkages they envisioned were not only sectional in scope but also national, ties that would transcend ethnic and religious differences. The old feudal empires of crime incessantly at war with opponents would give way to a confederation of stable organizations in which a democratic temperament and style would reign.

In 1927, that organization or combine came into being. It was called the "Seven Group"—not a group of seven individuals, but a group of power structures representing major syndicates in key population centers across the United States. Mutual cooperation was the strategic organizational cohesive force. From this central core, alliances were formed with gangs in Boston, Providence, Cleveland, and Detroit. Within the year, more than twenty-two gangs from Maine to Florida and westward to the Mississippi River were linked to the Seven Group, and much of the bloody competition that had marked the first years of Prohibition came to an end. The first tentative steps had been taken toward an interlocking criminal alliance of national scope. But the underworld does not live in a vacuum, unaffected by external events. When bootlegging emerged from its early chaotic competitions and matured into monopolistic, centralized organizations generating lucrative profits, the realization began to seep in among some racketeers that the wide-scale violation of the Volstead Act meant that Prohibition itself was increasingly perceived as a national aberration that could not last as demands for repeal mounted. It was only a matter of time before liquor became legal again.

Planning for a new and unknown future was a vast and complex undertaking, far beyond the scope of a single organization. In the late 1920s, gangster conclaves, much like international political summits, were held in Cleveland, Atlantic City, Chicago, and New York to discuss national cooperation in other vice activities, mainly gambling, and to explore the investment into and penetration of legitimate businesses.

During Prohibition, the cabarets, nightclubs, and jazz joints needed liquor supplies, and because the bootleggers were the only reliable source, they became involved in the nightlife business. Starting modestly, bankrolling dives and small speakeasies, the gangster bosses paid off the relevant police to avoid arrests and installed reasonably clean managers to front the operations. As they prospered, and as drinking in mob establishments became tolerated, the bootleggers attained a patina of respectability.

In African-American communities, white gangsters ran the better known nightclubs, such as the Grand Terrace in Chicago and the Cotton Club in Harlem. Capone's gang was behind the Grand Terrace. Earl Hines, who

FIGURE 2.1. The Roaring Twenties and Fallout from Prohibition:
Consolidation and Maturation—The Evolution and Development
of Criminal Syndicates

A. Loosely structured street gangs

↓

B. Clique formation and involvement   Incipient stage: coalescence
   in mercenary crime   and mobilization

↓

C. Criminal syndicate organization;   Maturation and
   production and distribution of illicit   federation
   goods and services; protection, infiltration into legitimate business

Key   A: Late 19th and early 20th century
      B: Prohibition: 1920–1934
      C: The 1930s

was to become a major jazz performer, in referring to his racketeer employers, said, "Our relations were always cordial and sometimes it paid to know
these fellows."[18] The Cotton Club was operated by Owney Madden's gang.
Madden managed to bring Duke Ellington's band to the Cotton Club with
minimum persuasion—given his reputation in the New York underworld. In
New Orleans, the spectacular career of Louis Armstrong was largely shaped
by ruthless white criminals until he achieved international fame. Throughout
most African-American communities, white gangsters controlled establishments that operated on the edge of legality; they had the power to influence
police and impose their will almost indiscriminately in communities that lacked
the political clout to oppose them. This process produced an immense suc-
tion of capital out of the communities. There were, of course, exceptions. In
Detroit, African-American gangsters banded together and forced the white
syndicates to come to terms with them. And because they were able to maintain some independence, agreements were reached that allowed them to retain internal autonomy and share in racket profits.

With Repeal, several syndicates transformed themselves into legitimate
enterprises, while others dissolved, using their wealth to finance movement
into other rackets. Some penetrated more deeply into the upperworld of
politics, business, and labor unions.[19] In labor industry disputes, mobsters
functioned as goons, shamelessly working for both management and labor.
The mobsters turned these situations to their advantage by exploiting both
groups and emerged as power brokers, exercising considerable influence in
many labor unions and commercial enterprises.

27

The syndicates that were formed and survived operated outside the pale of the law and the courts, so that legal remedies were not readily available to them in the resolution of conflicts and problems. In order to protect themselves and their transactions against fraud, theft or "contractual" violations, they had to resort to informal alternatives.

Not surprisingly, groups of "problem solvers" and protectors would emerge to cope with the unique problems of illegal firms. A frightening example of this "corporate protection service" was Murder, Inc. This murder machine was composed of contract killers employed by various syndicate bosses, who directed or contracted a troop of professional assassins to accommodate the needs of other affiliated gangs around the country and to provide enforcement service at home. When it was finally exposed in the early 1940s and brought to justice, the hoodlums composing the group were mainly Jews and Italians working for the Lepke Buchalter/Anastasia crime syndicate.[20] The trials and convictions of Murder, Inc. members stunned the nation. Some of its members had murdered more than fifty individuals; these were, in the shocking slang of the underworld, "contract hits"—cold-blooded murders on order, carried out with professional skill. A major crime leader in New York City, the only high-level gangster ever to be executed, Louis "Lepke" Buchalter, was sentenced to death for his complicity with the group.

Murder, Inc. was a key component of a "power" syndicate. It provided no illicit product or service to ordinary citizens who wished to drink, gamble, fornicate, or do drugs; it was an operation internal to the crime syndicates, designed to protect criminal activities from criminal predators and informers—anyone who might jeopardize a crime group's operation; and while it functioned, it did so with cool efficiency: Murders were committed all over the United States and no competitor or opponent of the syndicates could feel secure. Crime syndicates had evolved in the 1930s in such a sophisticated manner that distinctions between them could be made.[21]

Figure 2.2 illustrates the key characteristics of power and enterprise syndicates. Power syndicates provided protection services in the operating environments of enterprise groups. Also, power syndicates preyed upon legitimate businesses and industries, and as they exhausted upperworld victims, they turned to extort their criminal colleagues. In the greater New York area in the 1930s, the Buchalter–Weiss power syndicate sold violence and labor peace to legitimate textile and garment firms to insure against theft, vandalism, and union employee unrest. Eventually, intimidation tactics worked so well that the labor racketeers would become partners and owners of several businesses. The Buchalter syndicate of violence spread downward into narcotics and other purely criminal activities, imposing itself into illicit businesses by the threat of its guns and killers.[22] Other power syndicates such as the Dutch Schultz and Costello–Erickson syndicates, enjoyed extensive contacts among politicians, police officials, and prominent businessmen and could for a fee or a partnership effectively neutralize police investigations or assist in promoting business opportunities for vice suppliers.

FIGURE 2.2. Characteristics of Power and Enterprise Syndicates

Syndicate Type	Service-Product	Size	Longevity	Specialization	Clientele
1. Enterprise syndicates					
a. Free-lance, or integrated criminal entrepreneurial activities	Gambling, theft, robbery, loansharking, prostitution, extortion	small	short-lived	variable	small; variable
b. Specialized, diversified monopolies and mergers	Gambling, Drug importation and distribution, loansharking	large	durable	variable	large; variable
2. Power syndicates					
a. Corrupter, brokers, bribers	Arrange and guarantee illicit transaction; protection	small	durable	none	small
b. Extortionist	Violence	small	short-lived	none	small
c. Financiers and fences	Capital: money laundering; illicit investment opportunities	variable	variable	none	small
d. Mediators and resolving racketeers	Violence	large	durable	some	variable

---

Source: Robert J. Kelly (1987) "The Evolution of Criminal Syndicates" *International Journal of Law Enforcement Intelligence Analysis*, Vol. 2, No. 1.

Figure 2.3 presents a chart of the major mid-1930s organized crime leaders, including their territorial locations and associations. This chart shows what much of the literature on organized crime overlooks, that after Prohibition, the underworld in the United States tended to be dominated by a coalition of Jews and Italians. Luciano's group was paramount over all La Cosa Nostra groups and with its multiethnic leadership, it acted as a link connecting Italian and Jewish organized crime across the United States. The new arrangements were drenched in blood. A vicious war had to be fought within the Italian underworld in order to bring about the "Americanization" or modernization of organized crime.

THE CASTELLAMMARESE WAR: BIRTH OF LA COSA NOSTRA

During Prohibition, the American underworld was a multiethnic set of enterprises composed of Jews, Irish, Italians, Poles, Germans, and WASPS. Conspicuously absent from the ranks of the gangsters were African Americans. Many, however, did have secondary roles in minority criminal activities, working as fronts and subordinates for white gangsters and operating small-scale prostitution, gambling, and policy rackets at the sufferance of the more powerful white criminal groups.

As we have seen, Prohibition was an organizational catalyst creating the conditions for consolidation, cooperation, and interdependence in an underworld rampant with petty ethnic rivalries and animosities. The lure of huge profits was a major factor facilitating the relaxation of jealousies and the setting aside of minor disputes over meager territories. Still, some traditionalists who thrived on exploiting small ethnic ghettos of Italian immigrants resisted modernization; they balked at forming partnerships with non-Italians. The feeling among the traditional mafiosi was that others could never be trusted. Refusing to join the syndicates did not mean, however, that they turned a blind eye to the enormous profits the alcohol syndicates and vice rackets generated. The two main Mafia leaders in New York City (and for all practical purposes, the United States), Joseph (Joe the Boss) Masseria and Salvatore Maranzano, demanded tribute from their "soldiers," the younger, more Americanized mafiosi such as Charles "Lucky" Luciano, Frank Costello, Thomas Luchese and others, who were part of the multiethnic Prohibition syndicates.

The gangland war in the traditional Mafia that would end with the death of the two opposing chiefs and give rise to a national underworld began in New York in October, 1929. As the national economy worsened, culminating in the great crash of '29 on Wall Street, desperation gripped the criminal groups, who became bitterly competitive as the economy contracted with business failures everywhere and widespread, unprecedented unemployment.

The two major antagonists in the struggle were both fellow immigrants from the Sicilian town of Castellammarese del Golfo. Both men, who

FIGURE 2.3. Organized-Crime Leadership in the United States (circa 1936–1937)

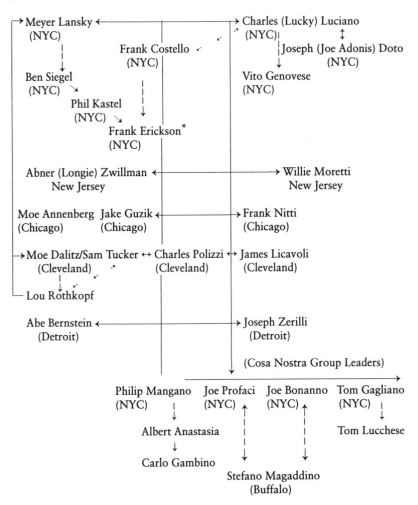

Jewish Leaders   *Italian-American Leaders*

Meyer Lansky ←————————————————→ Charles (Lucky) Luciano
(NYC)   (NYC) ↕
                      Frank Costello   Joseph (Joe Adonis) Doto
                      (NYC)   ↓   (NYC)
Ben Siegel   Vito Genovese
(NYC)   (NYC)
        Phil Kastel
        (NYC)
                Frank Erickson*
                (NYC)

Abner (Longie) Zwillman ←————————————→ Willie Moretti
New Jersey   New Jersey

Moe Annenberg Jake Guzik ←—————————→ Frank Nitti
(Chicago)   (Chicago)   (Chicago)

→Moe Dalitz/Sam Tucker ↔ Charles Polizzi ↔ James Licavoli
  (Cleveland)   (Cleveland)   (Cleveland)
        │
        Lou Rothkopf

Abe Bernstein ←————————————————→ Joseph Zerilli
(Detroit)   (Detroit)

                                                        (Cosa Nostra Group Leaders)
                ————————————————————————————————————→
        Philip Mangano   Joe Profaci   Joe Bonanno   Tom Gagliano
        (NYC)   (NYC) ↑   (NYC) ↑   (NYC)
                ↓   ↓
        Albert Anastasia   Tom Lucchese
                ↓
        Carlo Gambino
                        Stefano Magaddino
                        (Buffalo)

LEGEND: ↔ suggests mutual ties and strong association
          *(non-Jewish, non-Italian)
          ←--- suggests rank and position

Source: Peter Lupsha, "Organized Crime in the United States" in Robert J. Kelly, ed., *Organized Crime: A Global Perspective* (Totowa, NJ: Rowman & Littlefield, 1986).

came to the United States as adults, were inducted members of Sicilian Cosche and both aspired to the title "*capo di tutti capi*" (Boss of Bosses) in the American Mafia, and both expected their clients and colleagues to seize control of all rackets in which they were active. This meant crushing and repressing non-Italian competitors and collaborators. Neither boss fully appreciated that younger Italians and Sicilians, particularly those who had grown up in America, had formed friendships and alliances with many non-Italians during Prohibition and secretly despised the "Mustache Petes," the old world mafiosi who clung to their prejudices and their European customs and folkways. When the war between the Masseria and Maranzano factions began in New York City, it quickly spread and engulfed Italian hoodlums in all the major cities of the United States. After much blood and many lives were lost, the stalemate persuaded younger members of Masseria's gang to end the struggle by ending Joe the Boss's life. He was assassinated in 1931 and a truce (more of an interlude) followed in which Maranzano took the momentous step of reorganizing the Italian underworld into crime families with hierarchies of leaders, all of whom would pay tribute to him—the Boss of Bosses. From this came the famous term "Cosa Nostra" (Our Thing).

What Maranzano demanded, that the crime families take control of the American underworld, showed his ignorance and arrogance about the complexities of American society. Moreover, the younger men whom he putatively commanded had more in common with their non-Italian colleagues in crime than they did with him. Furthermore, fearing that he, Maranzano, might be deposed by the very men whom he persuaded to eliminate his rival Masseria, he secretly planned their assassination. Luciano, working closely with Meyer Lansky, Vito Genovese, Joe Adonis, and Dutch Schultz, seized the initiative and murdered Maranzano in 1931.

The death of Maranzano gave birth to crime as a fledgling national confederation in which everyone was to understand that cooperation, consolidation, and a sense of order would be the rules governing operations. A commission not only replaced a dictatorial authority figure, but also served as a regulatory mechanism for disputes among families. What remained intact as a legacy of the Castellammarese War were the crime families that were to become the nucleus, the core, of organized criminal activities on a national scale.

Technological innovation played a vital role in the expansion and modernization of criminal enterprises during the 1930s and 1940s. The national wire services not only facilitated the countrywide syndication of gambling, which made local bookmakers dependent on organized crime, but provided opportunities for the spread of bookmaking, sports gambling, and narcotics into all segments of American society. Because of their power, the organized crime groups affiliated with crime families felt free to move into new ethnic and racial territories. The African-American community in Harlem was a prime target for the Schultz gang. It eventually took over the policy rackets in Harlem through violence and politically manipulated

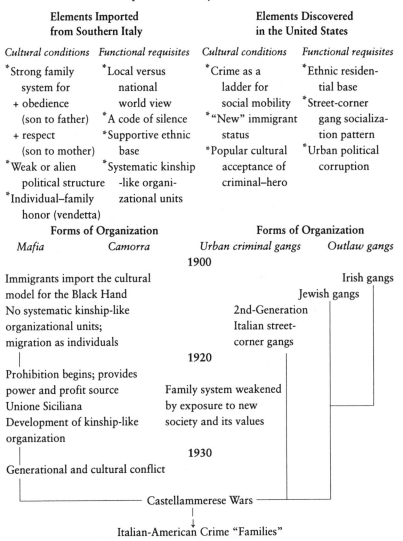

FIGURE 2.4. Developmental History of Italian-American Crime Families

Source: Francis A. Ianni, A Family Business: Kinship and Social Control in Organized Crime (New York: Russell Sage Foundation, 1972), 60. © 1972 The Russell Sage Foundation. Used with permission of The Russell Sage Foundation.

police pressure. When Rev. Adam Clayton Powell was a member of the U.S. Congress, he pointed out the realities of the Harlem crime scene and shocked everyone by speaking openly for the record what everyone knew.

On January 10, 1960, Congressman Powell said, "I am stating one unchallengeable fact, the Mafia and the syndicate are in complete control of Harlem." A week earlier from the House floor, he had launched a series of ten weekly speeches accusing the New York police of being involved in protecting organized crime, especially the numbers racket in Harlem.

Powell launched his crusade by charging that the police were corrupted, and that the illegal activities they protected were taking millions of dollars out of poor communities. Specifically, he wanted it known that as long as the illegal racket operated, then African Americans should have their share of the profits. He told a rally at his church: "I am against numbers in any form. But until the day when numbers is wiped out in Harlem . . . I am going to fight for the Negro having the same chance as the Italian."[23]

THE POSTWAR PERIOD

The late 1940s and 1950s saw two major developments within organized crime: (1) the growth of casino gambling in Nevada, especially Las Vegas; and (2) massive labor racketeering, especially the manipulations of Teamster pension funds. The other milestone event was the Appalachian Meeting of 1957, which revealed the nationwide power of La Cosa Nostra.

The discovery of a gangster conclave renewed interest in the underworld. Subsequent hearings in the U.S. Senate produced the sensational testimony of a Mafia defector, Joseph Valachi, who broke the code of silence and revealed the nature and structure of the Genovese Crime Family, one of the more powerful Mafia families in the New York area. What Valachi further disclosed was the extent to which the old Prohibition gangs had been subordinated to the Cosa Nostra and the spread of organized crime activities beyond the traditional vices of alcohol, narcotics, pornography, gambling, and prostitution.[24]

During the 1950s and 1960s security thefts and stock frauds increased, and along with the drug trade the internationalization of organized crime continued. In response to these alarming growth trends, the President's Task Force on Organized Crime in 1967 presented a blueprint for control and containment.[25] One of the principal outcomes was RICO (Racketeer Influences and Corrupt Organizations) statute (18 United States Code Sections 1961–1968). As part of the Organized Crime Control Act of 1970, RICO defines "racketeering very broadly and it includes offenses involving murder, arson, gambling, bribery, extortion, narcotics trafficking, loan-

FIGURE 2.5. An Organized-Crime Family

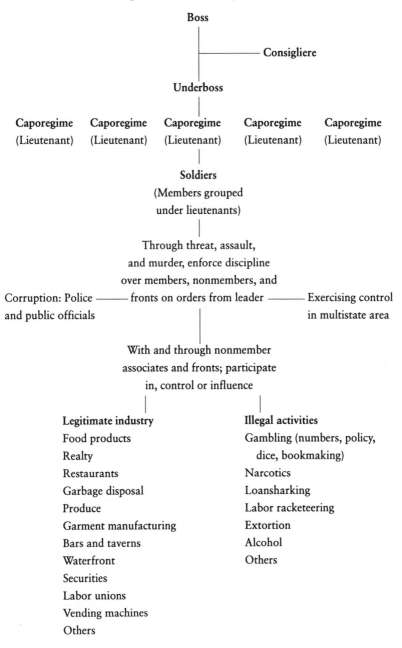

Boss
├──────── Consigliere

Underboss

Caporegime   Caporegime   Caporegime   Caporegime   Caporegime
(Lieutenant) (Lieutenant) (Lieutenant) (Lieutenant) (Lieutenant)

Soldiers
(Members grouped
under lieutenants)

Through threat, assault,
and murder, enforce discipline
over members, nonmembers, and
Corruption: Police ——— fronts on orders from leader ——— Exercising control
and public officials   in multistate area

With and through nonmember
associates and fronts; participate
in, control or influence

Legitimate industry   Illegal activities
Food products   Gambling (numbers, policy,
Realty   dice, bookmaking)
Restaurants   Narcotics
Garbage disposal   Loansharking
Produce   Labor racketeering
Garment manufacturing   Extortion
Bars and taverns   Alcohol
Waterfront   Others
Securities
Labor unions
Vending machines
Others

Source: Task Force on Organized Crime, *1967 Task Source Report: Organized Crime* (Washington, DC: U.S. Government Printing Office, 1967) 9.

sharking, and so on. The legal innovations in RICO are what really make it an effective crime-fighting weapon: Under the law, it is a crime to belong to an enterprise such as an organized crime group that is involved in a pattern of racketeering. Also, the criminal penalties for RICO violations are substantial and these include increased incarceration time, civil forfeiture provisions, and the removal of the leadership of a trade union (to be placed in government-sponsored stewardship) if it is determined by the Department of Justice that the union is in the hands of organized members or associates.

Since its passage into law in 1970 and its modifications in 1984, RICO has been quite effective in prosecuting, convicting, and imprisoning hundreds of major and minor organized crime figures.[26]

Other crime-fighting instruments, such as the Money Laundering Act, the Bank Security Act, the Witness Security Program, and the implementation of sophisticated electronic surveillance equipment, have vastly improved the capacities of the government to contain and frustrate La Cosa Nostra.

By the 1970s and 1980s, the traditional underworld of La Cosa Nostra had less clout in politics and lost some of its influence in labor unions. Still, even with most of the major bosses and *capos* imprisoned, the Cosa Nostra managed to sustain its familiar trades even as younger groups of criminals from the new immigrant population began to compete with the Cosa Nostra chiefs. Chinese, Vietnamese, Israeli, Russian, Nigerian, Colombian, Mexican, Dominican, Cuban, Jamaican, indigenous groups of whites (outlaw motorcycle gangs), and African Americans began to assert themselves criminally not only because American society was closed to them but also for quite the opposite reason. Coming from countries in tight economic straits, under draconian police methods, they found in the United States relative freedom to act in criminal ways: Police and prosecutors in America are diffused among city, state, and federal jurisdictions and are often in conflict and split further across a bureaucratic labyrinth of agencies. The space of America, the ease of speed and travel, the Constitutional protection and anonymity of urban life made it simpler to engage in crime and melt away in the protective ethnic enclaves that mushroomed in many cities as a consequence of the 1965 Immigration Act.[27]

The trial and conviction of John Gotti, head of the Gambino Crime Family, on murder and racketeering charges marked not just the fall of the country's most celebrated gangster but, as many law enforcement officials and academic authorities see it, the decline of the American Mafia as a whole. The sensational proceedings served as a showcase for the problems besetting this once invincible organization. One expert informed us that we were witnessing the "twilight of the dons."

Indeed, La Cosa Nostra's prospects appeared so bleak since the war on the Mafia began in the 1980s that it seemed inevitable that the crime families would be usurped by other ethnics, with the Chinese Ghost Shadows seizing control of some Teamsters Union locals, with the price of concrete now being fixed by the Jamaican Posses, and with the Albanians, Russians, and Nigerians becoming the secret force in hijacking and smuggling at Kennedy International Airport in New York City.

Television was especially guilty of inflating the Gotti myth. And just as Leroy "Nicky" Barnes, a major African-American drug trafficker and boss in Harlem once played and dressed up to his reputation as the "Black Godfather," Gotti introduced the style to La Cosa Nostra, whose bosses had historically avoided the spotlight of public attention as much as possible.

In the rush to corroborate the media blitz and enthusiasm of law enforcement over his conviction, few bothered to ask just what the Dapper Don did, what great power and influence the *capo dei tutti capi,* the Boss of Bosses, exercised. Gotti did not control New York's four other crime families, and there is not a consensus in law enforcement circles that the Gambino organization was New York's premier crime syndicate; the Genovese family was just as large, probably earning as much money, and exerting as much influence in other cities. The term "Godfather" may be something of a fraud, because it encapsulates the entire La Cosa Nostra into a single Boss of Bosses and fails to explain the complicated relationships among the New York and other crime families around the nation.

Despite a rash of convictions over the past ten years, La Cosa Nostra has shown a resilience rarely acknowledged by government officials. Historically the record shows that the conviction or death of a boss—whether Vito Genovese, Thomas Luchese, Anthony Corallo, Carmine Persico, Anthony Salerno, Philip Rastelli or John Gotti (the heads at one time or another of the most powerful families in the northeastern United States)—has meant little to the family entrepreneurs who seem well-positioned to survive the fall of a boss.

The very grassroots nature of the crime families (see Figure 2.5), with thousands of mob figures surviving a succession crisis, means that Mafia is still a viable enterprise. The imprisonment of leaders has been portrayed as a crushing blow, but the backbone of the crime families, its lowest ranking members, the "soldiers" and their nonmember "associates," are the real criminal masterminds; they still control industries, infiltrate unions and legitimate businesses, and run gambling and loan-sharking operations. The testimonies of many Mafia defectors such as Sammy Gravano, Joseph Chiodo, Joe Valachi, Vincent Teresa, Jimmy Fratianno, Angelo Lonardo,

Vincent Cafaro, and the work of courageous undercover agents show a large array of economic crimes that debunk repeated claims that successful prosecutions have mortally wounded the Mafia.[28] Every mob turncoat over the past thirty-five years has revealed the crucial role of associates in corrupting labor unions and influencing legitimate businesses. Associates come from a variety of ethnic and religious backgrounds and, therefore, are not eligible for initiation, but are key assets in the Cosa Nostra's criminal apparatus. Most associates front for gangsters: that is, they represent their secret interests in numerous businesses, and avoid the limelight in order to dodge prosecutions.

The economic terrorism of extortionate crime that Cosa Nostra soldiers and their associates exercise is not limited to large-scale businesses. They routinely prey upon local communities so regularly that the government cannot cope with the number of cases to investigate. Moreover, the fear of reprisals intimidates victims into silence. Without victim cooperation, extortions are not investigated, much less prosecuted. Together these circumstances makes dismantling the Mafia improbable.

Just as effective methods to combat widespread community extortion are few, law enforcement agencies have also been unable to effectively strike at the heart of the Mafia's money machine—gambling and loansharking—which generates hundreds of millions of dollars annually. As long as it can conduct bookmaking and loan-sharking operations, it is impossible for any Mafia family to be close to extinction.

From time to time, gambling operations are broken up, but bookies and gamblers do not ordinarily receive prison terms, nor do extortion victims cooperate with officials.

With ingenious moves to supplement their illicit income, mobsters have developed new markets for gambling (video poker) and new revenue sources—specifically gasoline-tax swindles with Russian hoodlums in New York City and elsewhere.

Over the last decade, the Mafia's position of preeminence may have eroded from unrelenting law enforcement pressures, but it remains deeply entrenched in many legitimate businesses, and its infrastructure of soldiers and associates has never slackened their activities so long as the attention focused on the Bosses.

THE NEW "MAFIAS": GLOBAL AND LOCAL

Today, many different mafiosi are at work in America—Colombian Cartels, Chinese Tongs and street gangs, Jamaican Posses, as well as gangs of Haitians, Pakistanis, and Nigerians. Like the Mafia, they rely on ethnic ties to give their projects coherence, solidified by racial and in-group loyalties. In other respects, the new syndicates differ markedly from La Cosa Nostra in their use of violence: their cruelty and brutality know no limits and are not tempered by sentiments toward children or wives of rivals. The new gangsters are further distinguished by their concentration on drug trafficking, which is the primary source of income for most of them. And the huge increases in drug use during the past twenty years have given rise to an international criminal network of unprecedented scope and sophistication.

In addition, a number of social, economic, and political trends have coalesced to form a new, larger space for organized crime: a vast hunting ground with no fixed borders and with entry permits available to the cruel and deadly.

The first trend is the development of computer and communication technologies. Billions of dollars from drug deals can whiz around the world in seconds; drug cartels have international banks ready to launder their narco-dollars. Second, the collapse of communism in the former Soviet Union and Eastern Europe, combined with the rebirth of market capitalism and weak governments reminiscent of the early twentieth-century immigrant conditions in America, contrive to form a devastating mixture that has spawned the genies of crime and unleashed an enormous structural corporation—a prerequisite for organized criminal conduct.

The third trend—itself a function of the first two—is the evaporation of national borders. In Western Europe, people, goods, money, drugs, and arms swirl around; Chinese and Latin American immigrants, many of whom are illegal, move through maze-ways of international smuggling rings that transport not only people but illicit goods.

In all of this, there is no worldwide conspiracy, no equivalent of a Mafia "Commission" ready to orchestrate criminal activity. Yet international criminal cooperation is growing, with Eastern European and Russian gangs selling arms to the Sicilian Mafia and the latter exchanging heroin for cocaine with Colombian cartels. Cocaine generates enormous sums of money that eventually corrupt the world's financial system and its law enforcement apparatus. It is estimated that at least $85 billion in drug profits are laundered through the financial markets each year.[29]

Never before has one type of criminal activity generated such sums of ready cash for investment in businesses, whether legal or illegal. It is the drug cartels and their global reach when mated with the postcommunist world economy that breeds the new organized crime.

The consequences of international drug trafficking have profound implications for the African-American communities in particular. The ghettos have been the targets of drug traffickers for decades and with the modest price of crack/cocaine many communities have been utterly ravaged by the drug.

Before the death of Pablo Escobar, the Colombian Cali cartel was believed to control nearly 85 percent of the world's cocaine trade. As with its great rival, the Medellin cartel, cocaine traffickers are highly organized, ruthless, and disposed to treating cocaine as a business like any other.

The Colombian cocaine syndicates manage a five thousand mile pipeline, the logistics of which are quite demanding, including all sorts of specialists. Similarly, heroin smuggling entails an equally sophisticated network in Afghanistan, Pakistan, Iran, Turkey, the Balkans, and in Asia, Chinese traffickers work out of Hong Kong, Burma, Laos, and Thailand across the Pacific to San Francisco and Vancouver, or through Triads in the Netherlands. There are not only more syndicates but there is more cooperation among them, and as profits from drugs accumulate, the possibilities of diversified portfolios and enterprise seem like the logical next step.

For example, Asian, more specifically, Chinese organized crime groups smuggle heroin and people into the United States, Canada, Europe, and Latin America. Indigenous gangs working with Chinese Tongs in the Chinatowns located in major cities engage in extortion racketeering across the spectrum of commercial businesses in these communities.[30] In all of this, one can see similar patterns with the immigrant experiences at the turn of the century. Among the Chinese and Latin American gangs, the same anatomy as the Italian-American crime families appears to be unfolding: local predatory crime, then expansion beyond the ethnic enclave into the larger society. Amid the proliferation of immigrant crime groups, two of the new underworld groups, bikers and African-American gangs, are homegrown. Outlaw motorcycle gangs consist of hoodlum clans with no definite ethnic or geographical base.[31] The prototype, the Hell's Angels, were founded in 1950 in the working-class areas of Southern California. Other groups sprang to life within a decade. The Pagans, the Outlaws, and the Bandidos formed a loose brotherhood of rootless petty criminals that eventually moved into stolen cars, narcotics, extortion, and drugs.[32] In the 1980s, the major motorcycle gangs affiliated with Mafia crime families, carrying out murders, arson, assault, and loan-sharking chores for mafiosi.[33] In effect, the motorcycle gangs became the street enforcers of Mafia soldiers. In time, as they accumulate experience and skill in criminal enterprises, the gangs themselves may rebel and compete against their mentors.

The recent explosion of African-American street gangs in Los Angeles, New York, Chicago, St. Louis, and other urban areas came out of the social upheavals of the 1960s.[34] One sees here a complex history of organized crime in the African-American communities. There appears to be a rupture with the past in criminal activity that is not as evident among white ethnics. To say the least, the standard account assumes that for decades minor African-American hoodlums worked local neighborhoods dealing dope, women, and running numbers as low-level employees of Mafia families. When formerly Italian inner-city neighborhoods changed, and when the civil rights movement encouraged African Americans to consider their own possibilities, that message was not limited to legitimate citizens: African-American gangsters moved up and seized control of their own turfs. In Buffalo, where the numbers gambling was controlled by the Magaddino family, African Americans at first paid a token tribute of 10 percent of the profits, then no tribute at all. In Newark, they snatched numbers gambling from the local Genovese family *capo,* even to the point of violence.[35]

Along with most organized crime, the drift from gambling into narcotics was inevitable. In the late 1960s, the major narcotics rings that were put together in African-American neighborhoods were different from all others in that they were not just street dealers but wholesale importers and distributors.[36] Attempts to organize nationally occurred in 1970, when Frank Matthews, a New York drug dealer loosely affiliated with the Gambino and Luchese families, called a meeting in Atlanta in order to coordinate a national drug-trafficking organization among African-American gangs.[37]

In turn, Matthews yielded to Leroy "Nicky" Barnes, who actually succeeded for a time in creating a seven man "Council" of Harlem drug lords. The Council controlled a significant part of the heroin traffic in New York, Pennsylvania, and Eastern Canada. Barnes was arrested in 1978 and eventually cooperated with federal authorities. He believed that a lack of trust and loyalty, and greed among his closest associates, led to his downfall. "We weren't subject to any intimidation by an outside group," he said. "We competed by having the best powder."[38]

With Barnes imprisoned, another drug organization emerged—Papa D's Family—that lacked the grandiose ambitions of the Barnes "Council" but had learned some shrewd lessons from its Mafia predecessors and Barnes's mistakes. The operational center was protected by TV surveillance with around-the-clock, posted armed guards. Women were crucial to the drug scheme's success. They were used as couriers; children were also used for making local drops and collections, as they were legally immune from prosecution. Above all, discipline and retaliation were ruthlessly enforced.[39]

Imaginative techniques caught on in Detroit, where the Young Boys consortium employed 450 children, mostly under eighteen years of age, some as young as eleven.[40] Innovations included color-coded clothing (red for heroin, blue for cocaine) among the drug couriers, the stamping of drug envelopes with brand names, and the employment of specially skilled criminals who provided false identification papers, credit cards, driver's licenses, and birth certificates.

In the 1970s, some observers predicted an African-American succession in organized crime, with gangs growing increasingly strong and stable, eventually displacing or violently challenging the dominant Italian-American crime families. By the late 1980s, this ethnic recomposition of organized crime had not occurred. African-American groups held on to their communities, dealing principally in narcotics and vices. They never developed a national structure like the Cosa Nostra and its Commission. Why the ethnic succession failed to materialize in the ways anticipated is very speculative. It is assumed that among the Italian crime families, patrilineal kinship ties helped ensure the continuity and loyalty of the enterprise, whereas in the African-American underclass that spawned the gangs in the post–World War II period, family patterns were matrilineal and less orderly. Furthermore, it is believed that the intermarriage among mafiosi, which was quite common, provided the social and psychological bonding that enabled them to survive gang warfare, law enforcement efforts to eradicate them, and challenges from other criminal competitors. This is the standard account as to why African-American organized crime proves to be too short-lived and undisciplined to approach the power of the Mafia.[41] As we shall see, the social, cultural, and historical context in which African-American organized crime developed were those in which racism and its ugly legacies figured prominently. Unlike the traditional criminal groups that emerged out of the immigrant population, African-American organized criminality has had a different and unique historical evolution. Comparisons of La Cosa Nostra with a "Black Mafia" are invalid for any number of reasons. For example, could the Cosa Nostra have developed into a powerful force in the underworld? Could it have consolidated its power in an environment of RICO, electronic surveillance, and special law enforcement agencies whose sole mission is organized crime control? That possibility seems highly improbable today. And then there is the issue of the social and cultural past. The sordid notion of "families," modeled after patriarchal kinship systems with blood ties serving social hegemonic functions, worked well for Italian-Americans but seems irrelevant for African Americans. This fact looms large in law enforcement anticrime efforts, with crime control intelligence-gathering operations and strategic planning dependent upon models of organized crime derived from Mafia models. Indeed, law enforcement may not have a comprehensive, reliable picture of African-American organized crime for precisely these reasons.

To understand how organized crime developed its distinctive style in the African-American communities, we have to return to the early post–Civil War days, when the great masses immigrated from the South and the states that were part of the Confederacy. The men and women emancipated from slavery did not have much time for politics, which were snares best left to abolitionists and radical reformers; opportunities and possibilities for work and survival beckoned in the North and Midwest and prompted the great migration northward into permanent settlements. The repercussions of the African-American presence, en masse, in the white North produced a reaction whose shock waves are still apparent and which created a complex set of factors that molded criminal styles reflecting the dire social realities and conditions that had to be faced.

NOTES

1. 18 U.S.C. (United States Code) 1961(4).

2. United States v. Turkette, 452 U.S. 576 (1981).

3. Robert J. Kelly and Patrick Ryan, "An Analysis of RICO and OCCA: Federal and State Legislature Instruments Against Crime," *International Journal of Violence, Aggression and Terrorism* 9, no. 3 (May 1989): 49–100.

4. Michael Maltz, "Defining Organized Crime" in R. J. Kelly, R. Schatzberg and K. L. Chin, eds., *Handbook of Organized Crime in the United States* (Westport, CT: Greenwood Publishing Group, 1994). Maltz's discussion does not make any references to African-American organized crime. His discussions appear to be based entirely on the La Cosa Nostra and ethnic variations thereof.

5. G. Robert Blakey, "RICO: The Federal Experience—Criminal and Civil" in Kelly, Schatzberg, and Chin, *Handbook of Organized Crime in the United States,* 451–490.

6. RICO (Racketeer Influences and Corrupt Organizations) is the most potent legal weapon against organized crime.

7. The etymological speculations on the origin of the word *Mafia* are wrapped in misinformation, mystery, obfuscation, conjecture, and legend. Possibly it derives from the dialect of Palermo, Sicily, where it connotes pride, self-confidence and macho behavior. About the middle of the nineteenth century, the term *mafioso* became associated with crime. A Sicilian, however, will refer to such a person not as a mafioso but more euphemistically as a "man of honor," or "man of respect," as belonging to the "friends of the friends," or the "society of honor." As for the term *mafia*, it is likely that the word has Arab ancestry, sources probably being the Arab *mafie* (*maha* or *nahias hojoi*) referring to rock caves used by the Saracens in the areas of Trapani and Maisala, and later by secret groups of anti-Bourbon volunteers. The local dialect transformed the sound of *mahias* into *mafia* (see Gaia Servadia, *Mafioso*, New York: Dell Publishing, 1976).

8. In a seminal piece of journalism written more than half a century ago, Walter Lippmann described the two worlds, the upperworld and underworld, as wed together by mutual needs, none of which could be gratified without the existence and abiding interest of the other. See Walter Lippmann, "The Underworld as a Servant of Power," *Forum* (January/February 1931): 162–72.

9. A *cosche* is a group of mafiosi who work for a "man of respect," a *capo*

43

Mafia who himself enjoys prestige and power in a local community.

10. Salvatore Francisco Romano, *Storia della Mafia*, 2d ed., ed. Arnoldo Mondadori, (Verona: 1 Record, 1966); Pino Arlacchi, *Mafia Business: The Mafia Ethics and the Spirit of Capitalism* (London: Verso Press, 1986).

11. Barrington Moore, Jr., *Social Origins of Dictatorship and Democracy* (Boston: Beacon Paperback, 1967).

12. Raimondo Catanzaro, *Men of Respect: A Social History of the Sicilian Mafia*, trans. Raymond Rosenthal, (New York: The Free Press, 1992).

13. Daniel Bell, "Crime as an American Way of Life," *Antioch Review* (Summer 1953): 131–145.

14. Henri Pirenne, "The States in the Social History of Capitalism," *Social Science Reprints* (Indianapolis, IN: Bobbs Merrill).

15. Kenneth Allsop, *The Bootleggers: The Story of Prohibition* (New Rochelle, NY: Arlington House, 1968), 210.

16. Maldwyn Jones, *American Immigration* (Chicago: University of Chicago Press, 1960).

17. Virgil W. Peterson, *The Mob: 200 Years of Organized Crime in New York* (Ottawa, IL: Green Hill Publishers, 1983), 24–32.

18. Quoted in Stephan Fox, *Blood and Power: Organized Crime in Twentieth-Century America* (New York: William Morrow, 1989), 85.

19. Robert Kelly, "The Evolution of Criminal Syndicates," *International Journal of Law Enforcement Intelligence Analysis*, vol. 2, no. 1, (1987): 13–31.

20. Burton Turkus and Sid Feder, *Murder, Inc.* (New York: Manor Books, 1951).

21. Alan Block, *East Side/West Side: Organizing Crime in New York, 1930–1950* (New Brunswick, NJ: Transaction Books, 1983).

22. Peterson, *The Mob*.

23. Charles V. Hamilton, *Adam Clayton Powell, Jr.: The Political Biography of an American Dilemma* (New York: Atheneum, 1991), 430–431; *New York Times*, "Powell Sees Bias in Policy Arrest," Peter Kihss 4 January 1960: 9.

24. Peter Maas, *The Valachi Papers* (New York: Putnam & Sons, 1968).

25. Task Force on Organized Crime, *Task Force Report: Organized Crime* (Washington, DC: U.S. Government Printing Office, 1967).

26. Rudolph Giulini, "Legal Remedies for Attacking Organized Crime," in ed. H. Edelhertz, *Major Issues in Organized Crime Control* (Washington, DC: National Institute of Justice, U.S. Government Printing Office, 1987): 103–130.

27. Robert J. Kelly, Ko-lin Chin, Jeffrey Fagan, "The Dragon Breathes Fire: Chinese Organized Crime in New York City," *Crime, Law and Social Change* 19 (1993): 245–269.

28. Joseph D. Pistone, *Donnie Brasco: My Undercover Life in the Mafia* (New York: New American Library, 1987); Donald Goddard, *Undercover: The Secret Lives of a Federal Agent* (New York: Times Books, 1988); Ovid Demaris, *The Last Mafioso: The Treacherous World of Jimmy Fratianno* (New York: Bantam, 1981); Peter Maas, *The Valachi Papers*; Vincent Teresa and Thomas E. Renner, My Life in the Mafia (Greenwich, CT: Fawcett, 1973).

29. Elliott Currie, *Drugs, the Cities and the American Future* (New York: Hill & Wang, 1993).

30. Ko-lin Chin, Robert J. Kelly, and Jeffrey Fagan, "Patterns of Chinese Gang Extortion," *Justice Quarterly* 9, no. 4 (December 1992): 401–422.

31. U.S. Senate, Mid-Atlantic Region: Hearing before the Permanent Subcommittee on Investigation of the Committee on Governmental Affairs, *Profile of Organized Crime*, 98th Cong., 1st sess., (February 15–24, 1985).

32. President's Commission on Organized Crime, *The Impact*, 65.

33. Yves Lavigne, *Hello Angels: Taking Care of Business* (Toronto: Benoit & Wayne Publishers, 1987).

34. Cheryl L. Maxson and Malcolm W. Klein, "Street Gangs Selling Cocaine Rock: The Confluence of Two Social Problems" (Paper presented at the Society for the Study of Social Problems annual meeting, August 1986).

35. U.S. Senate Hearings before the Permanent Subcommittee on Investigations of Committee on Governmental Affairs, *Organized Crime and the Use of Violence* 96th Cong., 2d sess., (April 28–May 5, 1980).

36. President's Commission on Organized Crime, *Record of Hearing* (29 November 1983–26 June 1985), 1–7.

37. President's Commission on Organized Crime, *Report to the President and the Attorney General: America's Habit—Drug Abuse, Drug Trafficking and Organized Crime* (Washington, DC: U.S. Government Printing Office, March 1986); Donald Goddard, *Easy Money* (New York: Farrar, Straus & Giroux, 1978).

38. President's Commission on Organized Crime, *Organized Crime and Heroin Trafficking* (testimony of Nicky Barnes) (Washington, DC: U.S. Government Printing Office, 1985), 205.

39. Ibid., Papa D's Family, 220–260.

40. U.S. Senate, Great Lakes Region, Hearings before the Permanent Subcommittee on Investigation of the Committee on Governmental Affairs, *Profile of Organized Crime*, 97th Cong., 1st sess., (October 28–November 3, 1984).

41. Robert J. Kelly, "The Nature of Organized Crime and Its Operators" in H. Edelhertz, ed. *Major Issues in Organized Crime Control: Symposium Proceedings.*

3

THE SECOND DIASPORA

AFRICAN-AMERICAN MIGRATIONS IN THE UNITED STATES

*Gentle Reader; for the problem of the Twentieth Century is the
problem of the color line.*
W. E. B. Du Bois, *The Souls of the Black Folk.*[1]

In 1953, fifty years after this famous line was written in the Jubilee Edition,
Du Bois felt obliged to expand on the social prophecy of race and its career.
In a new Preface he added,

> I still think today as yesterday that the color line is a great problem
> in this century. But today I see more clearly than yesterday that back
> of the problem of race and color, lies a greater problem which both
> obscures and implements it: and that is the fact that so many civi-
> lized persons are willing to live in comfort even if the price of this is
> poverty, ignorance and disease of the majority of their fellowmen; that
> to maintain this privilege men have waged war until today war tends
> to become universal and continuous and the excuse for this war con-
> tinues largely to be color and race.[2]

Nothing Du Bois wrote provoked more concern and controversy than
this claim. Although he had been criticized by some for possessing a narrow
view, a tunnel vision about race, leaving untouched the complicated issues of
class and politics, Du Bois had modified and profoundly broadened his conceptions of racial problems in the United States and inspired social scientists
such as E. Franklin Frazier to examine class hierarchies and their economic
consequences on African-American communities. Indeed, it could be shown
that the ideas driving *The Souls of the Black Folk* have universal relevance as
the history of this century winds to its close. Our purpose is not to illustrate
the validity of Du Bois's claim but to see how his insights bear on the prob-

lems of crime in contemporary African-American communities.

Du Bois saw a relationship between crime and the impoverished conditions pervading African-American communities. He implied that the affluence of some segments of society relegates those less able and less acquisitive, and less familiar with the politics of opportunity, to a status of victimhood in which crime takes hold. That has been the legacy for the vast majority of African Americans since slavery: a life of scarce resources, with limited legitimate economic and educational opportunities.

Connected with these realities, African Americans experienced two momentous migrations in the United States: (1) their forced removal from Africa and transport to the New World as slaves, and (2) their migrations as ex-slaves after the Civil War—a migration full of hope and expectation. We begin with a review of the history of the internal migration out of the southern diaspora that changed the demographic structures of the major urban communities in the North and set the stage for subsequent social, political, and economic developments and patterns of African-American criminal opportunities.

AFRICAN AMERICANS IN EARLY NEW YORK

African Americans have been residents of New York City for 368 years. The first arrivals, eleven in all, landed in New Amsterdam in 1626, brought by the West India Company, a Dutch corporation chartered to manage the operations of the newly founded colony, New Amsterdam. Under Dutch rule, New Amsterdam permitted free African Americans to own property, engage in business, and follow any economic opportunities available.

These opportunities were avidly pursued: The municipal archives of the New York City Department of Records and Information Services holds evidence of property ownership by early African Americans. The term *man of color* usually followed the Dutch name of the African American involved in either the purchase or sale of real estate.

That was the Dutch practice: a benign paternalism that tolerated racial difference if these practices were carefully circumscribed by compliance with norms governing intersocial behavior. As the colony grew, attitudes began to change. A few years before the conquest of New Amsterdam by the English, personal ownership of slaves had become the accepted and acknowledged practice and was continued by the British. The British took control of New Amsterdam in September, 1664, renaming it New York. Thereafter, indentured servitude and slavery in New York State lasted for two hundred years, until it was abolished in July, 1827, half a century after the signing of the Declaration of Independence. Even from the very beginnings of the importation into New York, there had been a core of African Americans living freely in the colony.[3]

THE PECULIAR INSTITUTION AND ITS HAUNTING AFTERMATH

Modern American racial views have been shaped by slavery. To place our work in its proper historical social context, we wish to examine how Americans viewed legalized slavery. Although a small number of Americans owned slaves, the practice of legalized slavery concerned most people and as the nineteenth century wore on, slavery took center stage in national debates. In 1850, the total number of slaveholders in the 15 slaveholding states was 347,525 against a total white population numbering about 6 million. Thus, about 6 percent of the population in the slaveholding states owned slaves.[4]

Slavery, the *peculiar institution,* as it has been called by Kenneth Stampp,[5] posed a serious dilemma for freedom-loving early Americans. Many wondered how a relatively small group of slaveholders could treat human beings as mere possessions and at the same time uphold the high-minded American ideal of human equality. To justify slavery, religious, cultural, and racial explanations or, better, rationales, were generated that were scandalous in their attempt to vindicate the practice. Religious theologies of suffering and salvation, which were embedded in the Christian faith and offered some other worldly relief and expiation for both masters and slaves, were forced on slaves.

Quite possibly, many slaves found comfort in myths that claimed suffering on earth would be rewarded abundantly in Paradise. Moreover, the promulgators of Christian notions of God's mysterious will that explained the pain endured in this life as a precursor of glory in the next, also rationalized the system of enslavement for slaveowners. For those who sought to soothe their consciences and ease their guilt, Christianity became a useful intellectual device.

Millions of Africans were brought to the United States during the slave trade, filling the plantations of the southern United States, which utilized their labor in meeting the needs of the mills and factories of Great Britain and the populous Northeast. The ties between Great Britain and the United States, two of the more advanced economic states in the eighteenth and nineteenth centuries, helped to nurture one of the most oppressive and socially backward institutions—plantation slavery. By 1780, nearly 4 million slaves were located in the southern United States.[6]

Three years before President Lincoln issued the Emancipation Proclamation on January 1, 1863, the 1860 census showed the African-American slave population in the United States at about 3,953,760 and free

African Americans numbering some 488,070.[7] At the time, African Americans constituted 14.1 percent of America's population. (Interestingly, the Bureau of Census's *Statistical Abstract of the United States 1991*, showed that in 1989 African Americans represented 12.4 percent of the population, so that in the last 130 years the proportion of African Americans in the United States has actually decreased by 1.7 percent.) From the Civil War onward, general attitudes in the white population were mixed, depending on which section of the country one lived in, and what impact slavery and emancipation had on one's socioeconomic opportunities and values.

Du Bois's prophetic prediction that the twentieth century would witness an effusion of racism in America (and elsewhere) may have been rooted in his insight that slavery meant, among other things, cultural genocide on such a massive scale that its legal erasure from America's political covenants could not succeed completely in abolishing its legacies. It would linger and haunt the country until the former slaves, their ancestors, and the society that held them in bondage could spiritually and psychologically purge themselves of the stereotypes of "us" and "them." Indeed, as Du Bois knew, part of the success of white ethnic assimilation and integration into the American cultural system was the preservation among the immigrants of their ethnic identities and cultures. Perhaps we tend, naturally, to consider the alleged "races" most distant from ours as being the most homogeneous; to whites, all yellow people look alike, and the reverse is no doubt equally true. The real situation seems far more complex, for if former slaves appeared to whites as morphologically and racially homogeneous throughout the United States, nonetheless considerable differences existed among them culturally, linguistically, religiously, and socially. And these differences were almost as great between different ancestral tribes as they were between Africans and Europeans.[8] Contrary to what might have been thought, tribes themselves did not constitute biological unities.[9]

Slaves experienced the mortification of being deracinated and some sought to embrace a pan-African culture that never, in the strict sense, existed.[10] No white immigrants felt so threatened as to think of themselves as "European-Americans." All American immigrant groups draw cultural identity and a measure of spiritual strength from a sense of their original roots—in Sicily or the Ionian Islands, in Ireland or Cuba, in Poland, Russia, Germany, Norway, Holland, and so on. These sentimental questions of origins are powerful tribal instincts. But what the slaves sought in "Africa" was an imagined entity—a lost maternal paradise. Doubtlessly, even in the minds of modern African Americans, few would consider their cultural experience as resembling that of a citizen of South Africa beyond the fact that both have suffered the corrosive and demeaning effects of white racism. The idea of Marcus Garvey that a place was waiting for African Americans in some generalized "Africa" in any but a vaguely metaphorical sense, was mere cultural demagogy whose appeal was a measure of the rage in the minds of a despised minority. Neither blacks nor whites can go home again except as tourists.

The estrangement of the African American is revealed in many ways. Because he or she cannot be white, the African American in white psychological imagery and sentiment is a blank—or, as Ralph Ellison expressed it, an "invisible man." For many African-American artists in the second half of this century, the Aunt Jemima, Uncle Tom, and Sambo stereotypes, these dehumanizing caricatures, were dead. Others working before the civil rights movement saw things in starkly different terms. The painter, Romare Beardon, chose to depict rural and urban scenes of domestic and community life and work through the faceless images of his subjects.

One of the most powerful and celebrated statements of the problem of race and its social effects of isolation and rejection appeared when America was on the verge of entering the Second World War.[11] In *Native Son*, Richard Wright shockingly challenged the magnitude of America's racial delusion. The main character in his novel, Bigger Thomas, crystallized for Wright aspects of African-American life that had not been addressed head on. The book resonates with a cry of bitterness and despair. The explosive interracial scenes end in an act of murder—a taboo murder in which an African-American male involved erotically with a white female violates her sexually and inadvertently kills her from a confused and irrational impulse that silencing her would somehow conceal his act.

What is remarkable is how little we know about Bigger from the beginning of his journey in the tenement to doom and regret in his death cell. The sense of isolation is palpable in the text and perhaps that was Wright's intention: to create in his character a social symbol that is obviously revelatory of a social disease and at the same time prophetic of impending disaster.

The Internal Crossings

Several approaches to the study of the great internal migrations of African Americans have been developed by social scientists. Each focuses on causes and circumstances. In general, it can be said that the Civil War aftermath provided one of the necessary "pushes" that set the masses of newly emancipated slaves in motion. After the Civil War, most emancipated slaves became tenant farmers or sharecroppers, which proved to be a dependency of another kind—yoked to landlords, rents, and debt. Economic bondage was no more endurable than the former slavery; when the economic situation in the South worsened, the "pulls" from the North proved irresistible. As the South stagnated economically during the Industrial Revolution, which was accelerating in Europe and the American North, former slaves were enticed northward. The Ku Klux Klan's angry reaction to the defeated South's moral and social sterility also provided an incentive for African Americans to move on.

The streams of migration after the Civil War joined the large flood of immigrants from Europe. The emergent heterogeneous enclaves of socially diverse classes and races mixed and mingled in the milieu that forged modern African-American societies, replete with their own subcultures. More than 250 thousand African Americans left the South between 1870 and 1910 and of these 190 thousand moved to northeastern states. When the patterns shifted, larger numbers of African Americans moved into the north central states, following the pathway of jobs and opportunities. "The African-American population of the large cities of the North and West," *The New York Age* reported in 1907, "is being constantly fed by a steady stream of new people from the Southern States."[12] Between 1910 and 1920, the population increased from 5 thousand to more than 40 thousand in Detroit and from 92 thousand to more than 150 thousand in New York.

Those who moved North belonged to the post–Civil War generation of restless, dissatisfied people unwilling to accommodate the traditional subservient roles of Southern life. Du Bois wrote that, "the south laments today the slow, steady disappearance of a certain type of Negro—the faithful, courteous slave of other days, with his dignified . . . humility."[13] Young African Americans spoke loudly and unequivocally with their feet. They left the South in search of what Du Bois called the possibility of escaping caste, at least in its most aggravating constraints. Freeing themselves from the pale of slavery and Jim Crow, young people were thus able to imagine new possibilities for themselves in the North.

All over the South, African Americans were swept up by a migration fever like those from Europe, Mexico, and Asia. They were psychologically driven to Chicago, New York, Cleveland, and Philadelphia by the particular *pushes* at home. Still, by 1910, about one fourth of the country's African-American population lived in urban centers, and of this total, almost three fourths lived in Southern cities. There were approximately 750 thousand African Americans in the northern and north central states, and more than one third of these sojourners lived in New York, Philadelphia, Chicago, and St. Louis.

The growth of Harlem's African-American community followed the settlement patterns of the other large, racially segregated communities that evolved in the years preceding and following World War I. That Harlem became the symbolic center of African-American urban life was the result of fortuitous circumstances.

Chicago attracted its proportion of former slaves who were unwilling to accept life in the South. Many who came to Chicago as visitors to the Worlds Fair in 1893 stayed to work.

The First World War shook the nation and altered its racial demographics profoundly. In 1914, as the war gained momentum and ferocity in Europe, the tide of European migration was suddenly reversed. The war cut off the flow of European immigrants, drastically reducing their number to a mere trickle. At the same time, Northern defense industries were facing enormous labor shortages and clamoring for workers. The United States was facing a labor problem while it was transforming itself into an arsenal and granary for Europe's war needs.

Desperate Northern industrialists dispatched labor agents to the South to recruit labor. As with other immigrants, most African Americans followed employment opportunities. Their mass movement out of the South signaled a new era for race relations, an era in which the urban dwellers began to outnumber their rural agrarian counterparts.[14]

Prior to 1914, there had been little to encourage former plantation laborers to leave the South and face the uncertainties of life in Northern city streets. For the first time, Southern African Americans were actually being invited to come North to fill defense jobs. They responded eagerly, and as each wave washed up in Northern cities, the migrants wrote the folks back home about the available jobs and a number of relatives and friends followed. A bewildered South, facing the possibility of a land left desolate for lack of labor, attempted to halt the exodus. Drake and Cayton point out in their work on the migration that Southern states feared the loss of their African-American population and took rather drastic steps to slow down the demographic hemorrhaging. Action was taken in the following locations:

Florida—city fathers in Jacksonville passed an ordinance requiring labor recruiters from the North to buy a $1,000 license or take the alternative of sixty days in jail and a $600 fine.

Georgia—the Macon city council exacted a recruiting license fee of $25,000 and demanded that the labor agent be recommended by ten local ministers, ten manufacturers, and twenty-five businessmen.

Alabama—fines and jail sentences were imposed upon any *person, firm, or corporation* guilty of *enticing, persuading, or influencing* labor to leave Montgomery.

Mississippi—agents were arrested, trains stopped, ticket agents intimidated. At Brookhaven, a chartered car carrying fifty men and women was deliberately sidetracked for three days.[15]

THE URBAN CRUCIBLE

By 1930, some two million African Americans had moved permanently to Northern cities. "The migration is probably, next to emancipation, the most noteworthy event which has ever happened to the Negro in America."[16] For the first time in their experience, the former slaves were able to develop a viable society that was, for the most part, under their own cultural control. The social bonding and cohesion of values were so intense that by 1920 the Harlem community became renowned as "the recognized Negro Capital" of America.[17]

Although migration held out new hope, the flip side meant uncertainties and hardship. Adjustments and accommodations were difficult and were made more acute by the realities of job loss and housing competition. These fears materialized quickly in the economic slowdown following World War I, when women could often find work as domestics while men found themselves shut out of employment, not so much by their lack of skills as by fierce racial discrimination. Consequently, a disorientation of the African-American dream and its institutions began to set in.[18]

Conflicts over housing intensified as property values depreciated when African Americans settled in communities. The schools became racial battlegrounds, but it was in the factories and workplaces that fear, hostility, and rejection made clear the attitudes of the dominant white society. Managers and factory owners employed African Americans to exploit them with lower wages, and to subvert the union-organizing activities of white workers.[19] By cynically dividing the workforce racially, employers were able to take advantage of everyone.

So long as the larger white community practiced systematic discrimination, African Americans in Chicago were encouraged to establish their own self-sufficient communities that would include banks, insurance companies, retail stores, churches, and schools.[20]

Decades before, the European immigration brought substantial numbers of Irish and German immigrants to New York.[21] By 1850, they drove free African Americans out of menial labor and service jobs, with Irishmen taking over carpentry and Irish women, domestic service; German and Slavic immigrants dominated the construction industries. Shortly before the Civil

War, Irish longshoremen threatened to tie up the port if African-American dockhands were not summarily dismissed.[22]

Systematic occupational deprivation was often compounded by psychological mortifications in cities such as New York, Boston, and other ports with teeming immigrant populations. As their numbers increased and as they threatened to compete with white migrant labor, African Americans were rudely pushed aside from occupations they had traditionally held.

When the troops returned in 1919, the familiar patterns of racial discrimination resumed. High levels of unemployment became widespread; the low-cost housing stock built by speculators in Harlem that first lured African Americans now imprisoned them. Rents could be raised with impunity, owing to a deepening segregation throughout the city, so that housing markets were sealed off. In the 1920s, the experience of segregated real estate exploitation and African-American unemployment (high rents and low wages) spawned the urban slum.

Harlem and other communities in Chicago, Detroit, St. Louis, and Cleveland were the first step from a rural, folk-type existence into the vortex of urban industrialism. A move north across the Mason–Dixon line was a crossing from feudalism to modernism, and in every respect was as unnerving as the transatlantic migrations of millions of Europeans. But the naturally apprehensive European immigrants were filled with optimism, and for many the dream of success eventually materialized, even if deferred by a generation or two. What they possessed and were able to sustain was confidence that they would be accepted, which was more or less guaranteed by white skin. For African Americans, the internal migration was at once a psychological death and transformative rebirth. Indeed, it was now possible for a former slave, a farm laborer, to see a grandchild develop the sensitive hands of a surgeon, and grandparents who may have believed in tribal magic could watch their grandchildren prepare for a career in nuclear physics. In short, Northern African-American communities symbolized a fluid, shifting world in which the real and fantastic often merged. However, the grim side of life was and remained overpowering, with all of one's energy absorbed by the frustrations of race. Not quite accepted as citizens by the vast white majority, but more American than all except the Native American, the desperate search for identity was filled with tensions and conflicts that could neither be contained nor resolved. Some sought relief in alcohol and drugs; others, through religion, and still others, in despair, turned their resentment aggressively outward against others.

The Southern diaspora at the end of the Civil War read like a legend of a tragic people in a mythology: people escaping an unhappy homeland to the apparent peace of a distant mountain (a term with significant symbolic meaning for many African-American intellectuals). The pre–World War I population movement, the advance guard of the Great Migration, as the movement of African Americans during the First World War is commonly called, laid the foundations for present-day communities in the great metropolitan centers of Chicago, Detroit, and Cleveland, and it was driven in large part by dreams of freedom and social salvation.[23]

The movement north also meant abandoning a relatively static social order, but that caste system, as brutal as it was, enabled the individual to develop useful survival techniques tested in life-and-death encounters against the daily precarious experience of life in the white South. These supports and protections, no matter how quaint they may now seem, buttressed a system of social rationality of inestimable value. Exchanging these for the fulfillment of utopian dreams in the North, but confounded by the humiliations of exclusion, brought about a loss of more than economic opportunities and privileges; these realities opened even the most stable individual to despair and anxiety when subjected to segregation and discrimination. Instead, an individual was thrown back into the slum of filth, disorder, and hate. Families disintegrated, churches splintered, and individuals found themselves displaced and emotionally adrift.

Still, the dreadful living and working conditions of millions, exacerbated by prejudice and discrimination, did not dim the visions of Southern newcomers who were hopeful and ambitious, much like their European counterparts. In spite of the growing apartheid and caste-like quality of social life, an African-American Harlem community emerged as the center for what Langston Hughes called the "New Negro Renaissance."[24] The great irony of racism, the ghettoized slum, was transformed into a Harlem with its cabarets, artistic and literary activities.

Harlem

In the 1920s, Harlem as an African-American community bulged with individuals of all social classes, from unskilled Southern farmworkers and West Indian migrants to professional elites. Many literary works refer to this period as the "Harlem Renaissance."[25] It was a period characterized by vigorous literary and artistic activity. For African-American intellectuals, Harlem was a cultural magnet drawing people from all sections of the world. Six notable literary talents, the writers and poets, blossomed in the postwar period: James Weldon Johnson, Langston Hughes, Sterling Brown, Claude McKay, Jean Toomer, and Countee Cullen.

As the sections inhabited by people of color became suitable areas for business expansion, and as the European immigrant population swelled, the need for housing displaced the former, who were rudely forced to seek living space in other sections of the city. In 1840, the bulk of the African-American population lived in the squalor of the Five Points District, located in the vicinity of New York's City Hall. Within two decades, the Five Points District became overwhelmingly Irish. There followed a movement up the West Side of Manhattan to an area between the west Twenties and the west Fifties, known as the Tenderloin District; others located a little farther up Manhattan in the west Sixties.

From 1902 to 1905, when underground mass transit was installed (the subway), real estate fever seized New York. The frenzied speculation in property permeated the air and speculators grasped at opportunities to make money by investing in property accessible to the subway system, betting that it would increase land values. In 1904, the year that the Lenox Avenue Line opened at 145th Street, practically all the vacant land in Harlem was built over. The Equitable and Metropolitan Life Insurance Companies invested heavily in Harlem real estate. "The existing speculation in flats and tenements surpasses anything of the kind which has previously taken place in the real estate history of the city."[26] Through the efforts of African-American real estate agencies, Harlem became the community's center of gravity.

At the beginning of World War I some white groups, such as the City and Suburban Homes Company, built homes in Harlem and rented to African Americans, but the real effort was carried by African-American realtors. A celebrated African-American realty firm, the Afro-American Realty Company, headed by Philip A. Payton, was hailed by James Weldon Johnson:

> When Negro New Yorkers evaluate their benefactors in their race, they must find that not many have done more than Phil Payton for much of what has made Harlem the intellectual and artistic capital of the Negro world is in good part due to this fundamental advantage; Harlem has provided New York Negroes with better, cleaner, more modern, more airy, more sunny houses than they ever lived in before. And this is due to the efforts made by Mr. Payton.[27]

In short, Harlem provided some of the best housing facilities available. "In fact, Harlem offered the colored people the first chance in their entire history in New York to live in modern apartment houses."[28] To describe Harlem merely in terms of its middle-class inhabitants and their neighborhoods, like "Strivers Row" or "Sugar Hill" would be a disingenuous distortion of class occupational realities, and the conditions under which most Harlemites lived.

Manhattan in 1925 had an African-American population density of 336 persons per acre and a white population density of 223 persons per acre.[29] Although Harlem contained its share of poor housing, many observers would agree that it was the "home of the best-housed Negroes in the world."[30] Better housing brought social stability by attracting the more affluent to Harlem.[31] And by 1920, 45.2 percent of New York City's 152,467 African Americans lived in Harlem.

Constrained generally by the white community's restrictive, unwritten social codes and economic apartheid, Harlem developed its own world—a segregated world, a world with its own churches, associations, entertainment facilities, and cultural life. Nonetheless, despite the segregation, Harlem's microcosm complied with the basic social pattern of New York City. Life in Harlem and Bedford-Stuyvesant moved to the patterned institutions of the larger society, but by the very fact of their exclusion from the wider community, those living in Harlem gave their own meaning to the dominant culture of white society.[32] To be sure, these were only minor variations on the dominant social values. Still, as Richard Bardolph claims, the communal life was a "black replica of white American culture on his own side of the line."[33]

Harlem is Nowhere

Nowadays, to live in Harlem[34] is to dwell in the bowels of the city, as Ralph Ellison put it. There are churches, many of them small, modest, and some lavishly appointed, such as the Abyssinian Baptist Church from whose altar Martin Luther King and some of the most charismatic religious leaders of the time have spoken. And today, in the midst of Pentecostal houses and grand churches are stately mosques in which some of the same hopes and dreams are given a new voice and sense of a future.

Much of the surrounding community, however, is a ruin. For James Baldwin, who grew up in Harlem and whose autobiographical novel *Go Tell It on the Mountain* is set in the ghetto, its ordinary aspects—the crime, the casual violence, the dilapidated buildings and littered streets—are indistinguishable from the fleeting images haunting the overcrowded and exploited scene that is the essence of alienation. It all folds, dream-like, in upon itself—hope and despair, and then resolve and determination and more hope. It is an uneasy, fragile psychology that grips the community.

It would be easy to conclude that the cultural and social institutions of the community then and now are simply the product of a racist-inspired social pathology, as Gunnar Myrdal asserts in his *American Dilemma*. Myrdal's solution to this is to urge African-American assimilation into American culture, which means acquiring the traits held in esteem by the dominant white society. The assumptions and implications in such recommendations are worth examining closely because the realities of community life are suggestive of how African Americans dealt with these issues. James Baldwin put the question succinctly: Why should we want to be integrated into a burning house? For Myrdal and others, it may not have occurred to them that African-American subcultural styles may be as much a rejection of the larger mainstream white culture as a contorted reflection of it.

A complicated dualism is at work where African-American culture (to the extent that it is distinctive) is a partial turning away from white patterns. Exclusionary practices do indeed give rise to counter or alternative values and lifestyles. However, the short of it is that no people can live in a perpetual state of "reaction." Consequently, the institutional organization of African-American communities is both an appropriation of mainstream culture and an invention of its own.

It is in this context that the examination of organized crime should illuminate some of the cultural and institutional dynamics at work in the community. For chronological purposes, we begin with the dynamics of the informal economy and then turn to the evolution of gambling activities in pre–World War II Harlem. In this social, economic, and political incubus, organized criminality emerged. Over time, as we shall see, crises transformed the communities. The earlier folklorist solidarity that knitted African Americans together into socially coherent wholes crumbled. Community life became more complex, chaotic, and more violent and, paradoxically, more stable and strong.

NOTES

1. W. E. B. Du Bois, *The Souls of the Black Folk: Essays and Sketches* (New York: The New American Library, 1969), xi.

2. Idem., *The Souls of Black Folk* (New York: Fawcett-Jubilee Edition), xiv.

3. James W. Johnson, *Black Manhattan* (New York: Alfred A. Knopf, 1968); (New York: Arno Press and the *New York Times*, 1940 reprint), 4–11; James E. Allen, *The Negro in New York* (New York: Exposition Press, 1964), 11–12.

4. J. G. Randall and David H. Donald, *The Civil War and Reconstruction*, 2d ed. (Lexington, MA: D.C. Heath & Co., 1969), 67.

5. Kenneth M. Stampp, *Peculiar Institution: Slavery in the Ante-Bellum South* (New York: Alfred A. Knopf, 1956).

6. Vincent Harding, *The Other American Revolution* (Los Angeles: University of California Center for Afro-American Studies, Monograph Series No. 4, 1980).

7. U.S. Department of Commerce, *Historical Statistics of the United States: Colonial Times to 1970* (Washington, DC: Bureau of Census, p. 1, 1975), 18.

8. Basil Davidson, *Africa in History* (London: Cambridge University Press,

1984); and Roland Oliver, *The African Experience* (London: Cambridge University Press, 1991), esp. chap. 10.

9. Claude Levi-Strauss, *The View from Afar* (New York: Basic Books, 1985), chap. 1.

10. Eric J. Hobsbawm, *The Invention of Tradition* (New York: Cambridge University Press, 1983).

11. Richard Wright, *Native Son* (New York: Harper & Row, 1966, originally published in 1940.)

12. Ronald Takagi, *A Different Mirror: A History of Multicultural America* (Boston: Little, Brown, 1993), chap. 13.

13. Du Bois, *Souls of the Black Folks*, 310.

14. U.S. Department of Commerce, *Historical Statistics of the United States, Colonial Times to 1970, Bicentennial Edition.*, 12. In 1910 there were 2.76 million African Americans living in urban settings and 7.45 million in rural areas. By 1920, the African-American urban population increased to 3.68 million and the rural population decreased to 7.2 million. By 1930, the African-American urban population rose to 6.1 million and the rural area population increased to 7.79 million. In twenty years (1910–1930) the urban population increased 119 percent and the rural population increased 4.5 percent. It may be presumed that the African-American urban increases in population were caused by blacks entering the United States. The rural population seems to have remained fairly constant during the period.

15. St. Clair Drake and Horace R. Cayton, *Black Metropolis*, vol. 1 (New York: Harper Torchbooks, 1962), 58–59.

16. Allan H. Spear, *Black Chicago: The Making of a Negro Ghetto, 1890–1920* (Chicago: University of Chicago Press, 1967), 157.

17. Johnson, *Black Manhattan*, 3.

18. Lee Rainwater and William L. Yancey, *The Moynihan Report and the Politics of Controversy* (Cambridge, MA: Howard University Press, 1967).

19. Gunnar Myrdal, *An American Dilemma* (New York: Harper & Row, 1944).

20. Spears, *Black Chicago*, 221; Drake and Cayton, *Black Metropolis*, 80.

21. Herman D. Bloch, *Circle of Discrimination: An Economic and Social Study of the Black Man in New York* (New York: New York University Press, 1969); Johnson, *Black Manhattan*.

22. Jim Sleeper, *The Closest of Strangers: Liberation and the Politics of Race in New York* (New York: W.W. Norton, 1990), chap. 1.

23. Gilbert Osofsky, *Harlem: The Making of a Ghetto* (New York: Harper Torchbooks, 1968).

24. Nathan I. Higgins, *Harlem Renaissance* (New York: Oxford University Press, 1971).

25. Johnson, *Black Manhattan*; Jervis Anderson, *This Was Harlem—A Cultural Portrait* (New York: Farrar, Straus, Giroux, 1982); David L. Lewis, *When Harlem Was in Vogue* (New York: Vintage Books, 1982).

26. Osofsky, *Harlem*, 78.

27. Johnson, *Black Manhattan*, 148.

28. Ibid., 147.

29. Thomas J. Woofter, *Negro Problems in Cities* (New York: Doubleday, Doran & Co., 1928), 79.

30. Seth Scheiner, *Negro Mecca: A History of the Negro in New York City, 1865–1920* (New York: Syracuse University Press, 1965), 35.

31. Ibid, 35.

32. Ibid, 37.

33. Richard Bardolph, *The Negro Vanguard* (New York: Vintage Books, 1961), 12.

34. The title is freely appropriated from Ralph Ellison, *Shadow and Act* (New York: Random House, 1964).

4

THE UNDERGROUND ECONOMY

INFORMAL INFRASTRUCTURES

In his often blistering study of the rise of the African-American middle class, E. Franklin Frazier alludes to "policy" as a criminal racket that was more than just an illegal enterprise that came to life in poor communities.[1] For Frazier, the class divergence with traditional folk culture was apparent in the lifestyles and consumption patterns of a "Black Bourgeoisie" immersed in the "sporting life" of racket bosses and criminal underworld figures. Indeed, the relationships between an emergent middle class and a ghetto underworld went deeper than the adulatory imitation of conspicuous consumption habits. Many African-American professionals, identifying themselves as middle class were involved in gambling activities, and not just as players.[2]

Frazier's moral condemnations notwithstanding, until the passage of the civil rights laws in the 1960s, exclusionary customs significantly affected African-American participation in the local and national economy and in the national political process. In purely economic terms, policy is a form of gambling; it is also a capital resource being circulated throughout a community, generating a livelihood for some and expectations for many others. It may also be understood as a response to the economic apartheid operating in the community. Being illegal, policy operated outside of the law but did not conduct its enterprises secretively: policy, or the numbers game, was openly played in the ghetto streets, storefronts, and social establishments. Few feared arrest; most played regularly and avidly, dreaming of winning to help pay bills, buy a refrigerator or radio, visit relatives in the South, or give the children a respite from the squalor of the big-city streets.

Throughout the 1920s, in Harlem and other emerging African-American communities in which policy number enterprises existed, it is instructive to note the role that numbers gambling played in those urban communities. The historic emergence of gambling and how it relates to the collective behavior of those communities may be understood as informal economic instruments that substituted for the legitimate commercial institutions that had abandoned the community.

LOTTERIES

America's earliest experience with lotteries dates from 1612 in the beleaguered settlement of Jamestown, Virginia.[3] From their inception, both legal and illegal lotteries had been popular in America. Many early American lotteries were private ventures that usually made money for their operators. In the middle of the eighteenth century, although popular and presumably honest, lotteries were banned throughout the colonies. According to Asbury, early lotteries were prohibited for moral reasons: "Principally for reasons similar to those given by the Rhode Island Legislature in 1733—by these unlawful games, called Lotteries, many people have been led into a foolish expense of money."[4]

But because colonial America urgently needed roads, defenses, bridges, schools, and churches, the political and economic reality of the period quickly changed colonists' attitudes toward lotteries as wasteful spending. The people wanted them, believing that they could be kept honest and that the funds derived could reduce taxes.[5] By 1744, lotteries were revived in all the American colonies. They thrived as another addition to the usual methods of public and private financing.[6]

Citizens were even willing to circumvent the law, if need be, when a church or a school would benefit. Asbury suggests that lottery playing was, "the only method of gambling that ever won the approval of all classes in this country."[7] By the first quarter of the nineteenth century, lotteries were an accepted feature of life in America. Interestingly, misuses and abuses attached to any phase of the business in this time period were not reported. No attempt will be made here to review the origins of lotteries; numerous authoritative accounts have done this.[8] What is of particular interest is the variety of lotteries, lottery policy, numbers, and the supportive structures necessary for their operations.

The Organization of a Lottery

Lottery, lottery policy, and numbers are all games of chance in which picking the right numbers decides the winners. However, each of the game's winners are determined differently. The term *lottery, lottery policy* (also referred to as *policy insurance*), and *numbers* are commonly misused. The term *policy* describes all number games in which numbers are used to pick winners.

Operating legal lotteries in the eighteenth and early nineteenth centuries usually involved a group of citizens who would petition the state government for permission to set up a lottery to satisfy a need for a religious or social improvement program that could not be readily financed by voluntary donations or taxes. With state legislatures, then as now, unwilling to levy new taxes to finance projects, a lottery might be authorized. Formal authorization would set the number of awards and the amount each winning ticket would receive.[9]

Fifteen percent of the total sales were deducted for the benefit of the lottery operators. The remaining money would be used to pay the winners. Illegally run lotteries followed the same formats except, of course, they were not sanctioned by state legislatures. The ventures that were not legislatively approved were usually endorsed by a local community organization.

A lottery started with a book in which each page was divided into three columns. The innermost column contained tickets numbered one to 13,350.[10] The tickets in the outermost column were cut out of the book and signed by one of the managers and handed to the purchaser. When all the chances in the outside column had been sold, the tickets in the middle column were clipped, rolled up, and put into a box marked A. The tickets in the innermost column were left in the book as a backup should frauds or mistakes be suspected.[11]

The prizes were determined in a second book containing two columns of 13,350 unnumbered tickets, in which 4,821 tickets would be designated as "fortunate" and had a prize printed across the ticket's face, and the remaining tickets were *blanks* with no prize. All the tickets were cut from the book and sealed in box B.

On the day of the drawing, the lottery managers publicly opened the two boxes and drew tickets from each box; the tickets from box A were matched to the ticket from box B. If the B ticket indicated a prize, the number and the prize were recorded. The drawing continued until the billets were exhausted. The "fortunate" numbers and prizes were published in local newspapers. This procedure generally took months to complete.[12]

Sometime during the 1820s, a new way of operating lotteries using the *ternary combination principle* was introduced. It was expected to save time and stop policy insurance. It did not stop policy insurance playing; it merely changed the way lottery policy insurance was played. Using this new method, winning numbers could be drawn in fifteen minutes.

The ternary combination principle prospered and survived as a gambling technique into the twentieth century. Twelve numbers were drawn at one time from a pool of seventy-eight numbers. The ticket bearing the first three numbers, drawn in order of their appearance, won the capital prize; the fourth, fifth, and sixth numbers drawn won the second prize, and so on, until the tenth, eleventh, and twelfth numbers drawn won the fourth prize. A combination of the second, third, and fourth numbers received the fifth award, and so on. Tickets with two drawn numbers won smaller prizes, as did those with one number. As many as thirty thousand prizes were offered in a single lottery. The remaining tickets that did not possess any of twelve drawn numbers were blanks and did not receive a prize.[13]

Besides buying a lottery ticket, players could place a bet on an individual number: one of the twelve numbers, or a combination of numbers picked from the seventy-eight numbers. This was known as buying a *lottery insurance policy*.

Lottery Policy Insurance Numbers

Sullivan suggests that this peculiar form of lottery policy, betting on individual numbers, was well known and in use as early as 1748 in the United States.[14] Other authors[15] indicate that the term policy started in the London lottery shops in the first half of the eighteenth century, when lottery ticket dealers—as a sideline to their business—sold insurance on numbers. The London shops tried to reach players who could not afford to buy a whole ticket or a share of a ticket, and sold players an insurance policy on numbers of their choice. The player could wager as little as a penny. The sales slips were called an *insurance policy* or a *lottery policy*. The clerks who recorded these bets and the runners who drummed up trade on the outside were known as *insurance solicitors*.[16]

Policy insurance attracted no particular attention until after the American Revolution. By 1800, although playing had not yet begun to reach into the lowest stratum of American society, taking the pennies of the poor became part of every drawing. Interestingly, during the late nineteenth century, many states outlawed lotteries without making betting on other state lotteries illegal.[17]

Before the development of the ternary combination system, the physical act of drawing out the tickets consumed weeks and even months, depending on how many tickets were drawn each day. On the day of the drawing only a certain portion of the "lots" were taken from the *wheel*. This allowed a person to bet that a particular number would be drawn the next day, according to a ratio of decreasing odds. The agent gambled one pound against one shilling, or a like amount, that the speculator could not name what number would be drawn. In another variation, wagers were taken on whether a ticket would be an *award* or a *blank*.

TABLE 4.1. Terms and Odds of Some Lottery Bets

Day Number—Any number from 1 to 78 played to be one of the numbers drawn, and to appear anywhere on the winning list. The odds paid 5 to 1.

Station Number—A number played to appear in a specified position on the list. The odds paid 60 to 1.

Saddle—Two numbers to appear anywhere on the list. The odds paid 32 to 1.

Station Saddle—Two numbers to appear at specified positions on the list. The odds paid 800 to 1.

Capital Saddle—Two of the first three numbers drawn. The odds paid 500 to 1.

Gig—Three numbers, to appear anywhere on the list. The odds paid 200 to 1.

Flat Gig—Three numbers to appear at specified position. The odds paid 1,000 to 1.

Horse—Four numbers to appear anywhere on the list. The odds paid 680 to 1.

Cross Play—A bet on any of the combinations, the numbers to appear on either of two drawings. The same odds prevailed as on straight plays, but 20 percent was deducted from all winnings.

Source: Herbert Asbury, *Sucker's Progress: An Informal History of Gambling in America from the Colonies to Canfield* (New York: Dodd Mead & Co., 1938), 92–93.

Lottery policy insurance is credited with being the cause of most of the fraud and dishonesty in lottery drawings. It made enormous revenues for the operators in which neither the state nor official bodies shared. The New York State Legislature in 1819 showed that in three days a New York City lottery office made $31,000 in insurance bets alone.[18]

The terms in Table 4.1 identify specific policy bet combinations used by players in the nineteenth century.[19] The terms are still in use where this type of lottery policy is played. The odds in Table 4.1 may vary with different houses. Complex combinations were designed to give the player more chances to win.

In the early nineteenth century, lottery brokers, similar to modern day security underwriters, became vendors for the sale of tickets. These representatives bought the tickets from a state "at a discount and marketed them at face value throughout the country."[20] The dealers who administered the promotion of drawings often received additional commissions.[21] These vendors became so expert in all aspects of finance that they resembled the role of mercantile bankers. Blakey reported, "The Chase National Bank and the First National Bank of New York City were founded by lottery brokers."[22]

THE ORIGINS OF CLEARING HOUSE BANK TOTALS NUMBERS

The beginnings and use of clearing house numbers in Harlem are blurry. How and when these numbers first came into use in policy has not been clearly documented. According to Claude McKay, "The early history of the founding and growth of the numbers industry in Harlem is unknown . . . it has a Mediterranean background . . ."[23]

McKay alleges that the origin of the numbers game in Harlem developed when African Americans in the early decades, 1910–1920, were joined by Puerto Rican and Cuban barbers who set up the operations in their shops. They had a large African-American patronage, chiefly those from the British West Indies, many of whom had worked in Cuba and Central and South America before coming to the United States and were familiar with Latino customs. He credits these African Americans in tagging the name "numbers" to the game. Originally, the pastime was known as "Bolita" or "Paquerita," so named by the Hispanic barbers. It was the West Indians' participation in the game that popularized it. McKay's commentary speaks to the popularity of numbers:

> It was introduced to Harlem by a Spaniard from Cataluna, who was nicknamed Catalan by the Spanish speaking Harlemites. Catalan devised his system of playing the numbers from the financial figures of the Stock Exchange. Familiar as he must have been with the method of the Spanish lottery, this could not have been a difficult job. The playing number was deduced from the totals of domestic and foreign sales . . . As the financial figures printed in the newspapers are exact, there could be no trickery. The numbers game has gripped all of Harlem precisely because there is no obvious trickery in it. It is an open, simple and inexpensive game of chance.[24]

The New York Age, a leading Harlem weekly newspaper with a large circulation, attacked in its headlines unlawful activities such as illicit alcohol abuse and gambling in the Harlem community. During the 1920s, they published a weekly list of over one hundred "Hooch Joints" (speakeasies) locations where illegal alcohol was being sold. These locations were reported to the police in an effort to have them closed. In 1924, the newspaper gave the following account of the genesis of the clearing house numbers game in Harlem:

> Data recently received by *The New York Age* indicates that the Clearing House numbers game in its present form is a modification of the New England Clearing House Lottery, which was operating three or four years ago, with the *Boston Globe* financial reports given as the official and final basis of settling. Promoters of this lottery sent out cards giving examples of how prizes were to be paid and two sets were given, for Boston Clearing House reports and another for New York. On the reverse side, these cards stated that: this new game is driving them all out. Being played in Massachusetts, Rhode Island, Connecticut, New Hampshire, Maine, and New York. Playing over a year now. And the data at hand extends back to 1920, indicating the Clearing House numbers gambling has been going on for at least five years. In the New England game a series of tickets is issued, numbered serially, offering four hundred and twenty daily and 1,620 weekly prizes. Tickets are fifty cents each. The New York bankers let the player pick any number or set of numbers they want to and any sum can be played on a number from one cent up. [25]

Redding gives another version of how the numbers game is alleged to have started in the Harlem community. He credits Casper Holstein as its author.

> No one seems to know exactly, where or with whom the numbers game originated, but the most authentic tradition has it that it began with a West Indian Negro—one Holstein, who combined the prosaic traits of a financier with the dizzy imaginative flights of a fingerless Midas. Though, the story goes, before his rise to affluence he seldom had one dime to rub against the other, he studied the financial press with feverish interest. Arriving in New York just before the old policy game was wiped out, he learned one rewarding lesson—that everybody everywhere desired to get rich quickly, and that this desire could be cashed in on. When he rose to wealth and position—contributing to Negro education, donating annually a substantial literary prize, and taking hundreds of the poorer Negro children up the Hudson each summer—he condemned the desires which his skillful manipulations had made a source of vast wealth for himself. But earlier he had not

been so mellow a philosopher, so kind-hearted a benefactor. He had been a Fifth Avenue store porter with an eye for the stock market reports and the shrewdness of a racetrack tout.

Came the day when, studying clearing house totals, an idea struck Holstein between the eyes. Tradition has it that sitting in his airless janitor's closet, surrounded by brooms and mops, he let out an uproarious laugh, and in general acted like a drunken man. That night when the pavement had been swept and the last clerk had gone, he sat in the basement until dawn studying the clearing house totals in the papers he had saved religiously. He had them from a year back. The thought that the figures differed each day played in his mind like a wasp in an empty room. It did not immediately occur to him how he was to use this information, so for six months he thought it over, meantime stacking the dollars he could pinch from his porter's wages. At last he devised the simple scheme of selecting three digits, two from the first and one from the second total by an unvarying rule, and having bets placed upon guessing the number. Thus, if the clearing house totals appeared 8,356,201 and 6,497,000 the winning number would be 567. He offered odds of 600–1.

In a year he owned three of the finest apartment buildings in Harlem, a fleet of expensive cars, a home on Long Island, and several thousand acres of farmland in Virginia.[26]

Holstein was considered by many to have been the foremost policy king in Harlem during the 1920s. In 1926, Carl Van Vechten depicted life in Harlem during the early 1920s. A character in the book, Randolph Pettijohn, the "Bolita King," is Van Vechten's fictional characterization of Casper Holstein.[27] In real life, Holstein was the owner of a popular club in Harlem, the Turf Club, located at 111 West 136th Street. In September 1928, Holstein was reported to have been kidnapped by white gangsters who demanded a $50,000 ransom for his release. The event was widely reported in the media. The Holstein kidnapping is discussed in chapter 5.

Clearing House Bank Totals Numbers Game

To know lotteries were administered before 1920 is helpful in understanding the changes that clearing house bank numbers made in the playing of numbers. The clearing house bank totals are published in daily newspapers. Using totals creates random numbers from 000 to 999. The lottery policy numbers were determined by a drawing conducted by its operators, whose results were then published and distributed to the players, a complicated process, to say the least, and one subject to manipulation and fraud.

The difference between lottery policy numbers (twelve numbers drawn from a pool of seventy-eight numbers) and clearing house totals numbers (a random three-digit number selected from the clearing house bank totals) significantly changed the policy racket. The differences in administration sparked the growth of the numbers business. In lottery policy numbers, a structured organization was necessary to figure out the winning numbers and then to distribute the information to the players; clearing house policy numbers, on the other hand, were published in daily newspapers, where anyone could figure out the winning number. This difference made it possible for individual entrepreneurial persons to start banking policy numbers without the necessity of a large administrative organization. Moreover, and most important, the players gained confidence in the clearing house operation.

To determine the winning number, the following procedure was followed: Using the last two figures from the millions column of the *exchange's* total ($831 million), for example, a *31* was selected, and the third digit, a *2* was selected from the last column of the *balances'* total ($92 million). These were combined to form the three-digit number *312*. The winning three-digit numbers paid 600 to 1. The "Bolita" numbers were determined by using the first two or the last two digits of the number 312, forming *31* or *12*. Winning a "Bolita" paid 80 to 1.

In the early days of the clearing house policy numbers game, it needed no more than a collector who picked up policy bets from players and a banker to finance the operation. Early bankers were also collectors who banked their own work, and some bankers eager to expand their operation would take on additional collectors.

Once the operation expanded to a point at which the volume of bets collected required an office staff to sort out the winning numbers, the banker was considered a "big bank." Collectors received 20 percent of their collection and another 10 percent of the winnings from winning players.

In the early 1920s, a local Harlem newspaper reported that about thirty policy banks existed in Harlem, with each engaging twenty to thirty numbers collectors.[28] In June 1924, a Cuban named Marcellina Cardena was alleged to have been the biggest clearing house numbers banker in Harlem, employing more than 100 numbers runners.[29]

Thus, the beginnings of a well-organized criminal enterprise were under way. It is important to note what policy was not, as well as what it involved in terms of criminal categories and activities.

Two structural factors are of particular interest because they represent a nuanced variation on standard definitions of organized crime that, since 1967 at least, possess the characteristics of the archetypical Mafia family. The La Cosa Nostra's (LCN) image of organized crime has been so powerful that it often blinds us to other potential forms of the phenomenon. Numbers was not a murderous or dangerous racket, such as drug trafficking or violent extortion. We can think of numbers/policy gambling as illicit entrepreneurial behavior at the edge of legality, where ambiguity and controversy were common attributes.

The Wickersham Commission pointed to the "spectrum of legitimacy" and criminal frauds as "the more important branch of organized crime." The description fits the policy operations that evolved in Harlem:

> Such criminal schemes shade off by imperceptible degrees into enterprises which are so conducted as to avoid criminal liability although employing unethical or even illegal methods of doing business; and "the line between the criminal and noncriminal activity is thus frequently a rather arbitrary one" . . . and the typical criminal of this class is not the bandit or the recidivist, but the business man gone wrong.[30]

Policy may be understood as a species of organized crime not comparable to Italian-American LCN crime families but rather as a form of illicit enterprise in that it extended legitimate business techniques and market tactics into areas normally proscribed (i.e., beyond existing limits of the law) for the pursuit of profits and in response to latent illicit demands.[31]

Conventional descriptions of enterprise tend to assume that the marketplace and business activity end at the lip of legitimacy. But policy shows that the legal boundary can change arbitrarily—abruptly shutting off segments of the legitimate marketplace or revealing market areas that had been previously hidden. As Prohibition demonstrated, the law does not necessarily end demand. Depending upon the nature of that demand, a market can continue to exist under proscription, as policy did. The question is whether policy was any less of an enterprise when it was declared illegal.

With Holstein's innovations, the clearing house number represented an innovative mediating technology linking clients and customers more closely. But, as we shall see, Holstein and other Harlem policy operators failed to protect their markets and core technologies adequately. This was not so elsewhere: In Chicago and Detroit, African-American racketeers shrewdly assessed their task environments and developed the necessary mechanisms to insure the viability of their enterprises. In almost all cases, with the exception of Harlem, buffering devices (joint operations with white syndicates; adequate payoffs to police; arming and hiring professional gunmen, etc.), and territorial agreements were reached with competitors and law enforcement regulatory agencies. In Harlem, the lack of political influence had dire consequences for the policy banks. Among other things, it meant that they could not neutralize police interference with their operations or control white syndicate forays against their banks. The objective sought was a level of stability or certainty that would contribute to the success of the enterprise. The vulnerabilities of Harlem policy operators, however, ultimately had to do with a crucial variable that could not be controlled: political influence. This narrowed the possibilities for stability and, along with a lack of violent force that could at least check the external threats of outside criminal organizations, the policy bankers found themselves at the mercy of corrupt politicians, police, and white gangsters. In terms of power brokering, security, and enforcement, the Harlem policy operations were simply no match for their opponents and challengers. Ballots as well as bullets were the prerequisites for sustained criminal enterprises.

THE FINANCIAL ASPECTS OF POLICY

Perhaps it was only natural that African Americans should operate policy for themselves. And the fact that at first white gangsters perceived Harlem's numbers racket (which they called "nigger pool") as a "penny" game of the poor; Harlem operators were initially free to develop the game, free of the threats of white syndicates. The white gangsters did not think there was any real money to be made from poor African Americans who were only betting pennies.

In reality, playing numbers was not just an escapist entertainment: It afforded the player a slim hope of relief from grinding poverty. Policy was also, and perhaps much more important, a financial institution—one that substituted for mainstream organizations that could not and would not provide financial services in poor communities. In the vacuum where there were few banks, credit associations, loan and realty enterprises, numbers gambling emerged.[32] It became a source of capital and, ironically, a means of savings, a device for personally accumulating some resources. And with the usury industry, policy banks offered the impoverished an alternative institutional system for the savings–investment cycle in the ghetto.

Harlem was not the only burgeoning community in which policy took hold. A cruder version of the Harlem racket, the "policy wheel" was brought to Chicago's minority communities from New Orleans at the turn of the century.[33] Policy in Chicago was operated primarily in the vice districts where the African-American population was concentrated. The prevalence of vice in the midst of the African-American population (which was virtually trapped by the opposition to integration among the city's real estate brokers and tenants' associations) inevitably linked vice and crime with color in the minds of whites.[34] A major reason for the success of the policy rackets was their political connections with the mayor's office and the Democratic Party machine that dominated Chicago politics.[35] Participation in organized crime and politics goes hand in hand.[36] The building of durable criminal networks is as much a political matter as are cunning and violence. Powerful political and economic cliques must be wooed and encouraged to support a criminal enterprise and relax their opposition to its development and operation.

As noted already, in Chicago, Detroit, New York, and Philadelphia—communities with sizable African-American populations in the 1920s and 1930s—at least two factors were at work that determined the viability of ghetto rackets: access to political institutions, and the use of systematic violence or the threat thereof.[37] But the staying power of a criminal enterprise, once it has taken definitive shape and formed an identity, depended not only on its connections with influential elites but also on its integration into the lifeblood of the community.

POLICY RACKETS AS CRIMINAL FIRMS

A potentially useful way of looking at organized crime in the ghetto is to see it as made up of "business firms" with their own strategies. The focus then departs from traditional perspectives that attempt to understand criminal activity purely in terms of violent, static organizations with elaborate structures and rituals, but with no particular purposes and an "economic" dimension as no more than an efficient device for exploiting in a predatory manner particular market opportunities.[38]

If, on the other hand, African-American policy is viewed primarily as a business venture involving a number of "firms," we may better appreciate their community significance, quite apart from their "criminality." First, we look in some detail at their assets, their wealth-generating capacities, and their roles in the general economic life of the community. Second, we focus attention on the dynamics of operations—how well or poorly they respond to pressures from law enforcement, from the community itself, and from competitors within and outside the community.

The simplest and most common conception about African-American organized crime and organized crime in general is that they are controlled and dominated by a single group with a tightly structured command system that directs member efforts in the production of illicit goods and services. The model is one of a criminal monopoly with a fixed, detailed operating strategy masterminded by those at the top. There are many reasons to be suspicious of this conception in general, and its applicability to the African-American policy rackets in particular.[39]

A great deal of evidence indicates that the policy firms in African-American communities were not monopolized by a single firm. Unquestionably, number banks and policy gambling were mainstays in African-American communities. Drake and Cayton concluded that the policy syndicate in Chicago's South Side employed five thousand persons and grossed at least $18 million in 1938.[40] Similarly, in New York's Harlem of the 1930s, dozens of policy banks were identified by Dewey's investigators.[41] As late as 1972, researchers in New York's Bedford-Stuyvesant section of Brooklyn examined numbers gambling volume and found that $300 million a year were wagered.[42]

THE COMMUNITY AND POLICY

The attitudes toward and participation of African Americans in numbers gambling suggest several cultural and sociological explanations. Carlson studied the numbers gambling of Detroit's African-American communities and found that the complex of motives included folklore, spiritualism, and dream interpretation—primary cultural sources of approval.[43] The portraits of policy players are quite fascinating. For example, Winthrop D. Lane's commentary on life in the mid-1920s portrays an African-American woman returning home after a day's work.

An unkempt woman, with hair graying, shoulders rounded and eyes rimmed with thick glasses, reads a newspaper on a subway car in New York City. She is colored. Her skirt is in rags, one toe shows through a shoe, an elbow pushes the lining of her sleeve into sight; perhaps she has just left her mop and pail in some downtown office building. Turning the pages hastily, she seems to be hunting for a particular place. At last she stops. Her forefinger runs up and down the columns. She is looking at the financial page. Finding an item, she gazes closely at it for a moment, and then throws the paper onto the seat beside her. She has a dejected look. Apparently, she is through with the paper.

She has been looking for the numbers. The numbers she wanted were the day's totals of bank exchanges and bank balances—announced each day by the Clearing House and published by the newspapers. On these she has been gambling. . . . It is the bright spot for her.

. . . All Harlem is ablaze with "the numbers." People play it everywhere, in tenements, on street corners, in the backs of shops. Bankers organize it, promote it, encourage it. They send their runners into flats and stores. You give the runner the money you are betting, write your number on a slip of paper, and wait. If the number you chose is the one that wins the next day, you get your money. Runners round up new business, stake off territory and canvass all the people they can reach. A person living in an apartment house may be the agent for the house. The names of these bankers are known in the neighborhood. One rides around in a twelve thousand dollar limousine and has a liveried chauffeur. Minor bankers abound; men and women, getting two hundred dollars capital, start in the numbers business. Recently, it is said, white men have been trying to wrest the control of the game from blacks; a Jew who formerly used his talents in the hooch business is spoken of as the leader in this effort.[44]

Sociological vignettes such as these bring to life theories as developed by Durkheim and Merton concerning the sociopsychological phenomenon of *anomie*.[45] Big prizes offer the possibility of immediate, immense wealth to winners; striking it rich overnight is an attitude congenial with *anomie* theory, which suggests that individuals will engage in deviant practices and take risks when the normal institutionalized means to success are blocked.

At the same time, the cluster of motives behind participation in numbers playing on a regular or daily basis could be explained solely by cultural or sociological theories. Given the structure of policy, the volume of betting, and the composition of the bettors pool, it seems that from the player's perspective number gambling served other personal needs besides the possibility of a big win: For many, no doubt, it was a means of personal interest in which placing a small bet is the most providential means of investment.[46] Moreover, the structure of the frequency of betting suggests that the players themselves adopted a long-range perspective about their activities. Most played daily with small amounts of money that would not be saved in bank deposits accounts. Policy with its "runners" (bet collectors) circulating freely and routinely in the local neighborhoods made numbers gambling convenient. Places where a bet could be made were numerous: newsstands, groceries, convenience stores, pool halls, bars, barber shops, beauty parlors, dry cleaning stores, pharmacies—retail establishments individuals use daily.[47] The availability and variability of betting outlets would indicate some degree of racial pride and community tolerance of numbers, despite its reputation in the larger public as a crime.

Numbers banks were also employers in the African-American community. The "banks" (collection points and payoff centers) could and did make credit available to their clients.[48] The liquid capital accumulated in the number banks derived from the daily plays; runners could make direct loans to players whom they knew and trusted to cover their bets or lend cash that would be used for other purposes. Indeed, the banks could lend monies to local businesses that participated in the numbers racket as betting "drops" so that the game functioned as a source of consumer credit and small loans circulating to local neighborhood retail entrepreneurs. These credit services provided to steady customers and small retail businesses served as a substitute source for the absence of mainstream banks whose lending and loan policies forbade making small loans to impoverished customers or making loans to businesses that could scarcely collateralize their debt.[49]

With the circulation of capital within the community, numbers bankers constituted the largest investors in ghetto real estate and the chief source of funding for African-American businesses.[50] Some of the bankers assumed philanthropic roles in depressed African-American neighborhoods, making donations to churches, providing scholarships to promising students, and helping to stimulate general social and economic developments.[51]

As Light observes, the large structural economic and social dynamics of color prejudice and poverty operated to partially legitimize illegal gambling enterprises. Light notes,

> Banks combine the savings of depositors to create a capital fund for business, mortgage and consumer investments. . . . numbers banks mimic this rhythm, first taking the "savings" of the poor, then returning capital to the poor community in the form of usurious loans, free loans, philanthropy and direct business investments by racketeers. Therefore, numbers gambling banks are an irregular financial institution.[52]

What mitigated the blemish of crime was the malfunctioning of mainstream financial institutions in low-income minority communities and their absence in the community. Of necessity, ghetto residents reached into their cultural repertoires and collective survival strategies for solutions. The institutionally induced deficits in finance credit, and capitalization in the ghetto were compensated for in some ways through the remedy of policy rackets. For other reasons, numbers gambling was attractive. First, it had no production costs when compared to illegal alcohol, prostitution or other vices. Second, when a bettor gave a number runner money, he or she became an accessory. Is it any wonder then that, in a cash-poor ghetto, policy was attractive. It became, for a while, the "mother racket," attracting white gangsters such as Dutch Schultz, Lucky Luciano, and Al Capone.

Two particular resources are needed to "organize" crime and sustain it. It was noted earlier that violence and credible threats thereof and the accessibility of political institutions were essential aspects of any criminal enterprise. These were not uniformly available in African-American communities throughout the United States in the 1920s and 1930s. Why they are important components of organized crime is a crucial question in the discussion of African-American involvement in the phenomenon.

With regard to the capacity for violence, there are at least three reasons why violence or the reputation for it is essential for the success of a criminal business. First, it allows the enterprise to conduct its business and hold onto its earnings without losing too much to criminal offenders and competitors who would take advantage of it.[53] Violence is also a means to intimidate tardy clients. As a rule, criminal markets require the enforcement of rules and territorial maintenance through agreements with other groups. In the absence of agreements—which must be enforceable through illegal means—or when agreements are violated, businesses will become disorganized. Violence then is a functional element in the maintenance of an orderly criminal market environment. Equally as important, the mere reputation for, and fear of, violence may be sufficient to maintain the market.

A second important dimension in the smooth operation of a criminal business is the capacity to corrupt or suborn law enforcement personnel, including prosecutors, judges, and politicians. In order to operate "peacefully" an organization requires the ability to impede, obstruct or deflect law enforcement attention away from itself. It is relevant to see that the capacity to corrupt enforcement agencies is as important as violence, if not more so, because politically powerful racketeers can harness the corrupted police to do their violence for them against criminal competitors. After all, illegal operations are also vulnerable to violence and theft by criminals. Finally, having the police on one's side or on the sidelines is useful, because in any violent showdown, the state will win by its ability to bring together an overwhelming preponderance of force. If a criminal organization's continuing capacity to operate is to be protected from the state, one of the most feasible ways to achieve this is to neutralize state power through corruption.

CALCULATING RISKS AND OPERATING STRATEGIES

A number of principles that guide legitimate businesses seem applicable in analyzing minority illegal firms. These develop around the question of how best to deploy assets so as to maximize the survivability and continuity of the criminal enterprise to make money.[54] This means that an illegal business, such as policy, must pay close attention to its reputation and capacity for violence. First, if it is weakened, the organization is endangered; second, the corruptibility of law enforcement must be carefully monitored, cultivated, and renegotiated as conditions in the enterprise's working environment change, which are sometimes occasioned by changes in community sentiments about the illegality of the enterprise, or because of challenges from new competitors, or because corrupt enforcement agencies demand bigger shares of profits. Within African-American policy rackets, violence and corruption were present among some groups but not others. In Chicago, the policy operators formed a syndicate by pooling their resources and by developing connections with William "Big Bill" Thompson, Republican Mayor of Chicago from 1915 to 1923, and then from 1927 to 1931. Urban politics and organized crime were wedded together in Chicago. According to Ianni,

> Kickbacks from the policy bankers to Thompson's political machine were estimated at $500,000 a year in the early 1930s. Although this was only one source of income for the Thompson machine, and by no means the largest, it was an important one.[55]

It is well to remember that during this time the Capone syndicate was the most powerful criminal organization in Chicago and in the surrounding counties. Capone's prestige was felt in Wisconsin, Indiana, Missouri, Kentucky, and Michigan in all of the vice industries, including, but not limited to, bootlegging. Although Capone could have crushed the African-American gambling syndicates, he did not. The policy syndicate managed to retain its autonomy through a combination of political influence and a capacity to fight for its territories and rackets. Hence, from a "corporate strategic" perspective, because the numbers did not interfere with the larger, more powerful criminal enterprises operating in the white community, and because the struggle to gain control and then sustain it over ghetto rackets would be too costly in terms of money, blood, and public apprehensions, numbers racketeers were left untouched.

The numbers syndicate also possessed another valuable resource. In Chicago, African-American communities were politically organized long before others in the nation. The policy bankers were a vital link between the white political machine and the African-American communities. At election time, both white and African-American racketeers mobilized their armies of underworld employees to turn out the vote for the machine. Registering voters, getting them to the polls, and voting were tasks efficiently performed by gangsters.

Similarly in Detroit, African Americans organized themselves against the violent threats of white competitors, such as the notorious Purple Gang. In this environment, violence more than politics mattered in keeping the numbers within the control of local African Americans.

It was not until after World War II, when significant political and economic changes occurred, that African-American control of Chicago's policy was jeopardized by white gangsters. Superior manpower, organization, and political influence enabled the Chicago "Outfit" (a legacy of the Capone organization) to challenge the ghetto entrepreneurs. African-American racketeers were murdered, kidnapped, and intimidated. In the post–World War II period, the electoral landscape had changed significantly, with African-American political power steadily diminishing as white influence and violence increased exponentially. Why this happened is not clear; our knowledge, unfortunately, is largely impressionistic: Perhaps the economic slump after the war weakened the political strength of African-American communities.

In any case, perhaps the very nature of numbers in Chicago and Detroit contributed to the eventual loss of control by African-American organizers. The racket lacked a centralized system of management, so that it could not adequately cope with threats to its various elements or properly monitor changes in the underworld and political environments in which it operated. As with New York in the largest and in many ways the most sophisticated policy operations, there was no "mafia"-type structure among these groups. In New York, in particular, the numbers operations did not evolve around a common code of behavior or rules governing relationships between and among various groups. The protection they paid to operate was not of a magnitude that would have significant political impact, nor were there examples of networks influencing an election, delivering a vote, funding a political candidate, or dabbling in union affairs. The scale of corruption was modest and was tied to the particular criminal activity involved.

The dispersed nature of numbers allowed the racket to remain in African-American control for some time. To the extent that there was organization, it was externally exposed, and when the corrupt political machines realized how lucrative penny and nickel gambling operations could be, they demanded more tribute in terms of graft in exchange for protection. And, when numbers became large and profitable enough to come to the attention of white syndicates in New York and Chicago, they moved in and absorbed numbers as part of their organization. In Chicago, white organized-crime leaders Sam "Mooney" Giancana, the heir of Al Capone, and Tony Accardo staged a takeover in 1952. Theodore Roe, who was Edward Jones's (the "Policy King" of Chicago) lieutenant, was executed gangland style.

The situation in New York's Harlem community is especially interesting because it illustrates the importance of political and criminal linkages in maintaining an illegal enterprise of some size. Initially, white gangsters in the 1920s lacked interest in numbers that they considered small scale.[56] Madame Stephanie St. Clair, a black woman who became the "Policy Queen" of Harlem in the 1920s and 1930s, made millions out of the small change bet daily on the numbers. Nor was she the only success. Joseph Mathias Ison and his brother Masjoe Ison, Wilfred Adolphus Brunder, José Enrique Miro, and Casper Holstein, whose innovations and reliability led to the growth and spread of numbers, became wealthy, prominent figures in Harlem—"Policy Kings and Queens." Holstein was also known as Harlem's only philanthropist during the 1920s and was also prominent in Black Elkdom, serving as the Exalted Ruler of one of Harlem's best lodges.[57]

As the game grew, it attracted white criminals. Again during the 1920s, Harlem numbers were not consolidated into a syndicate that pooled resources and assets; it was fragmented and lacked big layoff bankers who could handle a large "hit" (a win).

It was for precisely this reason—the need for ready cash to pay off a big hit—that "Dutch" Schultz, a powerful New York gangster, realized the potential profits: Schultz was able to lend a comparatively large sum of money to rescue a policy bank. Other larger loans, quickly repaid, led to the realization of just how much money was being transacted in Harlem's policy rackets. Thereafter, Schultz moved rapidly and violently to muscle in on and eventually take control of numbers. Stephanie St. Clair was forced to hide from Schultz's gunmen when she refused to work for him. In Harlem, the policy operators, unlike their counterparts in Chicago and Detroit, were unaccustomed to violence and ill-prepared to fight for control of their game. By 1935, the highest echelons of African-American bankers in policy had been driven out.

Schultz did use force and murder to persuade the policy operators to meet his demands, which amounted to relinquishing their control over numbers. But violence alone, although necessary, was not sufficient in gaining control. It was the political power of the white gangsters, protection payoffs to police, and the ability to mobilize votes that insured success. Those African Americans who survived the violence and police intimidation deftly orchestrated by Schultz and his political front man, James Hines, the Tammany Hall West Side leader, found themselves working as middlemen for white gangs. The lack of substantial political power and the inability or unwillingness to use violence in the organization and administration of illegal enterprises—weakened the competitive edge of the Harlem policy networks.[58] These two assets of illegal firms were virtually absent in the organizations that first emerged in Harlem. First, many of their direct participants were not career criminals with skills in violence, but individuals from all walks of life. Second, the political traditions of Harlem at that time were not synchronized with the overwhelming Democratic Party hegemony, and this weakened the community's ability to affect the political environment. The lack of political power within the ghetto produced the phenomenon of an "internal colony."[59] As a "colony," the African-American community was dominated politically and economically; it was subordinated to, and dependent upon, external power structures. Typically, the "colonizers" exploit the labor, capital resources, and assets of the colonized. This was no less true of Harlem and its criminal activities and enterprises. William Julius Wilson's study of class and social politics makes the point that "control by white ethnics of the various urban political machines was so complete that the blacks were never really in a position to compete for the more important municipal political rewards such as patronage jobs or government contracts and services."[60] Consequently, African-American leaders have been invested with little power to influence the economic conditions in their communities, or, in the case of organized criminal enterprises, to affect police activities that would inhibit crime or provide support for it. It was not easy for them to win concessions from the political machine that had, after all, no intention of giving its power away. Whatever concessions were made were won with the tacit social understanding that in return, constituencies would be influenced in directions advantageous to machine political interest. At best, leaders in the ghetto were in an impossible position. Historically, most found themselves in the extraordinary position of saying to whites, "Hurry," with reforms and improvements while saying to their constituencies, "Wait." This is of the utmost importance. The dilemma says a great deal about the situation that produced the fertile ground for organized crime, and, of course, it tells us a great deal about race relations and their effects on African-American life.

NOTES

1. E. Franklin Frazier, *Black Bourgeoisie: The Rise of a New Middle Class in the United States* (New York: Collier Books, 1962).

2. Drake and Cayton, *Black Metropolis*, 486–490.

3. George Sullivan, *By Chance a Winner* (New York: Dodd, Mead & Co., 1972), 5.

4. Herbert Asbury, *Sucker's Progress: An Informal History of Gambling in America from the Colonies to Canfield* (New York: Dodd, Mead & Co., 1938), 73.

5. John Samuel Ezell, *Fortunes's Merry Wheel: The Lottery in America* (Cam-

bridge, MA: Harvard University Press, 1960), 29.

6. Ibid.

7. Asbury, *Sucker's Progress*, 72.

8. G. Robert Blakey, "State Conducted Lotteries: History, Problems, and Promises," *Journal of Social Issues* 35, no. 3 (1979): 62–86; Asbury, *Sucker's Progress*; Ezell, *Fortunes's Merry Wheel*; George Sullivan, *By Chance a Winner*.

9. Ezell, *Fortunes's Merry Wheel*.

10. Ibid, 49.

11. Ibid, 57.

12. Asbury, *Sucker's Progress*; Ezell, *Fortunes's Merry Wheel*.

13. Asbury, *Sucker's Progress*; Ezell, *Fortunes's Merry Wheel*.

14. Sullivan, *By Chance a Winner*, 95.

15. Asbury, *Suckers Progress*, 88.

16. Ibid., 89.

17. Ibid.

18. Ezell, *Fortunes's Merry Wheel*.

19. Ibid, 82.

20. Blakey, *State Conducted Lotteries*, 68.

21. Harry B. Weiss and Grace Weiss, *Early Sports and Pastimes in New Jersey* (Trenton: Past Times Press, 1968).

22. Blakey, *State Conducted Lotteries*, 68.

23. Claude McKay, *Harlem: Negro Metropolis* (New York: E.P. Dutton & Co., 1940), 107.

24. Ibid..

25. *The New York Age*, 5 July 1924, 1–2.

26. Redding, "Playing the Numbers," 553–554.

27. Carl Van Vechten, *Nigger Heaven* (New York: Grosset & Dunlap, 1926).

28. *The New York Age*, 5 May 1924, 1–2.

29. *Ibid*, 7 June 1924, 1–2.

30. National Commission on Law Observance and Enforcement, *Report on the Cost of Crime* (Washington, DC: National Commission, 1931), 406 (emphasis added).

31. Dwight C. Smith, Jr., *The Mafia Mystique* (1975; reprint, 1990 Lanham, MD: Press of America, 1990).

32. Ivan Light, "Numbers Gambling among Blacks: A Financial Institution," *American Sociological Review*, 42 (December 1977): 892–904.

33. Francis A. J. Ianni, *Black Mafia* (New York: Pocket Books, Simon & Schuster, 1975), 112–113.

34. Drake and Cayton, *Black Metropolis*, vol. 1; John Landesco, *Organized Crime in Chicago* (Chicago: University of Chicago Press, 1929), 31–38.

35. Lewis A. H. Caldwell, *The Policy King* (Chicago: New Vistas Publishing House, 1945); Virgil Peterson, "The Barbarians in Our Midst" excerpted in Gus Tyler, ed., *Organized Crime in America* (Ann Arbor: University of Michigan Press, 1962).

36. Robert J. Kelly and Rufus Schatzberg, "Types of Minority Organized Crime: Some Considerations" (Paper presented at the 39th Annual Meeting of the American Society of Criminology, Montreal, Canada, November 1987).

37. Mark Moore, "Organized Crime as a Business Enterprise," *Major Issues in Organized Crime Control* (Washington, DC: National Institute of Justice, 1987), 51–64. Frederick T. Martens, "African-American Organized Crime: An Ignored Phenomenon," *Federal Probation* 54 (December 1990): 43–50.

38. Donald R. Cressy, *Theft of the Nation: The Structure and Operations of Organized Crime in America* (New York: Harper & Row, 1969).

39. Robert J. Kelly, "The Nature of Organized Crime and Its Operations," 17.

40. Drake and Cayton, *Black Metropolis*, 481.

41. Thomas E. Dewey, *Twenty against the Underworld* (New York: Doubleday & Co., 1974), 99.

42. Harold D. Lasswell and Jeremiah B. McKenna, *The Impact of Organized Crime on an Inner City Community* (Springfield, VA: U.S. Department of Commerce, National Technical Information Service, 1972), 112.

43. Carlson, "Number Gambling: A Study of a Culture Complex," 89–114.

44. Winthrop D. Lane, "Ambushed in the City: The Grim Side of Harlem," *The Survey* 53 (March 1925): 692–693.

45. Emile Durkheim, *Suicide* (Glencoe, IL: Free Press, 1951, originally published in 1897); Robert K. Merton, *Social Theory and Social Structure*, rev. ed. (New York: Free Press, 1957).

46. Commission on the Review of National Policy toward Gambling. *Gambling in America* (Washington, DC: U.S. Government Printing Office, 1975).

47. Carl E. Haugen, "Short Term Financing" in Eli Ginsbury, ed. *Business Leadership in the Negro Crisis* (New York: McGraw-Hill, 1968); Thomas C. Schelling, "Economic Analysis and Organized Crime," *Law Enforcement Intelligence Analysis Digest* 5, no. 1 (Summer 1990): 49–73, reprinted from the *President's Task Force Report: Organized Crime* (Washington, DC: U.S. Government Printing Office, 1967).

48. John R. Domingueq, *Capital Flows in Minority Areas* (Lexington, MA: D.C. Heath & Co., 1976), 38.

49. Robert Perucci, "The Neighborhood 'Bookmaker' Entrepreneur and Mobility Model" in Paul Meadoris and Ephraim H. Mizurchi, eds. *Urbanism, Urbanization and Change: Comparative Perspective* (Reading, MA: Addison-Wesley Publishers, 1969), 302–311.

50. Drake and Cayton, *Black Metropolis* Part II, 487; Whyte, *Street Corner Society*, 145.

51. Rufus Schatzberg, *Black Organized Crime in Harlem: 1920–1930*, chaps. 7 & 8.

52. Light, *Numbers Gambling*, 901.

53. Schelling, "Economic Analysis".

54. Kenneth R. Andrews, *The Concept of Corporate Strategy* (Homewood, IL: Jones-Irwin, 1971).

55. Ianni, *Black Mafia*, 112–116.

56. Fred J. Cook, "The Black Mafia Moves into the Numbers Racket," *New York Times Magazine*, 4 April 1971, 27.

57. McKay, *Harlem: Negro Metropolis*, 102.

58. Schatzberg, *Origins of Black Organized Crime*.

59. Robert Blauner, *Racial Oppression in America* (New York: Harper & Row, 1972).

60. William J. Wilson, *The Declining Significance of Race* (Chicago: University of Chicago Press, 1978), 148–149.

Du Bois's 1896 landmark study, commissioned by the University of Pennsylvania, focused upon the African-American people of Philadelphia. It was the first scientific study in African-American sociology and the pioneer effort in urban American sociology.[1] We shall not review this investigation other than to point out that Du Bois refers to an article in the *Public Ledger*, a Philadelphia newspaper, about a well-known policy shop, owned by an African American who had been writing policy for years. This early reference to an African American being involved in an organized criminal enterprise is rare.[2] The bank the policy writer was turning over his work to does not appear to be an African-American operation. The policy writer, the report alleges, was the president of a local African-American political club and, other than his policy writing, was a law-abiding citizen. This is of interest because his affiliation with a political club is consistent with the theory advanced in this study that political connections are an important adjunct for organized crime.

St. Clair Drake and Horace R. Cayton,[3] in their ethnographic studies of Chicago, indicate that nearly a century ago an African American, John "Mushmouth" Johnson, "King Foo," a Chinaman, and Patsy King, a white man, ran lotteries in Chicago's old First Ward. Another character, "Policy Sam," sometimes called the father of the game, operated a policy wheel as early as 1885. "Policy Sam" withdrew from the game when the antipolicy law of 1905 was enacted, but Johnson and others kept the game alive. In 1931, Chicago's African-American policy operators formed a syndicate of policy "Kings." St. Clair Drake and Cayton note that the relationships between some rackets and the community carry racial overtones:

> Highly important in strengthening the policy racket is the fact that
> Negroes are spatially separated and socially isolated from the remain-

der of the community, and are denied full participation in the economic life of Chicago. This permits every attack on South Side gambling to be interpreted as an attack on The Race—which is to an extent true considering that vice and gambling flourish unmolested in other sections of the city also. Bronzeville's civic leaders will rally to the defense of a Negro gambler if it seems that he is being made a scapegoat. A united front cutting across political and social-class lines emerges when there is reason to doubt the motives of some ambitious state's attorney or police chief, who can be accused of making political capital by attacking "Vice in the Black Belt." The policy kings know well how to exploit this feeling and rally their defense. . . . The Depression, with its devastating impact, weakened the legitimate Negro business institutions, the symbols of financial control and stability in Bronzeville. The policy kings emerged as one group who could point to the thousands of workers still employed by The Race. They were thus able to assume the role of Race Leaders, patrons of charity, and pioneers of the establishment of legitimate business. They were able to wield some economic control over community institutions through their power to withhold or grant gifts. [4]

Policy arrest records in New York City before 1920 show that there were no arrests made for clearing house policy numbers.[5] Perhaps this type of policy number (not to be confused with the type of lottery policy numbers used in Chicago) was unknown outside the African-American community.[6] In the early 1920s, African Americans in New York City, mostly in the Harlem area, operated large policy banks using clearing house totals. Kinship networks were the common organizational bonds that formed the social "glue" in the racket. An example of the growth of policy in New York can be illustrated by examining arrest records. In 1920, the New York Police Department reported only seven arrests for Policy Law violations in New York City, and by 1935 they were reporting 13,692 arrests yearly for the city (see Table 5.1). The Harlem court processed approximately 37 percent of New York City's total policy arrests between 1920 and 1930.[7]

The economic fixation of the African-American community with numbers may be explained by viewing numbers gambling as a substitute for the legitimate financial institutions that were conspicuously absent in impoverished communities then and now. Numbers players regarded this activity as a possible way of improving their economic condition.

	Male	Female	Total	Conviction	Percentage	Discharged

TABLE 5.1. Arrest 1920–1935 Police Commissioner's Annual Reports

	Male	Female	Total	Conviction	Percentage	Discharged
1920						
Lottery	57	2	59	29	49%	28
Policy	7	0	7	—	—	4
1921						
Lottery	110	11	121	49	40.5%	52
Policy	148	5	153	59	38.5%	22
1922						
Lottery	229	29	328	212	64.6%	70
Policy	620	34	654	116	17.7%	391
1923						
Lottery	382	43	425	246	57.8%	113
Policy	965	49	1014	118	11.6%	893
1924						
Lottery	657	55	712	496	69.6%	219
Policy	746	28	774	107	13.8%	489
1925						
Lottery	249	25	274	193	70.4%	60
Policy	1148	27	1175	115	9.7%	1192
1926 (In July Policy Laws were liberalized)						
Lottery	251	11	262	126	48%	61
Policy	1380	72	1452	121	8.3%	900
1927						
Lottery	262	17	279	219	78.4%	106
Policy	1938	298	2236	787	35.1%	991
1928						
Lottery	196	22	218	125	57.3%	106
Policy	2334	473	2807	1367	48.6%	1014
1929						
Lottery	193	18	211	89	42.1%	113
Policy	3017	480	3497	1681	48%	1438
1930 (Seabury Investigation Aug. 25, 1930 to Mar. 28, 1932)						
Lottery	351	27	378	118	32.2%	152
Policy	3852	482	4334	1896	43.7%	1262
1931						
Lottery	270	18	288	117	51.3%	110
Policy	1451	92	1563	1222	78.1%	782

(continued)

	Male	Female	Total	Conviction	Percentage	Discharged
1932						
Lottery	480	23	503	136	27%	224
Policy	3482	248	3730	1633	43.7%	862
1933						
Lottery	694	39	733	218	29.7%	334
Policy	6025	329	6354	4556	71.7%	1257
1934						
Lottery	296	15	311	146	46.9%	110
Policy	9808	552	10,360	6626	63.9%	1747
1935						
Lottery	297	23	320	72	22.5%	143
Policy	12,964	728	13,692	6340	46.3%	2719

Mainstream financial institutions have never been able to provide generally prevailing service levels in poor communities. In the resulting partial-service vacuum, blacks invented numbers gambling. Numbers-gambling banks became sources of capital and a major savings device of urban black communities. With the usury industry, numbers banks framed an alternative institutional system for the saving–investment cycle in the slum. Number banking illustrates the conjoint contribution of institutional and cultural causes in an analysis of poverty.[8]

Number players typically placed a small amount of money with a runner (an agent who takes the bets from players) whom they trusted, hoping to receive a generous return if they "hit" the winning number. As already noted, the numbers game or policy rackets can be seen as a substitute for financial institutions that were virtually nonexistent in early African-American communities. The fact that career criminals were not integral to the early African-American gambling organizations and management of ghetto gambling enterprises suggests that numbers were an indigenous response to the absence of economic institutions that could provide jobs, ready capital, and financial resources in a hard-pressed community.

Organized crime, then, is not simply a deviant activity within a community, nor is it a phenomenon associated only with some individuals having personality defects or pathological flaws. It is an innovative response to social contingencies and realities that define community life. That otherwise legitimate shopkeepers and upstanding citizens participated in the vice activity suggests that policy gambling, was a collective reaction in a community marked off and stigmatized by race.

These developments paralleled the genesis of the Mafia in Southern Italy, where government had all but abandoned the peasantry, and where corrupt police, an ambivalent church, and an aloof, aristocratic elite exploited the local population. The Mafia as an "alternative government" provided rough justice, jobs, finances for grain, and help to those who could not turn to official agencies. Similarly, in America's African-American ghettos, policy operators were not perceived as "criminals" in the usual sense, but rather as informal entrepreneurs prepared to meet the expediencies of local needs.

Light's comparative studies[9] of African-American and Chinese vice in the first half of the twentieth century illustrates the relevance of cultural factors in an illicit industry. (In fact, an examination of legitimate commercial activities operated by different cultural groups would show distinctive styles. Why, then, cultural overlays should not be apparent and relevant in illicit activities is a bit bewildering.) At any rate, Light's research reveals that both African Americans and Chinese had strong motives for compensatory illicit income, because legitimate opportunities were sharply circumscribed by social prejudice and xenophobia. Thus, the Chinese and African Americans were indirectly encouraged into illegal activity. As Light puts it,

> The black vice industry and the Chinese vice industry were internally different. The black vice industry consisted of streetwalkers and pimps who settled quarrels with fights. The Chinese vice industry consisted of syndicated brothels which resolved severe business rivalries by gang wars, but adjudicated individual quarrels. . . .
> Black pimps relied upon their reputation for violent prowess to intimidate workers and rival pimps . . . The black enclaves had high homicide rates, but no gang wars. Streetwalkers and their confederates frequently robbed their customers and, occasionally, robberies eventuated in killings. Chinatowns had low homicide rates, rampant gang wars, but no record of street robberies of visiting men. The implication is that the syndication of vice in Chinatown prevented petty robberies and unregulated conflicts among individuals, but encouraged collective struggles for business advantage. On the other hand, the free market organization of vice in black enclaves permitted individualistic killings and petty crime, but eliminated gang warfare.[10]

Light argues that Chinese prostitution organized through a Tong, and that the Tong in turn would provide organization and resolve conflicts. African Americans did not have available a similar cultural and historic tradition of "organized criminality." Consequently, the rough-and-tumble individual entrepreneurial style of the pimp or vice agent encouraged a free and open market competition generated by cadres of street pimps, and when the public demand for prostitution declined, the transition to alternative income-generating opportunities reflected their cultural and ethnic differences. The transformation to legitimate tourist industries among Chinese (restaurants, novelty-shops, and entertainment) was accomplished without much loss of earnings, because the Chinatowns did not pose the threat to visitors that later African-American ghettos did. The Tongs that had organized the brothels and opium dens facilitated the growth and operation of restaurants. In the African-American communities, on the other hand, the tourist trade for night clubs and entertainment, even though these were owned by white racketeers with affiliations in powerful crime syndicates, was stymied by the high volume of street violence and the threat of street thugs in the mid- and late 1930s. The threat of violence to tourists was not present during the 1920s. Harlem was, in the 1920s, New York's largest tourist attraction.

Whereas the demand for illicit goods and services encouraged minorities to respond, their particular method of meeting the demand is more clearly understood in terms of the provider and supplier's cultural and social characteristics. These seem to shape and mold the manner in which illicit activity is organized and affect its durability.

Light's studies on the ethnic and social organization of the vice industry concluded that sociocultural characteristics of provider subgroups are important factors affecting the manner in which responses are structured to meet consumer demands. Likewise, contemporary fieldwork on marijuana distribution networks in Brooklyn, New York suggested that retail-level traffickers were sensitive to the real or imagined racial and cultural backgrounds of those with whom they chose to do business.[11]

However, these issues do not address the internal organization of illicit activity within ethnic enclaves or ghettos that cater not only to outsiders but also to coethnic and ghetto dwellers. It would be a mistake to suppose that the collapse of quasi-legitimate tourist industries in the African-American ghettos and the decline of its vice industry meant that organized crime in the ghetto was under the exclusive stewardship of white criminals. Larger issues involving racism and alternative sources of vice services undoubtedly played a role in frustrating traditional organized criminal growth in African-American ghettos.

HOLSTEIN'S CAREER

On September 23, 1928, Casper Holstein was kidnapped by white gangsters.

After his release three days later, he failed to identify the five men who were arrested for his kidnapping. The case sparked national attention; it was the first time a wealthy African American was kidnapped and held for $50,000 ransom. The *New York Times* reported that Holstein, one of Harlem's wealthiest African Americans, had bet more than $30,000 on the races at Belmont Park in the week before his abduction.[12] His notoriety depicted a Harlem not engulfed in wretched poverty, but in affluence and deviance. A year later in Chicago, Illinois, Walter Kelly, an African-American policy banker, was also kidnapped by white gangsters and held for $25,000 ransom.[13]

In the early 1930s, when the Seabury Commission investigated corruption in the Magistrate's Courts of the Bronx and Manhattan, Harlem's policy operators came under scrutiny. Holstein is alleged to have dropped out of the policy racket to avoid public notice. He was arrested for the first time in 1935 for a policy violation. He maintained that it was his aggressive involvement in Virgin Islands politics, his homeland, that led law enforcement authorities to investigate his alleged gambling activities in New York. He claimed that he was framed. He received a penitentiary term and remained in prison for nearly a year.

Although he may have ended his career ignominiously, Holstein was one of many criminal entrepreneurs who operated a large-scale policy bank in the Harlem ghetto, employing hundreds of policy workers.[14] Apart from their chief purpose of generating money, numbers gambling banks created jobs for the unemployed and were a source of ready capital in African-American communities.[15] Those African Americans who were gainfully employed outside the Harlem community and brought their salaries back to Harlem, using part of it to play numbers, added to the economy of the area. In addition, a usury industry sprang up to serve the clientele of the numbers game. This species of an illegal, appended enterprise may have broadened its scope beyond the gambling needs of the minority community, taking on a life of its own.[16] The extent to which numbers became an integral part of the economy in African-American communities is suggested by Redding, who characterized the pervasiveness of numbers gambling as "the fever that has struck all classes and conditions of men."[17]

An indication of how lucrative the policy racket was in Harlem is evident from Internal Revenue Service prosecutions of several of Harlem's African-American policy bankers. In the early 1930s, Samuel Seabury's investigations uncovered large bank accounts belonging to Wilfred Adolphus Brunder, who deposited $1,753,342 between 1925 and 1930, and José Enrique Miro, who deposited $1,251,556 from 1927 to 1930.[18] Both men were convicted for tax evasion.[19]

Before the "Dutch" Schultz gang seized much of the Harlem policy rackets in the early 1930s, and consolidated their control, numbers were not a criminal monopoly or cartel operation. It was a local cottage industry, consisting of many independent bankers (mostly African Americans) who conducted the game, each providing the requisite operating capital and each taking the profits.[20] From the entrepreneur's point of view, the policy game appeared to be a sure way to make money. The large monetary returns available in a policy bank attracted some respectable African-American business people and politicians into the racket. To protect their interests, the policy operators employed reputable people to work in their banks. They reasoned that reputable people would take precautions against being arrested. If the workers were discreet and protective of their jobs, it follows that they would, in return, protect the policy operation. Teachers and unemployed wives of prominent community leaders, people who would feel a lasting shame to be arrested, worked in policy banks.[21] In 1925, *The New York Age* reported that a Harlem physician was arrested for operating a policy bank.[22]

In the mid-1920s and early 1930s, two separate attempts were made by white gangsters to wrest control of policy away from the African-American bankers. The first attempt occurred in the mid-1920s, when the policy bankers were able to resist the intrusions of white gangsters who used corrupt police officials as their major tools. This also included the insertion of several white Harlem bootleggers who, led by Hyman Kassell, entered the policy racket to increase their earnings. They were able to capture a share by using their saloons and Harlem's white shopkeepers to collect numbers for them. To force African-American policy runners to turn over their collections to them, or get off the streets, corrupt police were used to harass collectors employed by African-American bankers. The takeover effort had only limited success.

Kassell, identified by *The New York Age* as a leading white bootlegger in Harlem, operated as many as a dozen speakeasies in Harlem in the 1920s. By 1925, he was involved in the clearing house numbers racket as a banker.[23] He tried to set up a monopolistic stranglehold on the game. To do this, he employed all sorts of schemes and tricks to attract African-American numbers collectors to work for him. He bribed operators of cigar and stationary stores, ice cream parlors, and butcher shops to allow his collectors to use their establishments. [24]

THE STRUGGLE FOR CONTROL OF HARLEM

A strategic component of this bloodless gang war were the police and their manipulations through corrupt politicians who did the bidding of the Schultz syndicate. "Dutch" Schultz was a notorious gunman, widely feared in the New York underworld during the bootlegging wars. His organization extended through Upper Manhattan and the Bronx, and included gambling, night clubs, and extortion enterprises.

Schultz recognized the enormous potential of the Harlem policy racket. He also shrewdly calculated the risks in a takeover attempt. Because policy was an African-American game, and illegal, and because the policy operators did not have a reputation for violence, a takeover seemed relatively easy and not very costly, either in lives or in bribes.

The Harlem "coup" could be conducted, therefore, through a series of staged incentives that appealed to the common sense of his African-American competitors. Harlem became contested territory. The alignment of forces and resources clearly favored Schultz: He had important allies in the Democratic political machine who were influential with the police; Schultz commanded a sizable gang of experienced gunmen and could rely on his colleagues, Lucky Luciano, Frank Costello, Owney Madden, Meyer Lansky, and Bugsy Siegel for assistance, should the need arise. Pitted against the New York crime bosses, Harlem seemed vulnerable. Harlem policy operators paid the police but they lacked a crucial advantage—the political machine. Historically, African-American communities, especially Harlem, lacked political clout and could not easily neutralize the law enforcement apparatus of police, prosecutors, judges, and courts. More than removing law enforcement as an obstacle in criminal enterprises, Schultz mobilized police officers, bail bondsmen, lawyers, and court officials as active participants in his criminal enterprises and as appendages in his war for the numbers rackets in Harlem.

Tactically, the police would harass the street runners off the streets, thus forcing bettors to find collectors who were more accessible. The white bankers paid the police to arrest anyone who could not produce an identification card confirming that they worked for a Schultz-affiliated numbers bank. *The New York Age* published the following report:

> It is alleged that bankers who have an understanding with the police furnished their employees with a certain card bearing a cabalistic emblem of some sort recognized by the officer to whom it is shown and this card is to be used when the runner or collector unwittingly falls into the hands of the law. The card is supposed to show the fact the holder is with a banker who is "in right" and freedom or relief from further espionage is the immediate result.[25]

The other element was violence. The political protection Schultz could muster through his Tammany Hall links with Jimmy Hines, a Democratic Party boss in Manhattan, coupled with the firepower of his hoodlums, was the combination that forced African-American policy bankers to capitulate. James J. Hines, a powerful Tammany Hall politician in New York City during the 1920s and 1930s, placed his political power at the disposal of Schultz's criminal organization. This relationship between Schultz and Hines was the brainchild of J. Richard "Dixie" Davis, a lawyer. In the late 1920s, Davis practiced in Harlem's Magistrates Court, where he represented many of Harlem's African-American policy operators.[26] Davis saw the policy racket being exploited by the bondsmen because of their close relationship with the court's personnel and the defendants for whom they posted bail. The bondsmen were able to influence the defendants to accept their choice of a lawyer to represent them. Besides this, the bondsmen made it known that they could "fix" arrests for a fee. It was their familiarity with police officers and court personnel that made this possible.[27] Bondsmen over time become acquainted with police officers and could influence them to throw a case for a bribe. A loosely written complaint allowed the police to give the defendant an "out" at the trial. Political influence—asking a judge to dismiss a case—was possible too, but that influence usually had to come from within the judge's political organization. The most practiced technique employed before Hines became part of the Schultz organization was using the bondsmen to influence the police to throw a case.[28]

Dewey suggested that Davis believed he had the confidence of the top policy bankers in the Harlem numbers business because he represented them as their lawyer when they or their collectors were arrested. With his contacts in the policy racket, Dewey said that Davis "thought that with his brains, along with Dutch Schultz's muscle, he ought to be able to divert the golden stream of profits from the little bankers into a massive number racket."[29] Davis created a powerful policy combination in which he shared and used his liaison with Hines, who brought political protection to the newly formed Schultz policy combination.

The Schultz organization practically eliminated independent African-American policy bankers in Harlem. In doing so, he was able to have the African-American runners unwittingly join his organization by forcing their bosses to join his organization as salaried employees; the runners, believing they were working for an African-American banker, were in reality working for Schultz.

In the early 1930s, "forty murders and six kidnappings were laid at the door of policy gambling in the city."[30] By 1932, Schultz controlled a centralized policy racket in Harlem. He drained the profits out of the community whereas previously African Americans and Hispanic policy entrepreneurs had reinvested their profits back into the community.

Schultz's syndicate dissolved after he was murdered in 1935, but the lucrative profits and violence would not permit the policy racket to revert to its noncriminal entrepreneurial origins. Policy operators were susceptible to extortion and expropriation. The police had been prodded to action against Harlem's policy operators, so that if the game was to remain viable, it needed to reach out for white protection. When African-American policy bankers' had to pay off large "hits" with ready capital, wealthy white gangsters supplied loans for a percentage of the business plus repayment at a high rate of interest. Policy, as an autonomous African-American criminal enterprise, was compromised from then on and remained in the 1930s and 1940s under white criminal control.

Stephanie St. Clair, known as "Madame Queen of Policy," a black French woman from Marseilles, operated one of Harlem's big policy banks in the 1920s, from which she made a quarter of a million dollars a year.[31] She was arrested on December 30, 1929. She served eight months. St. Clair claimed that her arrest and sentence for eight months was in retaliation for her whistle-blowing. Outraged by the unscrupulous behavior of the police to whom she paid protection, she placed several paid advertisements in local Harlem newspapers, making serious charges of graft and corruption against the police. Almost immediately, she was arrested on what she termed a "framed charge" and was sent to the workhouse on Welfare Island for eight months.[32] The New York Age contained a report that, upon her release from prison in 1930, she appeared before Seabury's investigators (who were investigating corruption in the Manhattan and Bronx Magistrates Courts) and testified that she operated a policy bank from 1923 to 1928, in which time she paid members of the police department $6,000 to protect her workers from arrests, and that they double-crossed her and continued to arrest her workers. A lieutenant and thirteen men were suspended in December, 1930, because of her testimony about paying "protection money."[33]

In 1932, St. Clair claimed that she was being pressured by the Schultz gang to join their combination. She went to the mayor and the district attorney to protest how gangsters were trying to take over her policy business.[34] Her outcries were unsuccessful. St. Clair attempted to interest other African-American numbers bankers to join her in her fight with Schultz. They refused because they believed, correctly, that Schultz had the police and the politicians on his side. When Schultz lay dying of bullet wounds in a New Jersey hospital in October, 1935, a telegram arrived saying: "As ye sow, so

shall you reap." It was signed, "Madame Queen," Stephanie St. Clair is believed to have sent the telegram.[35]

Not all communities in the United States in which African Americans operated numbers banks succumbed to white gangster's threats. Gustav G.
Carlson identified at least thirty-five separate African-American policy organizations in the Detroit area. Several of these used the lottery-type policy
numbers (the twelve numbers picked from a seventy-eight number poll) and
some the clearing house totals. When the clearing house stopped publishing whole numbers in the early 1930s, they switched to the three-digit numbers derived from the mutual race horse results. These policy operations
controlled by African Americans also operated in cities such as Toledo,
Dearborn, Ann Arbor, Pontiac, Flint, and Saginaw. In 1928, a group of
Cleveland's Jewish gangsters attempted a takeover of the African-American
policy monopoly in Detroit and its surrounding areas. Realizing that if they
were to maintain control of the policy racket it would be necessary for them
to resolve minor individual differences and act as a group, the African Americans united and formed the "Associated Number Bankers." In addition to
its protective function, the organization served to regulate rates of payout
on winnings and the types of numbers games played. They also designated
the areas of operation in which different banks could operate. The associated bankers also retained a lawyer who was paid a monthly fee. His duty
was to serve as a bondsman and general consultant when the bankers or their
employees became involved with the law.[36]

In 1921, policy was introduced to Detroit by John Roxborough, who
years later was the comanager of Joe Louis, heavyweight boxing champion.[37]
In 1924, Roxborough formed a partnership with Monk Watson. The partnership between the two men lasted until 1928, when Roxborough was introduced to clearing house policy numbers by Casper Holstein, the Harlem
numbers banker. He adopted Holstein's method of determining winning
numbers. Both Roxborough and Watson, as partners and as individuals, were
two of the biggest African-American policy bankers in the Detroit area
throughout the 1920s and 1930s. Watson managed to maintain his independence through a cadre of gunmen and monthly payments of at least $4,000
a month to the mayor's office and smaller payments to various city officials
and police.[38]

With the election of William Dawson to Congress in 1942, Chicago's
policy men had a crust of protection not only from police but also from the
Chicago "Outfit"—the former Capone organization. For Dawson, who as

a criminal lawyer specialized in defending African-American gamblers and gangsters, his election and support from the political machine positioned him perfectly in the role of "minority middleman" for the community and his underworld supporters. Dawson's political organization was run efficiently, depending heavily on contributions from African-American policy men. Dawson's attitudes about gambling as an illegal enterprise were predictably apologetic and defensive, because he was in the early stages of his political career, a creation of a corrupt, urban political machine. For Dawson, gambling was, to put it charitably, a sustaining economic force in the African-American community. Bingo was played in churches and few complaints were raised; and why should the community not benefit from gambling that is conducted locally. Dawson rationalized gambling so that it was not a question of crime but an issue of economics.

Betting is a human frailty, but it isn't an evil in itself. . . . Negroes don't create money. They usually go outside their area to work for it and bring it back to their community. And a corrupt system, growing out of gambling, drains them dry. . . . If anybody is to profit out of gambling in the Negro Community, it should be the Negro. . . . I want the money my people earn to stay in the Negro community.[39]

When he moved on to Congress and secured his political base, his obligation and connection reached beyond the South Side of Chicago, and his role as a "race defender and advocate" diminished as his personal fortunes and celebrity increased. By 1942, with Dawson safely removed from the hurly-burly of Chicago's ward politics and into the comfortable halls of power and prestige in the U.S. Congress, the Chicago Outfit's Sam Giancana moved against a numbers operator. With the approval of Tony Accardo, Giancana kidnapped the Jones Brothers (who operated a successful policy bank and opened a department store in Chicago), demanded a hefty ransom, took over their policy business, and forced the brothers out of the county. With a minimum of violence and threats, by 1952, Giancana had control of numbers in Chicago.[40]

Money from numbers enabled Giancana to branch out into other enterprises and brought him to the attention of Tony Accardo and Paul Ricca, the principal bosses of the Chicago mafia. Thus, numbers was a stepping-stone for Giancana's career; it also suggests the fragility of organized criminal enterprises. Without political patrons and sponsors, few criminal projects endure over time.

In New York during the late 1930s, the Schultz gang collapsed.

Schultz's murder in 1935 did not restore African-American racketeers to positions of power in the underworld. Once compromised and intimidated, the policy racket became a joint enterprise, dominated by white criminals.

As in Chicago, Schultz's organization in New York, with its muscle, gunmen, underworld alliances, and political ties, could mobilize pressures to force concessions from opponents. Conversely, a criminal enterprise that lacked these vital resources and capacities could not endure over time, no matter how popular its community support base.

With the end of Prohibition and the Castellammarese War that consolidated the Italian underworld into a force to be reckoned with, many former bootleggers barged into policy through violence and sheer muscle, supported surreptitiously by the corrupted local political apparatus. When Schultz was murdered in 1935, "Trigger" Mike Coppola and "Fat" Tony Salerno of the Luciano Crime Family took over the Dutchman's numbers operation. Likewise, in Cleveland, Boston, Detroit, Philadelphia, and finally in Chicago, local Cosa Nostra members seized control of numbers gambling by 1940 in the African-American communities.

The pattern was fairly simple: Cosa Nostra members assumed responsibility for enforcement, profits, and police protection while Jewish associates and affiliates ran the business. African Americans did the footwork of collecting bets and making payoffs—relegated to minor-employee roles in enterprises that they had created and nurtured.[41] This was the trend through the 1960s, with African-American hoodlums working their neighborhoods, dealing dope, and running numbers as low-level employees of Mafia families. However, when formerly Italian inner-city neighborhoods went through a racial transition, African-American gangsters began to assert themselves on their own turfs. In Buffalo, for instance, African Americans seized control of numbers gambling from the Maggadino Mafia family; in Newark, they snatched numbers from the Genovese Mafia family, even threatening a gang war if the Mafia refused to yield.[42]

SYNDICATES, VICE, AND POLITICS

The tumultuous 1930s in New York ended with the conviction of James Hines, a major figure in Tammany Hall, the stronghold of Democratic Party politics in the city. Thomas E. Dewey convicted Hines after Schultz, a principal target of Dewey's racket prosecutors, had been assassinated four years earlier. But the end of Schultz and Hines did not substantially loosen the bonds between the underworld and the political machine. Frank Costello, a Mafia boss and close associate of Luciano, was gradually emerging as the "Prime Minister of the Underworld," a powerful behind-the-scenes influence in Tammany Hall, who would eventually play a role in the appointments of major political leaders and judges.[43]

Two basic types of criminal syndicates operated in New York City in the 1930s and 1940s. One type, described previously, was enterprise syndicates that provided illicit products and services such as narcotics, alcohol, gambling, and prostitution. Power syndicates engaged in extortion, protection, and racketeering activities in labor unions, and both legitimate and illegitimate businesses. Some syndicates, as Block suggests, displayed the characteristics of both power and enterprise.[44] On the scale of domination and terror, the enterprise syndicates, and this means African-American illicit syndicates, were weaker—at least in the pre–World War II period. As we have seen, in several cities where African Americans were better organized in terms of political connections and career criminals capable of violence, they were able to maintain their independence from white criminal organizations until the centralization crises that shook up the American underworld in the 1930s and 1940s. Once under white control, a new top was grafted onto policy and almost all the money taken in policy would never return to the community.

There were both weakness and strength in the African-American policy syndicates. It is clear that the policy syndicates in New York, Chicago, and Philadelphia were prey to extortionists. To achieve some security from their enemies, enterprise syndicates needed to protect themselves through their own security or through protection provided by politically connected law enforcement agents. In the case of Harlem and Chicago, underworld power brokers simply moved in on them by activating otherwise passive law enforcement agencies.

The major point is that in many instances the rise and fall of professional criminals, white or African American, seem intimately related to the political fortunes of district leaders and vice versa. Several who stand out are Schultz, Hines, Dawson, and the Chicago policy entrepreneurs.

Organized crime is more than just a criminal way of life; it is a viable and persistent institution within American society, with its own symbols, its own beliefs, its own logic, and its own means of transmitting these systematically from one generation to the next. Viewed in this way, organized crime is a pragmatic part of the American social system, and although successive waves of immigrants and migrants have found it a convenient means of economic and social mobility, it persists and transcends the involvement of any particular group and even changing definitions of legality and illegality in social behavior. Although organized crime appears to be a function of the social and economic life in the United States, it can also be viewed as falling on a continuum that has the legitimate business world on the other end.

Ianni's ethnographic study of African-American and Cuban networks in the late 1960s sought to show that the organized crime phenomenon is not unique to the Italian-American experience but that it has a logic of its own, manifesting itself among other groups poised to exploit the criminal opportunities American society thrusts upon them.[45] What seems clear is that the style of illegal activities is affected by the cultural and ethnic characteristics of the participants.

Ianni described conditions in the 1960s in Harlem that produced the bases for a Black Mafia.[46] For ghetto dwellers, one of their most important problems, one that confronted other ethnic immigrants decades earlier, was how to escape poverty through socially approved means, when these means were virtually closed to them. This problem is resolved to some extent by indulging in criminal activities. For most ghetto dwellers, the provision of illegal goods and services or the illegal provision of licit goods and services is tolerated widely because it is not seen as morally evil or socially disruptive. Poverty provides the moral climate for organized criminality in the ghetto, with the exception perhaps of drug peddling. But even here, escape from the bondage of poverty provides the context for widespread drug use. It is also the pervasive poverty of the ghetto that is the basis of recruitment into criminal networks.

The African Americans involved in ghetto policy networks were driven by aims similar to those that motivated the Irish, Jewish, and Italian criminals who preceded them: assimilation into, and accommodation by the larger American society. Apart from pervasive, cruel poverty, the cultural and structural forces that shaped the growth and evolution of white, ethnic-organized criminality may not yet be fully understood among African Americans and Hispanics. There appears to be no cultural ethos and cohesive kinship system among them that could be utilized for criminal purposes in criminal syndicates that have been characteristic of Italians. Certainly, African-American criminal networks can be expected to respond to their own subcultural imperatives, and in lieu of kinship and extended family solidarity, they may substitute peer relationships formed in street gangs and friendship ties forged in prison. These social bonds could be strengthened by a common sense of racial victimization that may form the catalyst necessary to generate and sustain an enduring criminal enterprise among African-American criminals. The next phase of the study examines the epoch between 1940 and 1970 that encompasses World War II, its aftermath, the Korean War, the beginnings of the civil rights movement, and Vietnam.

1. W. E. B. Du Bois, *The Philadelphia Negro*, reprint of [1899] manuscript with Introduction by Herbert Aptheker (Millwood, NY: Kraus-Thomson Organization Limited, 1973).

2. Ibid., 266.

3. Drake and Cayton, *Black Metropolis*, vol. 2, 484.

4. Ibid., 486.

5. The New York City Police Commissioners' *Annual Report* does not show any arrest for policy before 1920.

6. "Policy numbers" referred to here is a numbers game that is based on a three-digit number selected from the clearing house bank's totals. This method of choosing policy numbers in New York is alleged to have started around 1920. Later, in the early 1930s, racehorse *pari-mutuel* results were used instead of the clearing house bank totals to determine winning three-digit policy numbers.

7. This is an approximate average, because it does not include thirteen months (between 1920 and 1930) of missing Twelfth District Magistrates Court Docket Book arrest data when this search was made (the missing books could not be located). The Twelfth District Magistrate Court is one of two courts that processed all arrests made in the Harlem area. During this period Harlem became the residence of the majority of New York City's African-American population.

8. Ivan Light, "Numbers Gambling among Blacks," 892–904.

9. Ibid.

10. Light, *The Ethnic Vice Industry*, 469, 471.

11. Robert J. Kelly, "Field Research among Deviants: A Consideration of Some Methodological Recommendations," *Deviant Behavior* 3 (1982): 219–228.

12. *New York Times*, 23 September 1928, section 1, 2.

13. *The New York Age*, 12 December 1929: 1. Walter Kelly, reputed "King of Policy Operators," in Chicago, Illinois operated a 75,000 to 1 lottery wheel to determine winning numbers. Clearing house numbers were not used in Chicago at the time.

14. Schatzberg, *Black Organized Crime*, chap. 7. Marcellina Cardena, Joseph Matthias Ison, Wilfred Adolphus Brunder, José Enrique Miro, Masjoe Ison, Alexander Pompez, Stephanie St. Clair, John Diamond, Fred Buchanan, Charles Durant, Marshal Flores, Edward and Elmer Maloney, Moe Levy, Hyman and Pauline Kassell were several of the larger policy bankers operating in the Harlem area during the 1920s.

15. Light, "Numbers Gambling among Blacks," 898.

16. Henry R. Lesieur and Joseph R. Shelley, "Illegal Appended Enterprises: Selling the Lives," *Social Problems* 34, no. 3 (June 1987): 249–260.

17. Redding, "Playing the Numbers," 542.

18. Samuel Seabury, "In the Matter of the Investigation of the Magistrates Courts in the First Judicial Department and the Magistrates Thereof, and of Attorneys-at-Law Practicing in Said Courts," Supreme Court, Appellate Division, First Judicial Department. *Final Report*, 1932, 137–138.

19. Dewey, *Twenty against the Underworld*, 98–101.

20. Humbert S. Nelli, *The Business of Crime: Italians and Syndicate Crime in the United States* (New York: Oxford University Press, 1976), chap. 8.

21. Gunnar Myrdal, *An American Dilemma*, 330; Redding, "Playing the Numbers," 533–542, 536–537.

22. *The New York Age*, 31 January 1925, 2.

23. Ibid., 28 February 1925; 12 June 1926, 1–2.

24. Ibid., 12 June 1926, 1–2.

25. Ibid., 12 June 1926, 2; 26 June 1926, 1; 7 August 1926, 1.

26. J. Richard Davis, "Things I Couldn't Tell Till Now," *Collier's*, 22, 29, July; 5, 12, 19, 26 August 1939.

27. Craig Thompson and Allen Raymond, *Gang Rule in New York* (New York: Dial Press, 1940).

28. Davis, "Things I Couldn't Tell Till Now," 29 July 1939, 21, 37.

29. Dewey, *Twenty against the Underworld*, 320.

30. Herbert Mitgang, *The Man Who Rode the Tiger: The Life and Times of Judge Samuel Seabury* (New York: J. B. Lippincott Company, 1963), 204.

31. Ibid.

32. *The New York Age*, 13 December 1930, 2.

33. Ibid., 2.

34. Paul Sann, *Kill the Dutchman!* (New Rochelle, NY: Arlington House, 1971), 56–57.

35. Ibid., Thompson and Raymond, *Gang Rule in New York,* 325.

36. Carlson, "Number Gambling," 55–64.

37. Swanson D. Carter, "Numbers Gambling: The Negro's Illegal Response to Status Discrimination in American Society," Master's thesis, Wayne State University, 1970.

38. Stephen Fox, *Blood and Power,* 237–238.

39. James W. Wilson, *Negro Politics: The Search for Leadership* (New York: Free Press, 1960), 65; a quote from John Madigan, "The Durable Mr. Dawson of Cook County, Illinois," *Reporter,* 9 August 1956, 39–40.

40. William Brashler, *The Don: The Life and Death of Sam Giancana* (New York: Harper & Row, 1977).

41. U.S. Senate *Gambling and Organized Crime: Hearing before the Permanent Subcommittee on Investigation,* 87th Cong., 1st sess., (Washington, DC: US Government Printing Office, 22 August, 8 September 1961).

42. U.S. Senate, Mid-Atlantic Regions: Hearing before the Permanent Subcommittee on Investigation. *Profile of Organized Crime,* 98th Cong., 1st sess., (Washington, DC: US Government Printing Office, 15–24 February 1983).

43. Peterson, *The Mob: 200 Years of Organized Crime,* 251.

44. Block, *East Side—West Side.*

45. Francis A. J. Ianni, *Black Mafia.*

46. Ibid., 210.

RACIAL SERVITUDE AND MUTINY
IN THE UNDERWORLD, 1940–1970

You might almost say the numbers is the salvation of Harlem, its
Medicare, and its Black Draught, its 666 [two laxatives popular in the
South], its little liver pills, its vitamins, its aspirins, and its analgesic balm
combined.

Langston Hughes [1]

As the war years progressed, African-American criminal enterprises took on
various forms and developed connections with larger, more powerful organizations, such that some enterprises were dominated by white gangsters
while others remained exclusively controlled and managed by African Americans. In New York during the 1920s, African Americans controlled their own
policy operations. In the early 1930s Schultz absorbed the Harlem policy
rackets into his criminal confederation and African Americans were reduced
to salaried employees directly involved with seasoned, career gangsters operating Harlem's policy rackets. Even after Schultz's death, many remained
in the organization and were subsequently indicted along with James Hines
and Richard "Dixie" Davis in 1937, when Thomas Dewey, a special pros-
ecutor, arrested members of the Schultz policy cartel. Alexander Pompez,
Masjoe and Joseph Mathias Ison, José Enrique Miro, Marshal Flores, and
Wilfred Adolphus Brunder, key policy operatives in Harlem, were now
schooled in the abrasive ways that gangsters resort to in a policy racket.

After Schultz's murder in 1935, control of the numbers racket passed
into the hands of East Harlem La Cosa Nostra racketeer "Trigger Mike"
Coppola of the Vito Genovese crime family. When Coppola was implicated
in the murder of Joseph R. Scottoriggio, he retired to Florida and left the
racket in the hands of his lieutenant, "Fat Tony" Salerno.[2] "Fat Tony" controlled the numbers until his conviction in November, 1986, in what became
known as the "Commission Case." Salerno, Tony "Ducks" Corallo of the

Luccheses, Carmine Persico of the Colombo Family, Gennaro Langella, acting boss of the Colombo Family, Paul Castellano, boss of the Gambino Family, (who was murdered before he could stand trial), and four others were all found guilty as family bosses operating the national Commission of the La Cosa Nostra.

In Detroit, Philadelphia, Cleveland, and Boston the local mafiosi had generally seized control of numbers gambling by 1940. The African-American policy bankers in Chicago held on a bit longer. In 1940, while in prison, Sam Giancana met Eddie Jones, who, with his brothers, operated most of Chicago's policy wheels. The Joneses invested their policy earnings in legitimate businesses, purchasing a Ben Franklin store, four hotels, a food market, and several apartment buildings. Through Giancana's association with Eddie Jones, the "Outfit," Chicago's mafia, was introduced into the policy gambling racket.[3] In the usual underworld pattern, the Italian gangsters took charge of enforcement and profits while Jewish associates, such as Nig Rosen in Philadelphia, ran the business and counted the money. As workers for the Mafia, African Americans still did the footwork, roaming a given territory each day to make collections and payoffs to customers.[4]

In 1944, Gunnar Myrdal suggested that the African-American underworld appeared to have a "class" structure. He stated,

> [T]here is a Negro "underworld." To it belong not only petty thieves and racketeers, prostitutes and pimps, bootleggers, dope addicts, and so on, but also a number of "big shots" organizing and controlling crime, vice, and racketeering, as well as other more innocent forms of illegal activity such as gambling—particularly the "policy," or the "numbers," game. The underworld has, therefore, an upper class and a middle class as well as a lower class. . . . The shady upper class is composed mainly of the "policy kings." They are the most important members of the underworld from the point of view of their numbers, their wealth and their power. The policy game started in the Negro Community has a long history. This game caught on quickly among Negroes because one may bet as little as a penny, and the rewards are high if one wins (as much as 600 to 1). In a community where most of the people are either on relief or in the lowest income brackets such rewards must appear exceptionally alluring . . . During most of its history the policy racket in the Negro community has been monopolized by Negroes.[5]

Myrdal described the "culture" of the African-American criminal enterprise built around policy, with its hierarchical structure of "big shots," policy "Kings and Queens"—descriptive language markedly different from that referring to the Cosa Nostra "crime bosses" and "crime Czars," which imply sinister, cunning characteristics typical of career criminals. Al Capone ("Scarface" to many) had a reputation for explosive violence and acted brutally toward his enemies and partners alike when it was advantageous. Luciano of New York, and recently, John Gotti, career criminals also, were not noted for their diplomatic, genteel ways.

In contrast to the images of white gangsters, African-American gambling and alcohol entrepreneurs during World War II and the postwar years were not perceived of or defined as dangerously violent individuals, as were their Mafia counterparts. They projected a more benign type of "criminal" and even the term "criminal" must be loosely applied, because their enterprises enjoyed widespread community support, as Myrdal indicates. Others, not connected with gambling enterprises in the communities, operated individually, and these persons in drugs, prostitution, robbery, and other criminal activity were more readily perceived of as dangerous and violent. Overall, however, the power of white organized crime proved irresistible.

In the 1960s, concerns about African-American family breakdown, with birthrates of children born to unmarried mothers at about 26 percent, began to worry many observers. Since then (in 1994), illegitimacy has reached 68 percent of all African-American births and often over 80 percent in inner cities. It is widely believed that as illegitimacy increases, schools deteriorate and communities collapse. These conditions of urban decay correlate with drugs, illiteracy, welfare, and homelessness, and a rising incidence of crime where the cultural values of unsocialized children (mostly male adolescents) coupled with rampant physical violence and predatory sex become the norms, making illegitimacy and female-headed households an important social problem. From the 1940s through the 1970s the problem of the underclass and its disruptive effects on community life was not as clear as it is today.

COURTIER POLITICS IN THE GHETTO

World War II did little to improve the integration of African Americans into the political and economic mainstream of America. Bruising court battles had to be fought before the Supreme Court in *Brown v. The Board of Education* (1954) overturned the segregationist philosophy enshrouded in the Court's 1896 decision in *Plessy v. Ferguson,* which found that segregation did not, in itself, jeopardize the constitutional rights of African-American school children. In the United States armed forces, a Presidential Executive Order had to be issued in order to integrate military units that until then remained segregated and discriminatory, with white officers commanding African-American units.

After the War, former scandalous racist policies appeared to have a second breath and resumed throughout most communities in every region of the United States. This meant that social mobility for African-American war veterans would not materialize, as would be the case for millions of white veterans and their families. Prior to the War, the alienation that was so widespread throughout the depression years resulted in the formation of large criminal syndicates that were, from a sociological standpoint, desperate attempts by those closed off from legitimate institutional pathways to material success to carve out nothing less than expedient ways to circumvent obstacles—even if it meant embracing crime to do so. In the postwar period and throughout most of the 1950s, African-American communities were simply ignored and abandoned; and, most important, they lacked access to innovative and even organized criminal resources that enabled whites to avoid and neutralize class prejudices and deterrents to upward social mobility. In the virulent climate of overt racial discrimination ("Jim Crow") throughout the South and less obvious forms of segregation—but no less pernicious socially, economically, and psychologically—in the North, the African-American communities appeared to be economically stagnant. Able and fortunate African Americans, whose skills, talent, and luck enabled them to escape the crushing confines of the community, hastily abandoned it for the middle-class lifestyle. For millions of others, trapped in deteriorating communities, increasingly dependent on public assistance, or barely surviving as working poor people, the threats to the institutional integrity of the family, school, and church seemed utterly insurmountable.

Along with the family, the African-American church must be credited with holding together and sustaining the social bonds of the community prior to the civil rights movement and thereafter. It was the African-American church and ministry that became the epicenter of the civil rights movement, which may be thought of as a social revolution. Even before the War, the church served as a moral compass in the community and most played a significant role through their ministries as agents of crime control. It seems doubtful that the policy racket could have been tolerated had the church opposed it. Although most criminological accounts seem inclined to play down the power of the African-American church as an influential force in everyday life, ignoring its social and political roles in shaping norms and standards is perilous to any comprehensive social analysis.

The church in the African-American community has always been the place where protest and condemnation could be most vividly articulated and, at the same time, has functioned as a kind of psychological sanctuary. Most ministers could not hope to effect any objective change in the lives of their congregation, nor did the people expect them to; all church members came to find, and all they could receive, was the moral sustenance for another day's journey. But some ministers, notably Dr. Martin Luther King and the Southern Christian Leadership Conference (SCLC) did make a difference—a profound difference in everyone's life.

With few exceptions, during the 1940s and 1950s, the political captivity of African Americans and the dilemmas of their leadership were transparent. African-American leaders in the ghettos had been vested with little power because their vote had so very little impact in electoral politics at large. It was not easy to win concessions from people at the bargaining table who had, after all, no intention of relinquishing their power.

One can characterize the medley of professionals within the African-American community—the minister, the journalist, the lawyer, and the politician—as courier politicians who were hired, selected, or elected to arrange the truth into its most flattering and convenient poses, mediating between their patrons and the rudeness of the world beyond the ghetto.

The talented courtier possesses what Plutarch called "the soul of the acrobat" and once instructed in the correct forms of expedient behavior and speech, it is a relatively simple matter to survive as a "leader." Naturally, as the meaning of their lives and careers becomes synonymous with the pieties of meeting the requirements of the power structure, they know themselves to be superfluous. The art of survival and servility in a compromised racially sensitive world consists in the maintenance of the facade of government. But talents are needed to survive as a "mainstream" politician, one skilled in the ritual language of the issues.

Smiling and accommodating, many pre–civil rights movement politicians and religious ministers found themselves prepared to deny or distort the truth out of necessity. Preachers developed a certain refined simplicity. Unfortunately, this exegetical style has become so stereotyped a formula that the affectation of frankness was (and is often) more suggestive of a polite fiction than the time-honored expectation of honesty and truthfulness.

Today, in many instances, that same sense of helplessness and frustration affects African-American political leaders. For example, while many of the housing projects erected in African-American neighborhoods are stimulated by perpetually embattled leaders and local media, these community influentials find themselves in an impossible position. Those motivated by genuine concern must maintain a facade of strength with heartbreaking dignity.

It is unlikely that anyone acquainted with ghetto housing projects seriously assumes that one playground more or less has any profound effect on the psychology of the citizens there; similarly with schools. Anyone taking ghetto schools at face value must realize that they do more to incapacitate than educate, but leaders must demand these, because it is better, after all is said and done, to have playgrounds and schools so that African Americans are not entirely forgotten.

Consequently, many see politics as no more than the art of the possible, understanding it much in the way that an eighteenth-century general saw war: a vast and elaborate set of parade ground maneuvers by armies that would never actually engage in conflict, but instead declare victory, surrender, or compromise as their apparent strength dictated in order to collaborate on the real business of sharing the spoils. This is not a cynical appreciation of conditions, in that the local political structure in communities where vice, drugs, and other organized crime are present are usually environments of uneven political sensitivity where the indigenous leaders are peripheral to the centers of real power. One outcome of this political marginality has been the growth of the underclass.

According to Wilson,

> The urban political machines, controlled in large measure by working-class ethnics who were often in direct competition with blacks in the private industrial sector, systematically gerrymandered black neighborhoods and excluded the urban black masses from meaningful political participation throughout the early twentieth century. Control of white ethnics of the various urban political machines was so complete that blacks were never really in a position to compete for the more important municipal political rewards such as patronage jobs or government contracts and services.[6]

and,

> The proliferation of jobs created by industrial expansion helped generate and sustain the continuous mass migration of blacks from the rural South to the cities of the North and West. As the black urban population grew and became more segregated, institutions and organization in the black community also developed, together with a business and professional class affiliated with these institutions.[7]

Thus, the lack of meaningful political power within the ghetto produces the phenomenon of an "internal colony."[8]

In the later stages of the civil rights movement, when significant political gains had been achieved, the problems confronting African-American leadership and perhaps African-American officeholders at the municipal level, were not adequate in meliorating ghetto problems.[9] As Hatcher points out, terrain is now in the control of African Americans that was formerly beyond their grasp, but still the economic leverage ordinarily accompanying political power is missing.

The ghetto as a colony means that the African-American community is dominated as a political and economic unit subordinated to, and dependent upon, external power structures. Typically, the colonizers exploit the labor, capital resources, and assets of the colonized. And more than this, as Kenneth Clark described forcefully many years ago, the ghetto's subjective dimensions—resentment, hostility, rage, apathy, self-depreciation, and its ironic companion, grandiose behavior—create a situation in which those within the ghetto can never be sure whether their failures reflect personal deficiencies or the facts of race.[10]

In a curious way, however, the lack of social-class escalators that many social scientists see as an incentive to delinquency and criminal activity may be for some, especially those with limited options, a healthy response in that it signifies that oppressed people still possess sufficient strength to rebel and have not yet given in to defeat.[11] One may speculate that delinquency and crime are at least a measure of group ferment in that they reject, as exemplified by the inherent sense of rebelliousness characteristic of the criminal act, the inferior status imposed on them. The roots of ghetto crime, understood not as a form of pathology, but rebellion and rejection of the status quo, are diverse and many. They cannot be traced simply to bad housing, or lack of jobs, for by themselves, these crimes are not necessarily causative factors in sociopsychological disintegration. Taken together, they help to form patterns of instability that constantly threaten the emotional integrity of those caught in its web.

POLITICS AND ORGANIZED CRIME

The proliferation of African-American organized criminal groups in the post–World War II era seems to have also run aside the rise of African-American political consciousness and the awakening of political and social militancy. The links between politics and crime evident in the white community in the prewar era appeared to have emerged in the African-American communities. The general organized crime trends in the white community that seemed to rise slowly as alcohol and drugs became the dominant—and most profitable—illicit product of the 1920s and 1930s were not matched in the African-American community. Major African American traffickers in drugs surfaced in the early and mid-1960s, when pressures were mounted by African Americans for jobs, educational reform, fair housing, and a greater share of political power. Apparently, a combination of factors coalesced, some with unanticipated consequences that produced legitimate and illegitimate opportunity structures. In the wake of sweeping reforms, African Americans gained greater control over their communities, and as their political strength grew, criminal elements were able to take advantage of the correlative declines in white power. African-American influence within the ghetto crime scene increased, and gangsters were more able then than at any other time to wrest the ghetto's lucrative rackets away from white syndicates. They became less dependent upon La Cosa Nostra's political and police clout and could bargain independently with whites who were no longer able to operate as freely in the ghettos.

Organizations such as the Congress of Racial Equality in their 1967 annual convention publicly declared (facetiously, it may be supposed) that organized crime be reorganized in such a way that African Americans, not La Cosa Nostra, be permitted to monopolize organized-crime activities in their community and that those activities that were most harmful to the psychological health of the community be eliminated.[12] Adam Clayton Powell, Jr., minister and Congressman from Harlem, charged that New York police discriminated against African-American policy operators by arresting a greater proportion of independent African-American lottery operators than their Italian counterparts. Also, he wanted it known that as long as the illegal policy rackets operated, African Americans should have their share of the profits.

The civil rights movement set in motion social and economic mobility and inadvertently diminished the power of white crime groups that had dominated these communities until then. As the ghettos developed their newfound strength and accumulated political punch, the political agent, the operator, the machine functionary, not unfamiliar in white communities who had connections in the "administration" or City Hall, appeared on the scene. As the ghettos became more politically assertive and more economically viable, a host of new actors appeared: the "minority middlemen," the power brokers, those who were equally comfortable in the official world of government and business and in the shadows of opportunism and crime, where favors are arranged, deals are made, and money, when properly placed, can shield and immunize its possessors from the criminal justice system.

Despite the racist ideology conceived of African Americans, their underworld during the thirty years from World War II to the Vietnam Era was not a homogeneous, monolithic structure of power and influence but one that developed liaisons and partnerships with the power structures of the La Cosa Nostra, which it would eventually shed. Ellsworth Raymond "Bumpy" Johnson, a Harlem underworld figure (a bump on the back of his head gave him his nickname), worked essentially as a middleman and enforcer from 1940 to 1968 between the Italian syndicate (the Genovese Family) and African-American gangsters operating in Harlem.[13] If an African-American drug dealer wanted to buy a large quantity of drugs, Johnson arranged the sale. Italian gangsters knew him as a "persuader," one who could settle underworld quarrels before they erupted into violence, and overt violence they naturally wished to avoid. As such, Johnson was assigned to a place that for an African American in those days was considered high in the ruling circles of organized crime. When he was not in jail (where he spent twenty-five years of his adult life), millions of dollars in syndicate funds passed through his hands. He died in July, 1968, while free on $50,000 bail following a 1967 indictment by a federal grand jury on charges of importing narcotics from Peru to be sold in Harlem.

Since the early 1960s, federal and city law enforcement officials have described Raymond Marquez, also known as "Spanish Raymond," as one of the city's most successful numbers operators in the Harlem area. He is alleged to have built a gambling empire worth $30 million a year.[14] Marquez served a five-year sentence in federal prison in the early 1970s on gambling charges, but his network continued to flourish in his absence. Between 1950 and the 1970s, Marquez paid a percentage of his profits to Mafia boss "Fat Tony" Salerno, and today it is claimed that Marquez pays the Genovese crime family $300 a week for race track *pari-mutuel* results for his gambling operations.[15] It is apparent that the Mafia crime families still control the racetrack wire services, which are vital in illegal gambling operations.

In 1958, Marquez was involved in a publicized killing. "Spanish Raymond" who co-owned with Henry Lawrence an African-American/Puerto Rican policy bank operating in Harlem's Eighth Avenue section, was accused of killing David Peters, 28, the hoodlum son of an African-American minister. The shooting was alleged to have occurred over Peters' numbers-writing activities in an area where Marquez and Lawrence maintained ten "protected" policy spots. (In 1960, the *New York Post's* investigation of just ninety approved spots in a single section of Harlem indicated that specified payments to the police involved exceeded $200,000 a month, or an annual take to police of more than $2,500,000 annually.[16]) A grand jury failed to indict "Spanish Raymond" in the Peters homicide.[17]

During the Vietnam era, America began to experience an extraordinary fallout from the war. One movement or effect or outgrowth was "flower power," the protest generation and their blatant advocacy of drug use. At first, the "drugs of choice" during the Vietnam era were marijuana, amphetamines, and LSD, although gradually, heroin and cocaine replaced them. The Vietnam War opened the door for new opportunists to find underground trade routes to the heroin laboratories of Laos, Cambodia, and Thailand. Former African-American servicemen accomplished in a few short years what others had been unable to do under nearly two hundred years of white oppression. They broke the bonds that forced them to buy heroin from white importers in the United States—mostly La Cosa Nostra—and started their own smuggling and distribution networks, controlling operations from poppy cultivation to the selling of bags in ghetto streets. African Americans imported heroin in a ghastly but effective manner: in the caskets of servicemen killed in Vietnam. They distributed, marketed, and reaped the benefits and in the process got rich.

The Vietnam War grubstaked African-American organized crime and enabled it to grow exponentially. From these experiences, African-American organized crime has spread widely, much as La Cosa Nostra did in its early days. The crime groups include street gangs, the most notorious being the Los Angeles-based Crips and Bloods, and the violent Jamaican Posses, who have shown an uncanny ability to establish themselves in drug-free communities and create insatiable markets for marijuana and crack/cocaine.

By the end of the 1960s, the Vietnam War was at its height, the civil rights movement was actively promoting racial tolerance, and African-American pride was intense. It was in this setting that unintentional harm may have befallen poor, African-American inner-city youths by the antiwar demonstrations, which demanded the end of the military draft. Historically, conscription provided these youths with opportunities that took them off the street at a critical age—between eighteen and twenty—and provided a structured environment and discipline that they might otherwise never have known. Gangs offered street recognition, status, and support, all for the commission of crimes, whereas military service gave them the chance to learn a trade, something they could bring back to their neighborhood or take elsewhere when discharged from the service. Although service in Vietnam was the occasion for the organization of the drug traffic on an unprecedented scale, most of all, military service was a slim chance to achieve and to strive for the kinds of goals previously denied them.

Two of the most notorious African-American street gangs in the

United States were born in this tumultuous political and economic climate. Between 1955 and 1965, street gangs mushroomed in South Central Los Angeles and Compton, where neighborhood youths banded together to fend off other gangs. These gangs restricted their activities to their neighborhoods and high school sporting events, but they changed profoundly, becoming oriented to more criminal ways and lifestyles.

AN INNER-CITY COMMUNITY AND ORGANIZED CRIME: SYMBIOSIS

Lasswell and McKenna, between 1963 and 1970, studied the effects of organized crime on the inner-city community of Bedford-Stuyvesant in New York City.[18] Included in the project were studies of police archives, investigations of ongoing organized crime activity, and interviews with community residents—all focused on the development of an appropriate theoretical model of how organized crime interacts with the social process. The most important outcome of the research effort—a startling conclusion, but not unexpected—was that organized crime was the single most powerful force in the community. Organized crime activities grossed more revenue from its gambling and narcotics operations than the federal government collected in income taxes. Organized crime was also the largest single employer of community residents and effectively nullified whatever counterattacks were mounted against it by the government. No program, public or private, appeared capable of controlling or reducing major illegal operations in the community.

Although the authors did not propose a set of policies, a bridge from theory to practice, they carefully spelled out the practical implications from which organized crime problems may be viewed from a variety of perspectives. The researchers did not suggest that their study be used as a model in analyzing other ghetto criminal operations, because it was clear that it could not and should not be used to evaluate the effects of vice and criminality in other ghettos, whose circumstances were likely to be very different. However, one generalization seemed valid: Ethnographic studies of ghettos tend to confirm the idea that they are dysfunctional components within the larger society. Status frustration, cultural innovation, and their expression in illicit vice activities are the innovative responses to oppressive conditions and limited economic opportunities.

In the Lasswell study, the economic analysis of the data indicated that the hold of crime on that community had become sufficiently stabilized, so that for every dollar increase in per capita income in the community, there resulted a 10 percent diversion of that dollar to organized crime. Also, the authors showed a correlation between the narcotics traffic and the major crimes of robbery, burglary, and larceny. Every additional narcotics addict residing in Bedford-Stuyvesant increased the narcotics-related crime rate by a factor of at least .006 per 1,000 residents. Between 1963 and 1970, profits to organized crime from its gambling and narcotics operations in Bedford-Stuyvesant rose from a per capita figure of $25.50 to $214. By 1970, organized crime was grossing $88 million in current dollars from its operations.

Before 1936, Bedford-Stuyvesant was a fashionable, upper-middle-income section of Brooklyn. Residential development occurred between 1870 and 1930, but the depression hit the area at a time when there was an oversupply of houses available for sale. In 1936, the city extended a new subway line into Bedford-Stuyvesant that opened a rapid transit link with Harlem. The more prosperous African Americans began migrating from overcrowded Harlem and buying the oversupply of residential houses that were available.

By 1940, the Bedford-Stuyvesant racial balance hovered around 60 percent white and 38 percent African American. The community tipped to 51 percent African American in 1947 as a result of continuing migration drawn by the semiskilled job opportunities provided during World War II in the nearby, bustling Brooklyn Navy Yard. Through the 1950s and 1960s the racial composition of the community continued to change, so that by 1970 Bedford-Stuyvesant was overwhelmingly African American (82 percent).

And by 1970, Bedford-Stuyvesant was an economically depressed area. Its unemployment rate was double the national average. If the 1970 unemployment rate is added to the figure for area residents employed at less than a living wage, then the number jumped to 42 percent of the labor force out of work or marginally employed.

The two major activities of organized crime in Bedford-Stuyvesant, as in other inner-city areas, were the illegal numbers or policy game, and narcotics trafficking. Organized crime's other traditional operations, such as loansharking, hijacking, and the like, were not found to be a substantial criminal activity.

Policy Operations in Bedford-Stuyvesant

The New York City Police Department was arresting numbers operators in Bedford-Stuyvesant before African Americans arrived. By 1970, however, the scope of the numbers operation in that community had expanded to the point where five identifiable policy banks were servicing twelve policy combines, employing approximately 1,400 area residents and grossing $36.8 million annually. Of all the policy operators, only one of the bankers was an African American, but the police believed that even he paid a percentage of his profits to a white organized crime boss. The remaining bankers were white, and were identified as members of one of New York City's five (organized crime) families.

Methodologically, the Lasswell study suggested that the anatomy of any policy operation can be extracted from the "raid" data, and in the case of Bedford-Stuyvesant, there was a rich mine of policy bank documents seized by police. In the eight years between 1963 and 1970, the policy banks of Bedford-Stuyvesant were raided by the police seventy-three times. The composite picture of the policy operation in that community is reflected in Table 6.1. The data are hard in that they were painstakingly compiled from an inspection of the records seized during the period studied.

TABLE 6.1. The Volume of Policy Play in Bedford-Stuyvesant

Year	$ Volume of policy play (in millions)	Population (in thousands)	Banks	Number of controllers	Collectors
1963	$ 9.3	285	7	35	762
1964	10.3	281	7	40	892
1965	10.7	282	7	64	1039
1966	13.2	285	7	72	1068
1967	12.7	285	6	72	1140
1968	14.8	281	6	73	1239
1969	21.4	281	6	74	1269
1970	36.8	280	5	76	1345

Source: Harold D. Lasswell and Jeremiah McKenna, *The Impact of Organized Crime on an Inner City Community* (U.S. Department of Commerce. Springfield, Virginia, 1972), p. 112.

Between 1963 and 1970, the data indicate that the Bedford-Stuyvesant policy operation quadrupled its dollar volume and doubled the number of its employees. By 1970, the police could count 76 controllers and 1,345 collectors working in the policy rackets. These operatives were paid solely from policy proceeds. Gross receipts in actual dollars increased from $9.3 million in 1963 to almost $37 million in 1970. By 1970, the net take to employees and banks was at least $11 million.

Policy operations take ten cents of every dollar increase in community income. As the betting on policy increased by $1 million along with a

$10 million increase in community income, an additional thirty residents of the community (twenty-eight runners and two controllers) were recruited into the operation. The investigation discovered that to the extent that Bedford-Stuyvesant's gambling and narcotics operation are rooted in the community's social process, merely increasing the police deployed in the area or harassing the gambling and narcotics operation did not bring lasting results. It merely reduced the diversion of community resources into policy activity and perhaps slowed the rate of increase of drug addiction; but it did not eradicate the problem of illegal gambling or narcotics trafficking. Both illicit activities seem to have achieved an internal dynamics that is self-correcting and renewing.

The data in Table 6.1 point to these processes: for example, as the number of policy banks decreased over seven years from 1963 to 1970, and as the population declined, both the number of controllers and collectors increased, which may be construed as indicators of organizational consolidation and sophistication. The natural market forces of competition were apparently at work and those most able to neutralize police and protect their enterprise were able to survive and grow.

The data reflecting these trends are even more dramatic when examined carefully. Within a seven year period, the amount of money flowing in illicit gambling in the community increased fourfold; and the infrastructure (controllers and collectors) servicing this illegal activity more than doubled. All of this occurred as the unemployment rate in the community reached crisis proportions (42 percent).

Bedford-Stuyvesant Narcotics Trafficking

The narcotics traffic in Bedford-Stuyvesant may also be compared to a service industry (like the policy operation). In its basic structure it involves suppliers and consumers. The only narcotic drug of any consequence in Bedford-Stuyvesant in the late 1960s was heroin. The New York City Narcotics Register, which lists all persons coming to the attention of an official agency as a result of the possession, sale, or drug abuse, indicates that heroin was the drug for 99 percent of the area's drug abusers. There is also ample evidence in the public record that the importation and large-scale distribution of heroin in New York City was a monopoly of organized crime.

Lasswell recognized that intelligence gathering concerning the dimensions of the narcotics traffic lacked the hard database of policy bank operations. A raid on a heroin-cutting mill does not produce the same detailed records as does a policy bank. In fact, a major problem of the entire effort to control the heroin traffic in New York (and elsewhere) has been the lack of quality intelligence. However, it is possible to fit several pieces of information together to produce reliable estimates of heroin traffic in a particular area. The first step is to count the number of addicts in that community.

The Narcotics Register reported a total of 10,977 new addicts registered between 1964 and 1970 in the Fort Greene and Bedford health districts, which embrace an area slightly larger than, but including, all of Bedford-Stuyvesant. Police files of known resident addicts indicated that more than 6,000 heroin users frequented the area. A formula developed by Dr. Michael Baden of the New York City Medical Examiner's Office, which calculates a specific number of live addicts for every addict verified to have died from narcotics abuse, indicated that there were 6,125 heroin addicts frequenting Bedford-Stuyvesant in 1970. Two other officially sponsored scientific surveys of the addict population for the area found even greater numbers of addicts. Finally, the city's Addiction Services Agency indicated that by 1970, over 2,000 heroin addicts from the area had enrolled in methadone maintenance programs. Therefore, the lowest estimate of 6,125 resident heroin addicts in Bedford-Stuyvesant in 1970 probably errs on the conservative side. Numbers of addicts were matched to the median heroin habit. Police estimates of median addict habits were checked with known addicts, interviewees at local methadone centers, and surveys performed by Narcotics Register personnel; Table 6.2 summarizes the results of that survey.

The analysis shows that although the price of a single glassine envelope containing heroin had remained stable, there was a steady dilution of the drugs' purity in each bag. Economically, the results have been an actual tripling of price over an eight-year period. Socially, the addict population in the area had just about doubled every two years. This indicates that the addict population, after reaching a certain critical mass in numbers, develops its own dynamism and draws more and more people into its subculture. The data relative to number of pushers were obtained from narcotics squad intelligence files. It included primarily nonaddict sellers operating just above the street level on up to middle-echelon distributors. At one time or another, most had been arrested for the possession or sale of heroin. The numbers do not include importers or kilo distributors who drive the narcotics distribution networks in the community.

Unlike numbers betting, the cost of heroin to a community transcends the gross purchase price. The enormous amount of cash required to support the narcotics traffic, ($51 million in 1970) cannot be generated by the depressed economy of the area. The typical crimes committed by addicts are, in descending order of seriousness, robbery (mugging), burglary, and larceny.

These offenses are commonly included under the rubric, narcotics-related crime.

TABLE 6.2. Narcotics in Bedford-Stuyvesant

Year	Number of addicts	Median bag habit*	Price per bag	Median number grains per bag*	Median annual cost	Total annual cost	Number of known pushers in Bedford-Stuyvesant
1963	1,866	1.5	$5	3.0	$2,920	$5,448,720	47
1964	2,076	1.5	7	3.0	4,015	8,335,140	73
1965	1,836	2.0	5	2.0	3,650	6,701,400	48
1966	2,028	2.0	5	2.0	3,650	7,402,200	65
1967	3,936	4.0	5	1.5	7,300	28,732,800	23
1968	3,900	4.0	5	1.0	7,300	28,470,000	113
1969	6,036	4.5	4	1.0	6,570	39,656,520	225
1970	6,125	5.5	4	1.0	8,395	51,419,375	321

*Those are mathematical medians. It is recognized that in actual purchase it would be a whole bag, containing one or more whole grains of heroin.

Source: See Table 6.1.

Table 6.3 shows that there is a definite correlation between narcotics-related crime and area increases in the addict population. However, the number of crimes upon which the statistics are based involved crimes reported to the police. It has long been known that crimes reported to the police are only a fraction of the crimes actually committed. Some surveys have estimated that the actual count of robberies and burglaries is nearly twice the number reported.

The Lasswell study produced interesting findings from its analysis of the narcotics traffic, which conflicted with some commonly held impressions. When the increase in the welfare population in the area and the increase in welfare funds flowing into the area were examined in connection with narcotics figures, no significant relationship was found, other than the fact that an increase in the level of welfare payments increased the per capita income. The racial factor, namely, the rate of increase in the African-American population in Bedford-Stuyvesant, had no significant correlation with the rate of increase in the narcotics traffic. As mentioned earlier, there was a strong correlation between the number of addicts and the crimes of robbery, burglary, and larceny. An increase of one addict in the area showed an increase in the narcotics-related crime rate by a factor of .006 to .007 per 1,000 population. On the other hand, if the price per grain of heroin were to increase by one dollar, an increase in the narcotics-related crime rate would occur on the order of 9.5 crimes per 1,000 population.

TABLE 6.3. Narcotics-Related Crime

Year	Narcotics-Related Crime Rate*	Number of Addicts
1963	9.2	1,866
1964	11.68	2,076
1965	13.22	1,836
1966	24.04	2,028
1967	30.80	3,935
1968	47.05	3,000
1969	46.65	6,036
1970	52.47	6,125

* Per thousand population

Source: See Table 6.1

The extent of gambling and drug economies in Bedford-Stuyvesant affected not only law enforcement but also all the institutions in the community by depleting their scarce assets in criminal justice operations. The consequences for individuals and families living in such a crime-ridden environment are ominous, to say the least. In Harlem's numbers operations, the illicit income generated tended to circulate back into the community, such that gambling functioned as a substitute for scarce legitimate economic enterprises. In the case of Bedford-Stuyvesant, there is no evidence that illicitly generated capital stayed within the community. On the contrary, the fact that organized crime families of La Cosa Nostra dominated the vice industries of drugs and gambling meant that illegal profits flowed out of the community and were not transformed into capital wealth for internal consumption. The outcome was a steady decline in the economic viability of the community, characterized by an exodus of middle-class African Americans and an expanding destitute, helpless underclass overwhelmed by crime.

Throughout the history of minority urban ghettos in the United States, the currencies of the informal economy are heroin and now crack/cocaine. The gangs that developed around them reflect the dynamics of the trafficking systems. In these respects, modern minority criminal groups, particularly African Americans, have little structural resemblance to La Cosa Nostra crime families. Still, these groups are no less dangerous, nor are they likely to be short-lived or only drug-dependent, because the gangs may thrive beyond the demand for drugs and transform themselves to meet the illegal market conditions of other illicit commodities in demand. Drugs enable minority groups to generate essential criminogenic assets (the use of violence and the availability and distributions of illegal commodities). Once established, these groups can explore other criminal opportunities in much the same way that the criminal groups that emerged to serve the demand of illicit alcohol did during the Prohibition era.

Since crack and heroin are to ghetto entrepreneurial gangsters as booze was to the white ethnic gangsters during the Prohibition era, it is conceivable that Prohibition, which made the alcohol gangsters rich, may now parallel the commodities of crack and heroin as a contemporary lucrative modus vivendi for today's drug dealers. Crack is more available to small-time ghetto gangsters than heroin, mainly because the initial investment is within their financial reach. Moreover, the chemical process that yields crack is no secret: References to the recipe that uses heat and baking soda to turn cocaine into hydrochloride, or powder, and then into the smokable form of freebase called crack appeared throughout the late 1960s and early 1970s in underground literature, media interviews, and congressional testimony. What turned crack into a craze was mass marketing. Cocaine powder required an investment of at least $75 a gram, but a "hit" of crack costs as little as $5. Enormous profits are made by converting cocaine into crack.

Three classes of criminals created the crack epidemic. One was composed of anonymous kitchen chemists and drug traffickers in the United States, who used rudimentary science and marketing savvy to help hundreds of small-time criminals set up operations. The second group consisted of indigenous crime organizations, common in most medium-sized and large American cities, that seized local markets from smaller operators. The third group were gangs on both coasts who franchised crack operations into every corner of the country using African Americans and Latinos as their subordinates.

Survey research similar to the Lasswell study of Bedford-Stuyvesant found that organized crime activities were deeply rooted in impoverished

African-American communities. In the Illinois Crime Survey conducted at about the same time as the Lasswell research, it was found that in terms of race, over 40 percent of the African-American population surveyed (which included a household survey of citizens in the four most populous areas of Illinois and a systematic analysis of court records), bet illegally on sports events, and more than 30 percent bet on policy numbers. Furthermore, over 95 percent of African-American respondents believed that organized crime was operating in their county.[19]

The study identified independent (i.e., not affiliated with the Chicago "Outfit," the local Mafia organization) policy wheels controlled by African Americans on the South and West Side of Chicago and in Waukegan. The Illinois study supports the notion that the control of gambling in African-American communities, which was originally under the control of whites, was shifting.

JAMAICAN POSSES

Since the late 1960s in New York City, New Jersey, Baltimore, Maryland, Washington, D.C., and cities in Florida, California, and in Toronto, Canada, the Rastafarians have engaged principally in marijuana, cocaine smuggling, and gunrunning on a comparatively large scale.[20] The Rastafarian movement originated in Jamaica in the early 1930s. It centered on the quasi-religious belief that Prince Ras Tafari Makonnen of Ethiopia was the prophesied Black King and that his coronation as Emperor Haile Selassie I portended the time of deliverance for African people everywhere. "Ganja" (marijuana) is used within the community of believers as a religious sacrament. A close-knit group centered in this religious ideology that deifies Ethiopia's former emperor, the "Rastas" have achieved something of a detente with white organized crime families and other African-American criminal groups. They have gained territorial control over the criminal economy (temporarily, at least) in the West Indian and Jamaican communities in many cities of the United States. "Posses," as these gangs are known, appear to have hierarchically organized structures with descending positions from boss downward to the street worker. It is probable that, as with other ghetto-bound criminal groups, a flexible system of patron–client relations exists.

The term *posse* was adopted by Jamaican gangs from Hollywood westerns. The gangs evolved as an informal mechanism for gaining local community control. The posses matured criminally and embraced a doctrine of political nationalism that emerged in the late 1950s and 1960s. Neighborhood street gangs were aligned with either of the two leading political parties, the Jamaica Labor Party and the People's National Party. The groups interacted closely with activist Rastafarians in various violent endeavors, drug, and weapons trafficking. What has become known as criminal posses in the United States originated with Jamaican street gangs, and many active organizations in the United States still bear the names of streets or neighborhoods in Jamaica's cities and towns. The first U.S. posses were the "Untouchables" from Tecks Lane in the Raetown section of Kingston, and "The Dunkirk Boys" from the Franklintown area of Kingston. The "Shower" and the "Spangler" posses are two of the largest and the best organized of the posses operating in the United States today.

Jamaican criminals employ several methods to infiltrate a community. A common tactic is to select an African-American female and lavish her with gifts, money, and cocaine or crack. She, in return, permits the use of her home for a drug-trafficking operation. Another method is to pay selected individuals rent for apartments from which the posses operate. They also establish "gatehouses" for their drug distribution, which are usually vacant or abandoned buildings, fortified to make their activities more secure in case of police raids or robberies by criminal competitors. Their illicit drug organizations comprise individuals who package drugs, serve as wholesalers, retailers, lookouts, carpenters, and others whose jobs are to operate and protect the gatehouses.

Although Jamaican organized crime activity in the United States dates back to the 1970s, Jamaican posses emerged as a significant criminal threat in the United States in the 1980s. These groups are primarily involved in drug trafficking, especially cocaine and marijuana, but also in illegal arms traffic and other weapons violations. They have been successful at organizing and competing against other drug groups, perhaps because they have a strong vertical structure, enabling them to control costs and offer lower prices than competitors. Their aggressive marketing strategies have further enabled them to expand rapidly, mainly within inner-city African-American neighborhoods. The posses have a strong propensity for violence and use it freely to acquire and maintain territories. Some possess a multilayered structure; however, other less-structured Jamaican groups also exist, including some with family-based associations.

In 1991, an estimated forty Jamaican posses with 20,000 members were believed to be involved in illicit operations in the United States.

The two largest posses, the Spanglers and Showers . . . have been whittled away by successful prosecutions in New York and Florida. But their street operations have quickly been taken over by new groups: the Dunkirk Boys of Queens (N.Y.) has some 2,000 members,

Jungle Posse of Brooklyn's East New York section has 2,500 members, Samokan Posse also of Brooklyn, has 1,000 members. [21]

The *New York Times* reported that seventeen people were arrested by federal agents.[22] This gang of illegal aliens from Jamaica, known as the Gulleymen, operated a network of crackhouses, heroin dealerships, and transported illegal handguns purchased in the South and sold in the North. Federal agents allege that the gang made $60,000 a day in profits. (They take their name, Gulleymen, from a neighborhood in Kingston, Jamaica, called McGregor's Gulley.) Federal agents believe that the gang has sold franchises to street-level dealers, supplying them with crack and protection for a set fee. The group has been accused of killing at least twenty people, most of them rival drug dealers and former gang members who have crossed the gang's leader, Eric Vassell. Profits from the gang's drug and arms dealing have gone into legitimate enterprises, such as real estate in Brooklyn and Long Island, or have been shipped back to Jamaica to boost the campaign war chests of Jamaican politicians whom the posses support.

Another group, the Renkers posse, employ fifty workers selling crack in the Bedford-Stuyvesant, Crown Heights, and Flatbush sections of Brooklyn, and the gang has branched out to Philadelphia, Baltimore, and the District of Columbia.

UNEASY PARTNERSHIPS: JAMAICAN POSSES AND AFRICAN AMERICANS

Race may seem to provide a common bond between Jamaicans and African Americans, but the relationship has often been exploitative and violent. Seeing African-American communities as their natural criminal-market territory, conflict often erupts if African-American criminal groups are operating there. Clashes have occurred in Philadelphia, where a major African-American cocaine dealer was murdered by the Shower posse in a territorial dispute.

However, police reports also indicate cooperation between the groups. A fragile truce exists that confers benefits and advantages on both: Jamaicans need territories and associates familiar with local communities and police practice, and African-American criminals tap into drug supplies and the firepower Jamaicans command.

African-American women and children have been exploited by Jamaican groups. Like other middlemen selling drugs, they recruit neighborhood youths to serve in a variety of roles—as street dealers, runners, and lookouts. Women frequently serve as "fronts" in cocaine/crack trafficking. They rent apartments, recruit young street dealers, maintain an operation should the male be imprisoned, and some play more integral roles in the trafficking organizations. The prominence of women in both Jamaican and African-American crime groups stems from a cluster of sociocultural and historical factors. Impoverished life conditions in Jamaica and in African-American communities around the country have produced a high incidence of female-headed households. Consequently, women have embraced, or had thrust upon them, responsibilities and obligations traditionally relegated to dominant male figures. In addition, like other West Indians, Jamaicans understand "family" to mean a much wider circle than those within a single household. Common-law relationships are not unusual, nor are extended families and neighborhood friendships that provide a dense network of supportive social relationships. All of these factors add up to matriarchal families in which women as heads of household face chronic financial hardship. It is no wonder then, given the circumstances, that women sometimes play important supporting roles in criminal activities traditionally considered an exclusive male province.[23]

DRUG ORGANIZATIONS IN NEW YORK

Large, powerful drug syndicates, like those of Frank Lucas and Leroy "Nicky" Barnes, spread beyond the African-American ghetto in the 1960s and 1970s. The level of sophistication and scope of trafficking in the Lucas organization show that its operations were planned carefully. Frank Lucas and his brothers (Vernon Lee, Lee Van, Larry, and Ezell), known as the "Country Boys," employed relatives as a hedge against security breeches in their international narcotics-smuggling operations.[24] Lucas did not restrict his trafficking to wholesaling, but sought to control a network from Indochina to street-level sales in America's ghettos. All the trademarks of astute organization resembling La Cosa Nostra operations were apparent: Personnel were selected because they were trustworthy or reliable blood relatives—not because of some sentimental friendship or childhood attachment.[25] A division of labor existed in the organization whereby participants knew only what was necessary for them to function, and state-of-the-art technologies in transport, processing, and packaging were vigorously exploited in drug transactions.

"Mr. Untouchable"

Leroy "Nicky" Barnes, once known as "Mr. Untouchable" because of his seeming invincibility from prosecution, was also one of the most notorious drug kingpins in New York City's history. In January, 1978, he was sentenced to the longest possible term for trafficking—life in a federal prison without the chance of parole. One of the charges for which Barnes was convicted was operating a "continuing criminal enterprise"; the government charged that he had engaged in criminal rackets, including a series of narcotics violations "with five or more other persons, with respect to whom he occupied a position of organizer, supervisor and manager." Three years after his conviction, Mr. Barnes offered to act as an undercover informer for the government.

In his notorious career, he formed a murderous drug syndicate that created some of the largest African-American drug rings in New York City, bringing together the heads of the seven largest trafficking organizations that controlled a substantial segment of heroin and other narcotics sales in Manhattan, the Bronx, and Brooklyn. The syndicate, called the "Council," employed hundreds of millworkers, distributors, and street dealers. At the Barnes trial, five defendants were described as the "chief lieutenants" in the organization, and eight "lower echelon" defendants were also indicted on trafficking charges. The jury convicted all but one, whose case ended in a deadlock among the jurors. Two defendants were acquitted.

In testimony before the 1985 President's Crime Commission, Barnes revealed that he had taken an "oath of brotherhood" in this Council, which had been formed to assure cooperation between its member narcotics dealers in their distribution of thousands of pounds of heroin.[26] The Council was suspected of ordering the murders of at least five suspected informants and several drug dealers for "mere larcenies or insubordination." Further evidence brought forward in the 1985 hearings suggested that African Americans were highly organized in other illicit activities, with an organizational sophistication approximating La Cosa Nostra operations.

Since his conviction, Barnes has become a state's witness, resulting in the indictment and conviction of numerous defendants who were former partners in the drug trade. Among them were seven leaders of New York City's largest drug rings, who were convicted of drug charges and received long prison terms based on his testimony. Barnes is credited with providing information resulting in the indictment of 48 other defendants, according to federal prosecutors.

In June of 1992, the U.S. State's Attorney in Manhattan filed court papers seeking a reduction in Mr. Barnes' sentence because of his cooperation. The request indicated that he provided undercover evidence at tremendous risk to himself, which resulted in the convictions of scores of major narcotics dealers, including five defendants who received the same sentence he did: life without parole. If and when he is released, he is expected to be placed in the Witness Security Program. In 1946, Charles "Lucky" Luciano was released from prison after serving ten years of a thirty-to-fifty year sentence and was deported to Italy after cooperating with government officials. Almost fifty years later, we now see the first African American being considered for release from a life sentence without chance of parole for cooperating with government officials.

Before his conviction, when he circulated in Harlem, Barnes was a legend in the drug subculture. His appearances either on the streets or at drug locations invariably attracted attention. Prior to his arrest in 1977, Barnes was never convicted of charges that the federal government brought against him. Whether the failure to put Barnes in prison was the result of bad police work or court cases that lacked proper development and a structure of hard evidence is difficult to know. Whatever the reasons, the failure to make an arrest stick earned Barnes the street name "Mr. Untouchable."

Barnes had a record of thirteen arrests dating back to 1950, when he was eighteen years of age. For more than a decade, the police labeled him a "major narcotics violator" and investigated him, tapped his phones, bugged his cronies, and conducted around-the-clock surveillance. Not only was he listed as a "Major Black Violator" in police and FBI intelligence files, he was also found in the "Italian Major Violators" file in recognition, perhaps, of his reported ties to Cosa Nostra sources of narcotics and his fondness for patterning himself after his conception of the way Italian organized criminal groups worked.[27]

Police intelligence records also showed acquaintances with "Crazy" Joe Gallo, a member of the Profaci Crime Family, who Barnes met during a 1965 stay in Greenhaven prison, and Carmine Galente, a future Boss of the Bonanno Crime Family, who was also an important figure in the heroin pipeline from Sicily, Marseilles, and Montreal.

These Cosa Nostra criminal connections doubtlessly enabled Barnes to secure a reliable supply of heroin and to create an organizational structure (The Council of 12) modeled along Cosa Nostra drug-selling networks, with their many administrative layers, that provided a protective shield between himself and street sellers that, for all practical purposes, became an almost arrest-proof operation.

Barnes's early life is somewhat sketchy. He grew up in Harlem and could not fail to be impressed by the flashy lifestyle of drug dealers. An early arrest as a street junkie sent him off to a rehabilitation program where he kicked his habit. Back on the street in the late 1950s and early 1960s, Barnes pieced together his network. In 1965, he was arrested and sentenced for drugs to a twenty-five years-to-life sentence. While in prison he met Joey Gallo who was serving a five-to fifteen-year term for extortion. They became friendly and Barnes learned organization from an expert career criminal who was initiated into the Mafia. Police intelligence sources believed that the friendship struck up between the two served the ulterior motives of each.

Gallo needed troops for the gang war in which he planned to overthrow his crime boss, Joseph Profaci, and establish himself as a dominant force in the New York underworld, which he correctly saw as going through profound changes involving minorities as not just subordinates to Italian syndicates but as equal partners. Barnes was needed to recruit African Americans and to insure cooperation between Italian and minority gangsters.

When Barnes was released on a technicality, he created a drug empire facilitated by his Italian connections. He began by importing pure heroin and setting up a web of cutting and packaging mills and distribution points in several states around the country, including Canada. Gradually, his organization took over the street operations from mafia groups that had controlled drug trafficking in Harlem until then. The conflict that might have been expected never materialized and this is of interest, because it illustrates that racial antipathy was secondary to profits. As long as Barnes made money through his mafia connections, it did not matter who controlled the streets. If one could generate wealth, racial ideologies that got in the way were quickly discarded or ignored.

Barnes began investing his drug profits in real estate, travel agencies, car washes, and gas stations—following the practice of Cosa Nostra gangsters who sought to conceal their money and protect it in legitimate businesses.

In 1976, Barnes was indicted by the United States government, along with five of his associates, for conspiracy to sell 44 pounds of heroin to undercover agents. In 1978, he was found guilty and sentenced to life without parole. What he did in his criminal career was to show that African Americans could be independent and conduct large-scale, sophisticated criminal operations. Had he avoided arrest, his drug syndicate might have opened up vast new territories ripe for criminal domination in labor racketeering and in the infiltration of legitimate businesses that could conceivably have competed with the established La Cosa Nostra crime organizations. In his way, the wily "Mr. Untouchable" created a school for criminals who otherwise might have legitimately developed influence in labor unions and other industries as racial obstacles to employment and business enterprises eroded under the moral force of the civil rights movement.

"The Black Luciano"

Frank Matthews migrated from Durham, North Carolina to New York when he was a young man. In the 1960s, he worked in Bedford-Stuyvesant as a collector for an Italian-owned numbers operation before becoming a drug trafficker. As the Mafia's grip on African-American neighborhoods in New York loosened, narcotics distribution in Brooklyn's minority areas was being taken over by the people who lived there. They were no longer content to remain in the pay of Cosa Nostra importers and wholesalers. Many were now customers, looking to their former employers not just for supplies but for working capital and management expertise as well. African-American drug dealers were organizing, much as the Italian-American gangs had done in the 1920s and 1930s, with the purpose of ratifying one another's territorial claims and spheres of interest and eliminating competition.

Leroy Barnes pursued these objectives in Harlem, but the first tentative steps toward forming a "Black Mafia" (for want of a better term) had been taken in the early 1960s by Leon Aiken who was, in his day, the dope king of Harlem.[28] Establishing one of the first significant African-American drug distributions operations to coexist with the Mafia, Aiken made a fortune from narcotics and cleverly converted much of it into real estate around the country. He also diversified, like his Mafia exemplars, into all kinds of legitimate business, from fish-and-chips fast-food restaurants to neighborhood dry cleaners, using them not only to launder his drug money and provide a legitimate front for the Internal Revenue Service, but also as a springboard into New York's social and political life. As a "successful" African-American businessman in the early, tumultuous years of the civil rights movement, Aiken was much in demand among the liberal establishment until 1966, when he was convicted and imprisoned for twenty-five years.

Aiken's mistakes were largely ignored by other ambitious African-American drug dealers. The wealth, power, influence, and above all, the respect he enjoyed—albeit temporarily—through running a fairly tight, orderly operation inspired others who were quick to see advantages in good working relationships with the Mafia. Barnes was first to respond. When he fell in with Joey Gallo during a state prison term on drug charges, together they dreamed up the idea of organizing African-American gangs into a national syndicate along mafia lines. Of course, Gallo had his own agenda, needing "soldiers" in the war for Cosa Nostra power that he planned to launch upon his release. The project, however, came to nothing, not because African-American mobsters objected in principle to the idea of organizing themselves—to some extent they had already done so, driven by the nature of the illegal markets in which they operated into loose alliances and fluid partnerships—but because they disliked the idea of racial integration with Cosa Nostra. After all, for years they groveled in the dust as subordinates, often humiliated by Mafia power brokers who took few chances in the streets while amassing millions of dollars behind the scenes, and who insulated themselves from police and the murderous competition of street crime. For many, the question was why could they not do their own thing in their own way without strings attached to Mafia families? Indeed, the demographics favored African-American independence in the underworld. Communities that had traditionally been the domain of white ethnics were changing rapidly as African Americans and Hispanics expanded beyond their ghetto boundaries. Cosa Nostra soldiers could no longer command respect in the streets as they once had in Harlem, East New York, Brownsville, Newark, Philadelphia, Baltimore, Chicago, and Washington, D.C.

In practice, this meant that while they avoided the dangers of being exploited by mafiosi who had few compunctions about sacrificing others to law enforcement to insure their own security, African-American criminals were likely to face a prolonged period of gang strife similar to what the Cosa Nostra experienced in the 1930s as it sorted itself out during the Castellammarese War. Although the bloodbath the Mafia endured during its birth pangs was traumatizing, the purge produced a national confederation of complex alliances and hierarchies among the top Mafia families that tightened discipline, streamlined rackets, and for the rank and file offered a heightened sense of identity through Mafia membership.

Barnes was disappointed but never abandoned his hopes of national consolidation. The problem was a reliable supply of drugs. Although there were African-American narcotics entrepreneurs, none could develop independent sources outside the United States. What Barnes had to do was form a liaison with mafiosi suppliers, if only temporarily. The future would take care of itself.

Following precedent and seeing narcotics rather than the more modest rackets in gambling and prostitution as the gold mine of quick millions, Frank Matthews examined the Brooklyn drug markets, took inventory of what was required to gain control of some territory that could function as a supply base for out-of-town networks, and approached Cosa Nostra drug dealers for supplies and finance. The standard terms of Cosa Nostra drug deals were 30 percent down and the balance on the delivery of heroin—in cash. Only a handful of African Americans possessed the resources to transact business with the Mafia on credit consignments and then only at the risk of their lives. Matthews, like Barnes, had contacts in both the Bonanno and Gambino crime families, but they declined to help.

The Mafia crime families may have had a monopoly on heroin—for the moment—but had no such import control on cocaine, or over the Cubans who brought it into the United States. Undaunted, Matthews changed his tactics and made contact with "Spanish Raymond" Marquez in the policy business, who introduced him to some of the important cocaine traffickers in New York.

Within a year, Matthews built an organization, mainly of "home boys" with connections in a dozen Eastern and Southern cities. The former chicken thief from North Carolina soon impressed the Cosa Nostra, who reconsidered selling him heroin, partly, it must be acknowledged, to preclude his dealing directly with the Corsican Mafia, the main suppliers of the American Mafia, and partly to retain some sort of influence over Matthews's rather reckless business methods. Quickly thereafter, he created a drug mill for processing and would pay premium prices to any kilo supplier in order to keep his business flourishing. Many of the principals in Matthews's organization worked behind a legitimate front that at first shielded them from police surveillance.

Through 1969, 1970, and 1971, Matthews adroitly expanded his narcotics business in city after city, state after state. Where no dealers were operating, he established a business, and where one did exist, he absorbed it, making offers that no local dealers could refuse. With a partner, he established headquarters in Atlanta, Georgia and sank millions into local real estate but maintained his New York base of distribution, which enabled him to fan out in the Northeast in Connecticut, Rhode Island, and Massachusetts. Through another partner, he serviced wholesale drug outlets in Detroit, Chicago, and Los Angeles. By 1972, not including the territories that he controlled directly, Matthews formed alliances to avoid law enforcement attention and to prevent costly wars with competitors.

Sometime toward the end of 1971, Matthews put together a national conclave in Atlanta of top African-American and Hispanic drug dealers. The main business item of the meeting was to discuss ways and means of breaking the Mafia's stranglehold on heroin imports. Preferably, it should be done peacefully, so that existing supply arrangements would not be interrupted or jeopardized. The need for an independent source was critical, because in the minds of these narcotics racketeers, a competitive alternative to Cosa Nostra drug supplies might achieve several desirable goals. It would remove the brake on expansion and keep Cosa Nostra wholesale prices reasonable. It would also provide a margin of safety in the event that Cosa Nostra traffickers were arrested, which loomed as a real possibility as the country's fears and concerns over drug abuse put pressure on the government to do something to control the expanding drug problem.

The discussions concluded with Matthews exploring Corsican drug sources through Cuban networks. The Cosa Nostra was still the principal source of supply but tolerated the fact that African-American traffickers sought multiple wholesale sources. The Corsican connections temporarily turned wholesale drug dealing into a buyer's market. As African Americans consolidated their hold on distribution territories and sources, Cosa Nostra crime families astutely plugged into the expanding drug networks as investors and advisors.

The racial detente and fragile alliance between the two underworlds could easily have unraveled because of Matthews's sensitivities and his threat of gang violence should Cosa Nostra soldiers continue to insult his people. Intimidation came not only from the Cosa Nostra, police, and other drug enforcement agencies, but from African-American competitors and opponents of narcotics. Matthews could and did make credible threats against Cosa Nostra soldiers who interfered with his associates, but with African-American extortionists the tactics in coping were complicated. According to Goddard,

> In New York, Philadelphia, and several other cities, his [Matthews] organization—indeed, the drug trade as a whole—was under attack by self-styled Black Muslim commando groups seeking to collect a 10–15% "tax" on sales. By preying on dealers in no position to holler "cop" when victimized by kidnapping and extortion, these so-called Muslim groups were out to get rich on narcotics without even having to handle them—and without forfeiting the goodwill of a black community appalled by the drug problem and inclined, like the police, to blame atrocities on narcotics gang warfare.[29]

But the Black Muslim commandos were in no position to resort to police protection either. Matthews declared open season on Muslims and the "Black Mafia" of Philadelphia. This latter group, according to the Pennsylvania Crime Commission Report of 1990, was an outgrowth of 1960s street gangs in Philadelphia's impoverished African-American neighborhoods. They controlled narcotics sales and distribution and engaged in extortion.

From their choice of name, "Black Mafia," Philadelphia's law enforcement authorities speculated that the gang hoped to establish an overarching organization that would emulate Cosa Nostra's organized criminal styles and practices in providing protection for its members and in attaining absolute power over their criminal markets.[30] The versatility of its criminal activities distinguished the Black Mafia from other groups such as Nicky Barnes's "Council" in New York, or the Philadelphia successor group, the "Junior Black Mafia."

The Black Mafia extorted numbers bankers and some legitimate businesses operating in the African-American ghettos of Philadelphia. White numbers bankers who were using African-American writers and sub-bankers in the ghetto were also targeted in "shakedowns," although they were careful to avoid Cosa Nostra–backed vice. Narcotics was their principal activity.

In terms of organizational structure, the Black Mafia formed an associational pattern—a confederation of gangs with a few top-level leaders, or influentials, at the top, commanding numerous lieutenants and associates. Unlike Cosa Nostra, which depended for survival on violence and corruption, the Black Mafia relied almost exclusively on the former and for that reason was doomed. Its most infamous incident occurred on Easter Sunday, 1972, when the elite of Philadelphia's African-American underworld converged at Club Harlem, a brassy nightspot in Atlantic City. Some of Frank Matthews's key people in Philadelphia were assassinated, along with five others, in an auditorium packed with six hundred people. The official explanation for the audacious act that produced the carnage was that Tyrone Palmer, one of Matthews's men, was murdered in fulfillment of a "contract" worth $15,000, issued by the associates of Palmer's underboss who had been murdered on Palmer's orders for some slight or indiscretion.

What this and other incidents show is that the Black Mafia was destined to self-destruct because of its heavy reliance on violence, which exposed the organization's members to danger from rivals and law enforcement agencies. To insure the collapse of the Black Mafia and the neutralization of the Muslim commandos, Matthews acquired a consignment of automatic weapons and dispatched his men to take them on.

In New York, the main threat to Matthews and others were street-level vigilantes who could not be bought off and who were not susceptible to violent countermeasures. Often, these self-righteous individuals were frustrated by lack of law enforcement activity in their communities or by corruption of the police, and had no other motive but to clean up their neighborhoods. Along with similarly committed Black Panthers and genuine Black Muslims, they had taken to shooting pushers on sight. But pushers were expendable. So the war of attrition instigated by otherwise upstanding citizens petered out from sheer exhaustion.

In July, 1973, the world came crashing down on Frank Matthews. He was due in Brooklyn Federal Court to plead to an indictment superseding one of six on narcotics trafficking already handed down against him. He failed to appear and has not been found since—nor has an estimated $20 million in cash. Police forces all over the world continue to search for him.

Speculations about Matthews's disappearance range from the reasonable to the preposterous. Some think he may be running a narcotics business in the United States by remote control, much like Charles "Lucky" Luciano handled the Mafia's heroin business in the United States from five thousand miles away in his Italian exile. Others think he was assassinated at the hands of the Cosa Nostra and their African-American associates. This latter speculation is persuasive in that the draconian penalties associated with the drug business have meant that the mortality rate of informers is very high. Ordinarily, the big operators, white or African American, covered themselves against informers though bilateral treaties in which they promised not to inform on one another in return for the same consideration. High-level gangsters would commonly unite to liquidate lesser figures or third parties who threatened them. This may have happened to Matthews—a victim of a cabal of drug dealers who feared that out of revenge and his innate need to survive, he would cooperate with law enforcement agencies in exchange for witness protection.

Unlike the Cosa Nostra with its obsessive concern for *omertà* (silence), which does not countenance human frailties, and its highly sophisticated methods of corruption, African-American mobs have primarily one method by which to enforce silence—violence. The alternative, not considered particularly dishonorable, given that African Americans could not create the web of corruption white criminals did, was to inform; perhaps this was not just a way of avoiding arrest but was of strategic significance, in that rivals could be eliminated as well. Several African-American racketeers bought themselves out of minor scraps with law enforcement by exchanging information about other dealers. As an alternative to bribery, becoming a "snitch" would appear to be the only effective means of dealing with straight police and prosecutors. Naturally, snitching had to be used with discretion, or, as in the case of Matthews, as a last-ditch effort to survive. The experiences of these two major African-American organized crime figures (Barnes and Matthews) of the 1970s raise the question concerning whether African-American crime groups could indeed achieve the capacity to become powerful, self-sustaining syndicates free of Cosa Nostra ties and capable of functioning autonomously. This is an issue that will be examined in subsequent chapters.

"Papa D" Washington

Shortly after Barnes entered federal prison, another organization gained recognition as a major importer and supplier of drugs. It operated out of a brownstone building located in Harlem and was headed by Daniel Washington, known as "Papa D," and his second-in-command, Clarence Wynn, who was responsible for the recruiting of personnel, workers, and enforcers.[31] The drug operation supplied Boston, Detroit, Pennsylvania, Chicago, Washington, and North Carolina markets.[32] The operation imported drugs from England and the Bahamas using women as couriers. Each woman smuggled two pounds of heroin weekly into the United States.[33] "Papa D" kept himself insulated from the everyday dealing, which was handled by his subordinate, Wynn. "Papa D" was eventually arrested in the early 1980s for tax evasion.

BLOOD TIES, FAMILY, AND CRIMINAL BONDING: ETHNIC SUCCESSION REDUX

Analysts who disagree on most issues concerning the Mafia and its structural features, agree that kinship and close family relationships constitute the strength and durability of Italian-American crime families—indeed, a major theme in the literature of the 1970s about Cosa Nostra emphasized the concept of kinship. Family attachments dominated discussions about the organizational culture of Mafia.[34]

The family was the basic core of Southern Italian social structure in which mafia originates and it reached out to include in an arc of relationships the full range of official and consanguineous relations. Nuclear families and lineages within this bounded network were tied to each other in a web of "honor."[35] Within the social membrane of relatives, mutual responsibility connects and tightens relations among members; similarly with mafia. If the social structure of Southern Italy is the family in macrocosm, mafia is that social structure in microcosm. There is no dissonance between the values of mafia and the values of the people in the Mezzogiorno (Southern Italy).

In terms of modern American Cosa Nostra families, some of these organized impulses persist in the notion of the "crime family," even among those who are members not genealogically related to each other. The interdependence of cultural traditions and kinship that gave birth to mafia-style secret criminal organizations in the south of Italy and structured Italian-American crime families creates the same norms of interdependence and reciprocity that characterize the kinship bond. Whether the fictive bond is formal or informal, the members of the criminal clan take on a kinship-like pattern of behavior and expectations of behavior from others. Although unrelated members openly and freely acknowledge that they are not genealogically related, they can and do learn to take on the rights and obligations that are expected in this type of kinship link. All of the rules of conduct, the requirement to place the family above all else, the injunction to protect the family honor by being a "man," and the code of silence where family matters are concerned, are voluntarily accepted in return for the security and certainty that go with family membership.

Artificially created bonds that are genuine substitutes for those inherent in kinship are possible if and when the anticipatory group provides security for and acceptance of the individual. Crime families meet this need by providing more security and access to resources than would be possible for the individual himself. In the crime family, the individual is immersed in a skein of alliances—he is "connected" and can operate in his sphere without fear, even fear of the police. *Omertà* (silence) provides the symbolic representation of the mafia code, and so long as the member abides by it he remains "in"; should he fail (and mafiosi have repeatedly betrayed their oath of secrecy), he is ejected and the dishonor must be washed clean in blood. It is this feature, the intricate pattern of ritual alliances, that sets Italian-American "crime families" apart from other gangs.

The web of actual kinship is also an integral component of the American crime families. Of the sixty-odd Mafia bosses identified as participants at the famous Appalachian meeting in November, 1957, almost half were related by blood or marriage, and even more if godparenthood is included as a kin relationship. At one point, according to Ianni, three of the five bosses of New York's Cosa Nostra crime families had children who were intermarried.[36] These relationships were a series of complex alliances binding together lineages in the families for the systematic exchange of services.

It is these structural characteristics of Cosa Nostra crime families that gave them formidable strength and survivability. But as American culture erodes the strength of family and kinship in Italian-American culture, the crime families will give way to the next wave of aspiring ethnics, just as the Irish and Jews did before them. The evidence for this displacement was already apparent in the 1970s. African Americans, Hispanics, and Asians were pushing aside Italian Americans in the policy rackets. In some cases the succession has been peaceful, as in parts of New York City and Philadelphia, when the Cosa Nostra "leased" rackets on a concession basis. The Cosa Nostra members supplied money and protection while African Americans and Hispanics ran the street operations. In other cases, the transition had not been easy: in Chicago, for example, Cosa Nostra syndicate members were pushed out of gambling and drug trafficking under the threat of war.

Ethnic succession does not mean that the Cosa Nostra is a carcass lying in the streets, destroyed by new ethnic and racial groups eager to challenge and acquire its hegemony in vice and criminal markets. And it is not that it lost its instinctive connection with the public it serviced; rather, that public has changed its color, culture, and needs. Furthermore, while the President's Commission on Organized Crime (1986) made some respectable inroads into areas of organized crime that heretofore had been ignored, it failed to address African-American involvement in any substantive degree. This occurred despite the fact that Leroy "Nicky" Barnes, a major New York drug kingpin in the 1970s, testified before the Commission outlining what was clearly an African-American crime syndicate. For many, the Commission's negligence was more than an oversight; it prompted ten of the nineteen Commissioners to state, "The Commission . . . has failed to address the roles of American black and Jewish organization in organized crime."[37]

One of the few to address the issue was New York City Police Commissioner Lee Brown, who took up the volatile question of street crime and drugs in the African-American community. Unfortunately, Brown made no connection among African-American criminal syndicates, drugs, and street crime.[38] This widespread inability to see organized crime as a far broader and more comprehensive phenomenon than La Cosa Nostra has blinded us to its variations and diversities. Too often, the public, law enforcement authorities, and even scholars are caught up in a narrow vision of organized crime in which it is synonymous with the Cosa Nostra. The mafia imagery is a common stereotype. As the 1976 National Advisory Committee on Criminal Justice Standards and Goals explained,

> . . . a number of families of La Cosa Nostra are an important component of organized crime operation, [but] they do not enjoy a monopoly in underworld activities. Today a variety of groups are engaged in organized criminal activity.[39]

The report, however, does not describe such groups, nor did it make any attempt to address the unique qualities of these other criminal organizations.

Regarding the issue of African Americans and organized crime, Mark Haller pointed out even earlier (as had Myrdal),

> There has, in fact, long been a close relationship of vice activities and Negro life in the cities. . . . In the operation of entertainment facilities and policy rackets, black entrepreneurs found their major outlet, and black politicians formed their chief support.[40]

Similarly, in their pioneering study of rackets in New York City's African-American community, Lasswell and McKenna provided the President's Commission and other law enforcement agencies with a probative document on what were certainly African-American crime syndicates. They concluded that, next to the federal government, numbers, an illegal gambling activity in which African-American syndicates were principally involved, was the largest employer in the Bedford-Stuyvesant section of New York City.[41] This study was conducted more than a decade prior to the President's Commission and four years before the 1976 Advisory Committee Report, yet it was cited in neither.

Despite the denials, skepticism, and mystification in official circles about African-American organized crime, there is a historic linkage between criminal groups that challenges popular imagery of racial and ethnic antipathy. In 1983, in testimony before the U.S. Senate Judiciary Committee, the New York City Police Department offered its assessment of the racial/ethnic situation among organized criminals:

> The American blacks have been employed within the Italian organized crime structure primarily at the lower levels of gambling operations in the inner-city areas. . . . Many law enforcement agencies have come to recognize that black organized crime is growing into a distinct, clearly definable structure that must be dealt with in those terms.[42]

After World War II, the crime picture changed dramatically, with Jewish and Italian racketeers gaining control of policy gambling through the use of police who functioned in African-American communities at the behest of corrupted politicians. Tactical arrest of policy bankers and systematic extortion meant that African-American racketeers ultimately succumbed to the political superiority of white racketeers. Today, we are witnessing a shift away from dependence upon white criminals in gambling and vice activities. The reasons are several. First, numbers gambling is a declining source of relatively safe revenue for African-American gambling syndicates because state and municipal lotteries are effectively competing with the scarce, but nonetheless always available, gambling dollar in the African-American community. Second, career criminals, attracted to more lucrative illicit enterprises, are drawn to the more profitable, albeit more risky, narcotics business. Third, narcotics trafficking marks a significant separation from Cosa Nostra dominance. Just how African-American racketeers organized themselves around the fickle and dangerous narcotics business will be examined in the remaining chapters. It is of interest, however, whether the late 1970s did indeed represent a milestone in the growing independence of African-American criminal groups.

In a field study designed to empirically test the implications of ethnic succession theory in terms of some of his earlier predictions about the movement of new groups into ascendancy in organized crime, Ianni concluded,

Among the Italian-Americans in organized crime . . . links were formed by the family and kinship system that dominate the culture. . . . Among blacks and Hispanics the family seems less important.[43]

Ianni's study was limited to field observation of criminal networks that circulated small amounts of stolen goods through associations of criminals, forming working alliances in prison and in ghetto streets. But there is another body of evidence, perhaps even more compelling, that casts doubt on the reliability and generalizations of these descriptive findings.

In his testimony before the President's Commission, Leroy "Nicky" Barnes referred to an "oath of brotherhood" within a council of high-level drug dealers. The Jeffers narcotics organization was referred to as "The Family;"[44] and "The Country Boys," a family in the blood-relative sense, describes an organization headed by Frank Lucas. The language of family terms is not a capricious emulation of La Cosa Nostra but reflects a desire to establish kinship as a bonding agent among these African-American criminal organizations. It is a deliberate technique designed to instill loyalty and trust among members that transcends routine and ordinary associations. It is not all that emotionally different from legitimate groups that often refer to themselves as "brothers." Fraternal, religious, and occupational groups also freely use these terms. It ensures that a common bond solidifies the groups, one based not just on common, instrumental goals, but on blood ties, or equivalent symbolic kinship relationships.

Oddly enough, themes of kinship and family have been largely ignored when looking into the backgrounds of successful African-American racketeers, many of whom were born in the South and built their enterprises around the family, much like their Cosa Nostra predecessors and for many of the same reasons. For example, Roland "Pops" Bartlett, a heroin dealer, was born in Georgia; Frank Lucas and his brothers came from North Carolina; Frank Moten, a policy racketeer and loan shark, sometimes called "The Black Godfather," was born in a rural section of Georgia; and the Chambers Brothers' organization of Detroit originated in Marianna, Arkansas.[45]

African-American Southern families and their extensive kinship networks, as Billingsley so vividly described, were sources of psychological strength and endurance that suffuse the culture and collective community feelings.[46] Especially important were long-term obligations and reciprocal relationships that generated a deep sense of interdependence. The notion of kinship that Ianni describes as the defining features of Southern Italian families and Mafia crime families was no less stronger in the agrarian South among African Americans. The rich history in the South of organizing to achieve a common goal is best illustrated by the civil rights movement—a southern-born and southern-based political and moral movement. Uniquely Southern, the movement relied on two bedrock institutions: the church and the family, and it changed the course of American history. The African-American family and its kinship ties anchored in morally centered values suggest an organizational motif in which legitimate and illegitimate networks could arise, be nurtured and perpetuated, and flourish.

The concepts of collective social bonding and solidarity that many commentators on African-American life have described as "deficient"[47] may, on the contrary, help us to understand the mastery of gambling, loan-sharking, and legitimate business entrepreneurial activity among traditional African-American racketeers. Light puts the issues aptly and is aware of these implications in which the transition from the legal to the illegal is sensitive to, and understandable in, the economic and political context of everyday life. Light says,

> In many cases, numbers gamblers and loansharks are the same individual . . . [and] have been the largest investors in black-owned business or ghetto real estate and the chief source of business capital.[48]

In an analysis of fifty-four major African-American racketeers in the New York metropolitan area, it was found that

- Legitimate investment in businesses were noted among 84 percent of the violators,
- Business investment included restaurants, delicatessens, car washes, nightclubs, racing shops, auto leasing companies, sporting goods stores, towing ships, liquor stores, record shops, cab services, social clubs, cleaners, laundromats, stationery stores, groceries, and apartment buildings.[49]

It is readily apparent that the movements of streams of illicit monies into legitimate investments are an essential part of African-American criminal operations, and in this respect they closely parallel the techniques of other ethnic groups, especially Cosa Nostra, in organized crime. The process may be illustrated in the career of one African-American organized crime figure in Pennsylvania.

Willie Price had been identified by the Pennsylvania Crime Commission, State Police, and FBI as a racketeer operating in the city of Chester, a small community in the southeastern part of the commonwealth, close to Philadelphia. He was a boxer and had been involved in the killing of a Black

Muslim, who he claimed broke into his home. Price had an interest in a grocery store, from which he conducted gambling and loansharking. He also financed his cousins in their narcotics business. Price emerged as a sort of local folk hero because he provided loans to local residents and workers at the Penn Ship Yard. He "bankrolled" numerous enterprises in Chester and maintained a partnership in a video poker and vending company with Joseph Iacona, who was a close associate of Santo Idone, a *capo* in the Bruno/Scarfo Cosa Nostra Family of Philadelphia and Atlantic City. Iacona was also a business partner with John Nacrelli, the former mayor of Chester, who was a convicted racketeer. Because of his relationships with the political system and his financial inputs into the economically depressed African-American community, Price enjoyed protection from local law enforcement and established a power base in the corrupted politics of the city. He cleverly constructed and intermingled legal and illegal enterprises that engendered local community support and protection. His keys to success were the alliances with local mafiosi and his reinvestment in the community, which gave him, among other things in addition to income, the appearance of propriety. Price represented a classic example of racketeers who are able to mask their illegal enterprises with legitimate "front" business interests. And his connections and associations with known mafiosi did much to enhance his prestige and safety in the local underworld of drugs and gambling. Price showed how criminal rackets are often integrated into the political and economic fabric of a community and his career also suggests that ethnic succession—at least in its incipient stages—was well under way in some parts of the African-American underworld.[50]

The emergence of African-American organized crime as a distinct phenomenon uninhibited by its dependence on larger, more powerful criminal organizations such as La Cosa Nostra, was evident toward the end of the 1970s. As the decade closed, the drug hysteria and the enormously profitable enterprises that fed off it were taking on a life of their own. Still, the belief persisted that no matter how wealthy African-American drug entrepreneurs became, they lacked the essential cultural and social assets necessary to organize crime on a durable, continuous basis. Italian-Americans, and Jewish and Irish gangsters before them, possessed the resources necessary to organize, as do, apparently, contemporary Chinese and Hispanics. La Cosa Nostra and United Bamboo exist independent of their particular criminal activities, but what of African-American criminal enterprises? Are they capable of surviving beyond the particular criminal activity engaged in? Or do they dissolve as an organizational entity when and if a criminal project is completed or disturbed by law enforcement? In short, are African-American criminal groups market-dependent, or are they similar structurally and temporally to other ethnic and racial groups whose life spans transcend the particular criminal enterprises they participate in? These comparisons may be unfair and irrelevant. The African-American experience is certainly different, making for a different organizational motif. The comparisons are irrelevant in another way. White crime syndicates, especially La Cosa Nostra, have their roots in centuries of tradition and in cultures that encouraged the emergence of secret societies. Furthermore, the fixation on other groups that are described as bureaucratically and rigidly structured may be more fanciful than factual. Credible research challenging the Cressey model of a "crime corporation" is abundant and persuasive. Investigation into the internal structures of what seem to be homogeneous criminal syndicates, such as the Japanese Yakuza or La Cosa Nostra, reveal that virtually every crime family is different, with local exigencies affecting both their structural forms and criminal methods. La Cosa Nostra is not homogeneous; geographical differences and internal variations are more the rule than the exception. Distinctions between "power" and "enterprise" syndicates may be one way of clarifying the evolutionary structural differences between La Cosa Nostra families and African-American criminal enterprises, but then these distinctions may be frivolous and may not matter much from the community's standpoint. Why would it matter so long as criminogenic conditions prevail in African-American ghettos where criminal activities thrive and grow despite the risks and the endemic violence?

A more realistic approach to the problem is to analyze African-American crime in its own terms, based on its own historical developments. Many of the enterprises, and principal participants, as we have seen, can trace their roots to the numbers and policy rackets and these, in their communal settings, epitomize the organization of crime. Organizing assets were present. Violence was used with appropriate discretion calibrated to the seriousness of the infraction. Corruption existed and was systemic but modest by Cosa Nostra standards; and access to financial resources through loan sharks and successful gamblers was prevalent. These community-oriented criminal enterprises were also linked with other ethnic criminal groups where a "lay off" to a Cosa Nostra–affiliated bank could be made. Payoffs to Cosa Nostra families were routinely made to guarantee political protection—a factor becoming less and less important today than in the past. Although formal positions such as "caporegime," "consigliere," and "soldier" do not dominate the underworld lexicon of African-American racketeers, there is little doubt about where power lies and who can expeditiously exercise it. The pertinent facts as far as the communities and neighborhoods are concerned are that the stable gambling and vice infrastructures may very well yield "investment" opportunities in new sources of revenue—drugs. Here we see criminal enterprises indigenous to local communities, independent of Mafia ties, proliferating and reshaping the landscape of the African-American racketeer.

The type of person attracted to this criminal marketplace may be, and usually is, quite different from those who entered the gambling and numbers rackets. He or she is likely to be younger, less socially mature, less able to function legitimately, and, above all, more willing to engage in violence. Systematic avenues to corruption are less developed and the likelihood of arrest and prosecution is enhanced by the nature of the criminal business and the law enforcement agencies deployed against it. Thus, African Americans involved in drug trafficking are more vulnerable but can in the short term become quite successful—if by success we mean the accumulation of large amounts of cash. Some, like Barnes and Matthews, achieved the status of millionaires before their downfalls and were, in fact, "bosses" of large, sophisticated narcotics enterprises that certainly represented a form of organized crime.

Finally, it cannot be emphasized enough that all types of organized crime shape themselves according to the structure of the communities in which they operate, and the nature of legal and illegal forces (police and criminals) aligned against them. There are lessons to be learned from a close look at organized crime in the community, many of which are plagued with predatory street crimes that represent the fallout from organized criminal activity. To ignore the pivotal functional roles of racketeering in the economic, political, and social life of the community is to guarantee tragic consequences for citizens caught up in it. More than this, because African-American organized crime may not quite match the threat of La Cosa Nostra, government may not be responsive to community demands for more protection. Any community exposed to uncontainable crime can only expect a deepening of the disaffection enveloping its inhabitants. To the extent that gangsters and racketeers serve as role models for youth, law-abiding, hardworking citizens must witness the spectacle of social mobility of racketeers because the government dismisses and disregards the omnipotent power of organized criminality, the message is clear and painful: Respect and dignity mean little next to wealth—however it is acquired.

Conclusion

The regrouping of populations in American cities and suburbs has undergone drastic changes during the thirty years between 1940 and 1970. Generally speaking, our larger metropolises with their suburban peripheries have followed a somber course. The white exodus from the central cities and its replacement with African Americans is a trend that has produced large, poor, ethnic African-American ghettos. In 1969, for every African American who moved into the central cities, three whites left for the suburbs. Between 1960 and 1970, the percentage of whites living in central cities declined precipitately, while whites living outside central cities increased by nearly 30 percent.[51] As the large cities became more populated with African Americans, it followed that control of activities both licit (with limited results) and illicit would come under their control.

The irony of continuing African-American poverty in the midst of a largely affluent white society served as a catalyst leading to deeper involvement in criminal activities. In the thirty years since World War II, the indications are that many African Americans saw race as a rallying point for expansion and consolidation of criminal enterprises.

At the opposite end of the spectrum, more affluent African Americans began advancing economically, socially, and politically—progress that was a positive legacy of the civil rights movement. On the other hand, this very progress provided other kinds of opportunities for criminal activities. Rackets that had been confined to racially segregated ghettos, built around somewhat scattered and loosely organized groups, consolidated around drugs and gambling. And as Cosa Nostra influence declined in the ghetto, African-American organization emerged to fill the vacuum.

As the exodus of talented African Americans from the inner city accelerated, young mobsters often became the most visible models of success. Drugs functioned as the means of launching major criminal enterprises in communities that destroys them in the process. The post–World War II years, the Korean and Vietnam Wars, and the civil rights movement set the stage for profound changes in the United States, not least of which was the nature of the crime problem. In the 1970s, although no African-American racketeer had faced a RICO indictment—a sure sign of importance in the underworld—that would change.

NOTES

1. Quoted in Thomas A. Johnson, "Numbers Called Harlem's Balm," *New York Times*, 1 March 1971, 1. Through a fictional character in "Simple and the Numbers," the poet Langston Hughes focused on the special relationship between the numbers racket and how many African-American communities viewed the numbers racket.
2. Francis A. J. Ianni, *Black Mafia*, 119.
3. Sam Giancana and Chuck Giancana, *Double Cross* (New York: Warner Books, 1992), 109–113.
4. Stephen Fox, *Blood and Power*, 349.
5. Gunnar Myrdal, *An American Dilemma*, 330.

6. William J. Wilson, *The Declining Significance of Race*, 148–149.

7. Ibid., 149.

8. Robert Blauner, *Racial Oppression in America*.

9. Richard G. Hatcher, "Minority Objections," *New York Affairs* 3, no. 3 (Spring); John Howard, "A Framework for the Analysis of Urban Black Politics," *Annals, Academy of Political and Social Science*, (September 1978), 439.

10. Kenneth B. Clark, *Dark Ghetto: Dilemmas of Social Power* (New York: Harper Torchbook, 1967).

11. Richard Cloward and Lloyd Ohlin, *Delinquency and Opportunity* (New York: Free Press, 1960).

12. Donald Cressey, *Theft of the Nation*, 197.

13. Ianni, *Black Mafia*, 119.

14. Selwyn Raab, "Faxes Produce Numbers Arrest in Harlem Ring." *New York Times*, 21 April 1994, 1.

15. Ibid., B4.

16. Ted Poston, "The Numbers Racket," in Gus Tyler, ed. *Organized Crime in America*, 262.

17. Ted Poston, "The Policy Racket," *New York Post*, 29 February–10 March 1960, 24.

18. Lasswell and McKenna, *The Impact of Organized Crime*.

19. Illinois Institute of Technology Research Institute, *A Study of Organized Crime In Illinois* (Chicago: Chicago Crime Commission, 1971), 61–77.

20. Testimony of the Police Department, City of New York, (July 11, 1983), before United States Senate Committee on Judiciary, "Report on Organized Crime in New York City," (Washington, DC: U.S. Government Printing Office).

21. Charles M. Sennott. *New York Daily News*, 17 November 1991, 33. A compiled account of efforts by Jamaican, Russian, and Asian syndicates in a related coverage of mob wars.

22. *New York Times*, 8 December 1990, 1.

23. Raymond T. Smith, *Kinship and Class in the West Indies: A Genealogical Study of Jamaica and Guyana* (Cambridge, MA: Cambridge University Press, 1988).

24. C. R. Taplin, "Lucas Family Troubles," *Sunday Bergen Record*, 5 January 1975, 1.

25. Ibid., 1.

26. The President's Commission on Organized Crime, *Organized Crime and Heroin Trafficking*, 194–218.

27. Fred Ferretti, "Mister Untouchable," *New York Times Magazine*, (June 5, 1977), 15–17, 106, 108–109.

28. Donald Goddard, *Easy Money*.

29. Ibid., 168.

30. Pennsylvania Crime Commission, *Organized Crime in Pennsylvania: A Decade of Change, 1990 Report*, (Conshohocken, PA, 1991), chap. 7.

31. President's Commission on Organized Crime, *Organized Crime and Heroin Trafficking*, 221–222.

32. Ibid., 236–237.

33. Ibid., 230–231.

34. Cressey, *Theft of a Nation*; Ianni, *Family Business*; Joseph L. Albini, *The American Mafia: Genesis of a Legend* (New York: Appleton-Century Crofts, 1971).

35. Raimando Castanzaro, *Men of Respect: A Social History of the Sicilian Mafia*.

36. Francis A. J. Ianni, "Mafia and the Web of Kinship" in Luciano J. Iorizzo, ed. *An Inquiry into Organized Crime* (New York: The American-Italian Historical Association, 1970).

37. President's Commission on Organized Crime, *Organized Crime and Heroin Trafficking*, 77; President's Commission on Organized Crime, *The Impact: Organized*

Crime Today, 177.

38. Lee P. Brown, "Crime in the Black Community," in *State of Black America* (New York: National Urban League, 1988).

39. National Advisory Committee on Criminal Justice Standards and Goals, *Organized Crime* (Washington, DC: U.S. Government Printing Office, 1976), 8.

40. Mark Haller, "Organized Crime in Urban Society: Chicago in the Twentieth Century," *Journal of Social History* 2 (New Brunswick, NJ: Transaction Press, Winter, 1971–1972), 221.

41. Lasswell and McKenna, *The Impact of Crime*, 10.

42. Senate Judiciary Committee, *Organized Crime in the Northeast*, U.S. Congressional Hearings, Testimony of the New York City Police Department on July 3, Organized Crime Control Unit, Intelligence Division, (Washington DC: U.S. Government Printing Office, 1983), 18–19.

43. Ianni, *Black Mafia*, 312.

44. R. Rudolph, "West Orange Man Held without Bail as Leader of a Large Jersey Drug Ring," *Newark Star Ledger*: 1988, 1.

45. I. Wilkerson, "Detroit Drug Empire Showed All the Traits of Big Business," *New York Times*, 18 December 1988, 42.

46. Andrew Billingsley, *Climbing Jacob's Ladder: The Enduring Legacy of African-American Families* (New York: Simon & Schuster, 1994).

47. Daniel P. Moynihan, *The Case of National Action: The Negro Family*, Office of Policy Planning and Research, U.S. Department of Labor (Washington, DC: U.S. Government Printing Office, 1965).

48. Light, "Numbers Gambling," 898.

49. Frederick T. Martens, "African-American Organized Crime," 43–50.

50. Pennsylvania Crime Commission, "Chester Pennsylvania: Racketeering at the Local Level" in *Organized Crime in Pennsylvania*, 309–322.

51. Judson R. Landis, *Sociology: Concepts and Characteristics* (Belmont, CA: Wadsworth Publishing Co., 1974), 208.

If the 1970s saw the beginnings of the African-American encroachment and partial domination in drugs, then the 1980s could be considered the decade of drug-related crises. This is also an area in which the increasingly thin line between foreign and domestic social issues is so often traversed that the very distinction itself finally had to yield to a higher truth: that events in Bogota, Colombia and Marseilles, France were directly related to the price and supply lines of drugs in Miami, New York, Chicago, and Los Angeles. Indeed, relations among drug suppliers, distributors, manufacturers, and users became part of a new mosaic—defined as illegal and, hence, played out on a "cops-and-robbers" stage—that was nonetheless global and local in every way.

In meetings between political, military, and law enforcement officials of Andean cocaine-producing nations and North American consuming nations, the big issue is where to place primary responsibility: on the streets of big cities where drug use is rampant, or on the cocaine-producing hamlets and villages of Peru, Colombia, Bolivia, and on the opium that is grown and harvested in Pakistan and the "Golden Triangle" of Southeast Asia.[1] This is hardly moral discourse, since at stake is a coordinated effort to eradicate drug use while not upsetting the economic stability of South American, Southeastern, and Southwestern Asian nations. To be sure, the availability of a product or a crop, whether it be petroleum or drugs, is crucial to market prices as well as political attitudes. A key element in the collapse of the distinction between foreign and domestic policy is the need to create scarce supplies in the face of heavy demands.[2] Once again, the United States found itself the dependent victim rather than the dependency creator.

The drug problem highlights the raucousness of much of what passes for sociological wisdom in this era. The fashionable belief that drugs were little more serious than cigarettes or liquor went up in the smoke of statistics showing the high correlations of crack use with arrest and conviction rates for serious crimes in U.S. cities.[3] The fashionable middle-class notions of drugs as a "recreational" phenomenon collapsed as usage and drug addiction among the affluent and the young spiraled. Drug addiction among American youths spiraled. In the United States in 1990, twenty-seven million Americans, or 11 percent of the population, used some form of illicit drugs at least once during the year.[4] And this, it is well to remember, is an area of acknowledged underreporting. Even if drug usage and drug abuse are not identical, the numbers are sufficiently staggering to cause all but the most confirmed advocates of the drug subculture to pause.

The notion of drug purchases in nonpunishable zones of sale and distribution, once so widely touted as a livable "Dutch" solution, foundered on the hard realities.[5] Clearly, such a policy proposal, whether in the name of legalization or *laissez-faire* libertarian economics, only served to sanction a two-tiered society of drug users and was not, in the opinion of many African-American politicians whose constituencies live with the full brunt of drug abuse, a broad social solution to drug abuse as such.[6] The advocates of drug decriminalization became trapped in a quagmire of antidemocratic political theory—in which permissiveness is transformed into a perspective allowing for tolerable levels of human waste.

One might argue that, in effect, using and selling drugs have become nonpunishable crimes. Thus, although these are crimes with victims, they have not been punished—at least to any appreciable extent. What happens is a crisis in advanced societies that cannot be mandated on policy grounds, except by raising the stakes: allowing higher prices for poorer drug services and goods, and higher risks in drug purchasing and acquisition. Part of this trade-off creates a sense of contentment among participants in the organized, international drug networks and markets, who settle back into an agreeable business equilibrium. Drug prices, like those for coffee, oil, or other legitimate commodities of high consumer value, become rationalized. Goods and services flow in a relatively uninterrupted fashion, and a new class of entrepreneur emerges and changes the character of global relations, without necessarily shaking the foundations of the social order. In brief, the explosion of drugs, from crop cultivation to street selling, involves many countries and people.

THE DRUG TRAFFICKING INDUSTRY: STRUCTURE, CONDUCT, AND PERFORMANCE
The way that economists approach questions about business processes and structure is through a field of economics called *industrial organization* that is concerned with giving an account or description of how some particular economic activity is put together. It is taken for granted that drug dealing is

organized in the sense that a large amount of activity is carried out in a co-ordinated manner by many individuals. The questions are whether it is organized in a special way because it is illegal and whether its activities are under the control and direction of a single individual. The answers to both issues are most probably "no." The drug markets are not like that—any more than the K-Mart business or General Motors is in the United States. There is an organized pattern of activities, but they are carried out in complex ways that are not necessarily under the total direction and control of a single individual.

Thinking about drug trafficking as an industry like most other business activities facilitates an explanation of its structure, organizational dynamics, and profitability. Ordinarily the empirical framework for analysis requires a great deal of data that is often difficult to obtain. The research process is even more arduous when an industry is not only illegal, but transnational in sweep, and multilayered.[7] From a business standpoint, illegality has other important ramifications: The illegal nature of drug trafficking makes it difficult to determine its scope, structure, and profits. Unlike legitimate business, there are no reports to shareholders that would provide information about the performance of specific firms and divisions within firms, or about trends within the industry as a whole. And unlike legal commercial enterprises, at the lower levels of distribution and retail, there are enormous variations from one location to another, according to the clientele, patterns of drug use, and law enforcement tactics.[8]

In spite of these limitations that in legitimate industries would spell the disaster of stagnation, the drug industry dwarfs most legitimate businesses, being larger, according to one commentator, than the global trade in oil. Interestingly, it is one of the few industries with profits so astronomical that even increasing tonnage seizures does not appear to have a serious impact on price.[9] The losses from law enforcement activities, which have steadily increased, can be regarded as overhead costs and do affect price;[10] still, it is difficult to imagine any other industry that could afford to lose significant segments of its product and other tangible assets, and emerge nonetheless with a very large profit.

Most conventional industries do not operate in total illegal contexts, so there are structural differences that set drug firms apart, but they share many characteristics in common, despite their illegal status. For instance, as can be seen in Figure 7.1, taking Colombian cartels as a model of a set of firms in the drug industry, they

- Possess a multilevel set of activities, including the cultivation and collection of the agricultural product into its final retail selling form, which parallels that of many legal products that are handled from the raw material through the transition, processing, production, transportation, importation, wholesale distribution, and finally, marketing and retailing states.

• Move through the chain from the growing fields to street sales, with the value of the product increasing at each phase of the process.

• Tend to specialize and vertically integrate so that the organization of the Medellin and Cali cartels (considered the most powerful) do not differ much in essentials from IBM or Xerox.[11]

Pictures and descriptive charts that neatly lay out the skeletal structures of drug firms as if they were no different than companies and corporations dealing in legal products can be somewhat misleading, however. And this applies at retail-level operations (especially there), where competition for street corners can turn into brutally violent struggles. As with Mafia groups that also developed organizational structures to rationally accommodate their lucrative heroin trafficking, cocaine cartels are also held together, or dismantled, by other factors that play into business transactions—such things as codes of honor, family bonds, friendships, and so on. Whatever the glue that binds groups together, all are driven by at least four major factors that ultimately affect profits, which are the only reason for being in business. These factors operate not only at the highest levels of the drug trade but also in the streets of American cities where "nickel and dime" bags of dope are sold in streets, schoolyards, offices, and playgrounds.

1. Every dealer must be cognizant of his or her competitors, the number of challengers, and how dangerous they might be.
2. The cost of drugs from suppliers and the quality of their supply is a serious consideration in that it affects the sales market.
3. Security of buyers or consumers.
4. There are the possibilities of more appealing, less costly drugs that could undermine or supplant one's business and livelihood.[12]

COMPETITION AND RIVALRY IN THE STREET TRADE

Evidence of cooperation among drug traffickers surfaced during the late 1980s, when New York Mafia families developed strong ties with Colombian and Cuban dealers in Miami, thereby facilitating arrangements with Mexican crime families.[13]

At the retail level, where street sales take place, competition rather than cooperative partnerships tends to be much greater and bloodier. Dif-

FIGURE 7.1. A Colombian Cocaine Syndicate

Typical Columbian Cocaine Organization

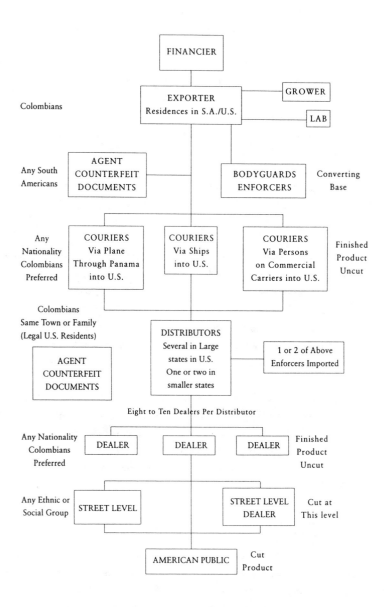

Source: New York City Police Department Testimony, Organized Crime Control Bureau, 1987.

ferent ethnic groups, who see drug dealing as one way of economic advancement, strive for dominance in the retail market. This process is another version of the phenomenon of ethnic succession, which one analyst describes as, ". . . the historical succession of ethnic minorities in organized crime [*that*] constitutes one of its most notable features, with no ethnic group retaining its supremacy in crime indefinitely."[14] O'Kane's insight helps to explain the intense competition in the drug retail markets, but it is insufficient as an explanation of intraethnic disputes, such as those that have occurred between rival Jamaican Posses, which are sometimes more deadly and violent than the conflicts among different ethnic groups. The "guerrilla wars" among street gangs may be explained by the struggle for preferential market spaces.[15] Harries notes,

> [I]n drug markets, like "normal" markets, rent is used as a means of sorting retailers. However, in drug markets, "rent" is paid in the form of violence with the greatest "price" paid for the best locations.[16]

The "drive-by" shootings that have been the signature of drug gangs engaged in the retail end of the business and testify to the violent conflicts involved in the competition for turf and lucrative outlets, should not obscure the fact that even at this level, tacit cooperation over "turf" and advantageous gang alliances are quite common. Cooperative trends may actually increase as the retail end of the drug business experiences "professionalization." O'Kane describes some of the initial steps in this direction:

> In Detroit, black gangs, such as the Pony Down and the Young Boys Inc. have evolved from opportunistic violent street gangs to sophisticated criminal enterprises. Drug dealing is their main business and their membership increasingly attracts middle-class youths as well as the traditional lower class members. They operate in secrecy, with a small tightly knit core of leaders whose style mimics that of corporate entrepreneurs more than the traditional style of urban street warriors.[17]

From another part of the country, San Diego, California, ethnographic research on African-American street gangs suggests similar conclusions: African-American gangs are primarily focused on making money in contrast to other groups, such as Mexican-American, Filipino, and Southeast Asian gangs. Drug sales and robberies constitute the main sources of income but other, ancillary criminal activities have become integral to gang activities, as an interview with a gang member illustrates:

> I was getting my money selling drugs—large amounts—drugs like
> sherm [PCP-laced marijuana], crystal [methamphetamine], weed
> [marijuana], and the main killer cocaine. We deal through Cubans
> and Mexicans in big events, then eventually to the Mafia. Gangs are
> all about money now. Pimping girls is also a popular way to make
> money. Drug dealers go days without sleep. Weed is the only drug
> that drug dealers use. Most [drug dealers] don't go to school, but the
> ones that do will go to school, and then sell drugs after school till
> sometimes 3 a.m. Then he will wake up the next day and start all over
> again.[18]

In Brownsville, a dangerously violent ghetto in Brooklyn, New York,
a piece of graffiti scrawled in public housing project stairwells reads, "Money,
ho's [women] and clothes."[19] It is the motto of the Lo Lifes, a street gang
that is not, in the traditional sense, an organization with a set membership
and turf. For the Lo Life members there is no ritual initiation, just a casual
shift from outsider to gang member. Each member of the crew receives a
street name that is a combination of the initial syllable of his first name and
the suffix "-lo." Sharron is thus "Shalo." Robbery and drug dealing are
major gang activities here, too, but a reason for organizing is self-protec-
tion, as a gang member relates:

> If you are nobody and somebody shoots you . . . then nobody is gonna
> come back for you. You just go out. Simple. But if you got props
> [friends, guns, support], you got respect and you got a crew. People
> think twice about cappin' you [shooting you] cause there are people
> who are coming back.[20]

In another more anthropological scenario of African-American adolescent street life involving drugs and guns, Williams provides a snapshot
of kids operating a small drug firm.[21] Most of the members spend sixteen
hours a day at the "office" (the Bronx streets, called the "dope stroll") serving customers out of an apartment crowded with teenagers doing a brisk
business in cocaine; others are out in the street selling "jumbo" crack in glass
vials, dodging the police and predatory stick-up boys. They are children who
have become a labor force in the drug industry as an unintended effect of
the "Rockefeller" drug laws in New York, which require that adults convicted of selling narcotics be given mandatory sentences of a severity intended

to be daunting. Being relatively immune from legal sanctions, children are more prone to risk taking, and because they are typically without money, they are conditioned to be acquisitive, and are, thereby, well-adapted to working in the retail drug business. It was not long before the local folklore had teenage African Americans and Hispanics buying expensive cars, walking around with large clumps of money stuffed in their pockets, and recklessly gambling hundreds of dollars on pickup games of basketball in local playgrounds.

Ironically, it was government success in the interdiction of marijuana that spawned the cocaine/crack trade and changed the drug industry's traditional networks of distribution. When the Nixon Administration's campaign to stop the importation of marijuana was implemented, it worked sufficiently well to raise the price of marijuana, which in the early 1970s was the staple commodity of the American drug culture. At about the same time, cocaine, which had been a speciality drug used by the affluent underground, crossed over to college campuses and spread into the American mainstream. When that occurred, the price doubled. The basic equation of dope economics changed; cocaine was easier to smuggle than marijuana and became more profitable.

As the huge American market for cocaine expanded and stretched from coast to coast, from Canada to the Mexican border, the proprietors of the drug supply, the Colombian cartels, figured out a way to bypass the industry's normal channels. Miami had become a Latin outpost on the North American mainland. As the Cosa Nostra's oligarchy relinquished its place at the top of the criminal underworld, with its influence on the urban American-outlaw culture receding in the face of African-American, Hispanic, and Asian groups muscling into gambling, drugs, and extortion, other models and other groups took up the slack. The Jamaican Posses brought their style of criminal enterprise to African-American neighborhoods throughout the Northeast and eventually into the heartland of the United States. Posses were organized, violent, astute, and cunning in their business dealings. Eventually, African-American youths became the foot soldiers in the drug trade.

When the cocaine market became glutted with oversupply in the 1980s, prices fell. When crack was developed into a consumer product, the price of cocaine further declined, which made the market more flexible and elastic. With deflated prices (Drug Enforcement Agency [DEA] estimates indicate a price drop from $100,000 a kilogram of cocaine in 1980 to $16,000 in 1988), freelance entrepreneurs, who had previously stumbled into the market undercapitalized and could not insure a reliable supply or support distribution organizations of their own, now found it easier to acquire control of their own underground economies within communities where drugs had become a formidable local enterprise and a major employer of neighborhood youth. Several major repercussions emerged from the bull market in crack that inundated African-American and Hispanic communities. The most troubling outcome, as Williams observed, is the essentially routine, ordinary character of drug dealing; it is simply taken for granted (as with any legitimate business of distribution and sales) that a crack business has much in common with owning and operating a small supermarket. It is, like a legitimate business, in the interest of the operators to maintain an orderly, stable business environment. Technically, because crack dealers are criminals, they cannot enter into contracts that can be adjudicated in the courts. They must do their own policing and enforcement either by violence or its threat against poachers, irresponsible associates, and recalcitrant clients who fail to meet their financial obligation. In effect, the climate of lawlessness breeds the attitude of resignation that death may be just around the corner at any time.

Being their own enforcement/security apparatus means that guns proliferate and with time homicide rates soared among young African-American males caught up in the maelstrom of drugs. The mortality rates among young African-American males are ghostly reminders of wartime casualty rates among combat troops. In 1986, the National Center for Health Services released information and findings that there were about twice as many African-American women as men in the United States, and so many young men died that the average life expectancy of the African-American population as a whole has been depressed.[22]

The Gruesome Logic of Crack: Desperation in the Inner City

Homicide has become the leading cause of death for African-American males between the ages of fifteen and twenty-four. They are dying at a rate that has increased by 67 percent in four years and is now six times greater than that for other Americans in the same age groups. Young African-American males are endangered—not only indirectly from societal neglect and abuse, but also directly by their own actions and activities. They are killing, maiming, and narcotizing themselves more than if they had been annihilated in wars or been felled by natural diseases. Not only are they destroying themselves, but they are also jeopardizing the institutional structures and lifestyles in communities that are already seriously destabilized by economic depression.

The drug menace is not recent, however; its history is decades and generations old. Several million people, mostly men who lived in the cities,

TABLE 7.1. Victimization Rates for Persons Age 12 and Older, by Type of Crime and Race of Victims

Type of crime	Rate per 1,000 persons age 12 and over		
	White	Black	Other
All personal crimes	88.7	110.8	88.3
Crimes of violence	29.9	50.4	23.7
Completed	10.4	21.4	10.0
Attempted	19.5	28.9	13.6
Rape	0.6	1.3*	0.0*
Robbery	4.7	15.6	5.1*
Completed	2.9	11.4	2.8*
With injury	1.2	4.9	2.1*
From serious assault	0.6	2.7	1.2*
From minor assault	0.6	2.2	0.9*
Without injury	1.8	6.5	0.7*
Attempted	1.7	4.2	2.3*
With injury	0.4	1.3*	0.6*
From serious assault	0.2	0.5*	0.0*
From minor assault	0.1*	0.7*	0.6*
Without injury	1.3	2.9	1.7*
Assault	24.6	33.5	18.6
Aggravated	7.8	18.3	5.3*
Completed with injury	2.7	6.7	2.1*
Attempted with weapon	5.1	11.6	3.2*
Simple	16.8	15.2	13.3
Completed with injury	4.5	3.0	5.1*
Attempted without weapon	12.3	12.2	8.2

(continued)

were infected by taking heroin in the late 1960s. Some died from overdoses of lethally adulterated drugs; many never fully recovered and are now in their thirties and forties, dying from AIDS, or have succumbed along the way to one or another of the predictable consequences of long-term addiction: jail, disease, social isolation, and financial marginality. The proportion of African-American men in the cities who are living within what the society at large considers its social and economic mainstream has been shrinking steadily for the past twenty years.

Things might have been different if members of this depleted, drug-ravaged generation should have survived to shepherd the seething young men

Crimes of theft	58.8	60.4	64.6
Completed	55.2	57.1	56.4
Attempted	3.6	3.4	8.2
Personal larceny with contact	2.0	4.6	2.5*
Purse snatching	0.7	1.2*	0.4*
Pocket picking	1.3	3.4	2.1*
Personal larceny without contact	56.7	55.9	62.1
Completed	53.4	52.5	54.3
Less than $50	21.7	18.3	19.6
$50 or more	28.5	29.9	31.9
Amount not available	3.1	4.4	2.8*
Attempted	3.3	3.4	7.8
Type of crime	White	Black	Other
Population age 12 and over	175,614,070	23,872,300	6,928,110

Note: Detail may not add to total shown because of rounding.

*Estimate is based on about 10 or fewer sample cases.

Source: *Criminal Victimization in the United States, 1992.* A National Crime Victimization Survey Report, Bureau of Justice Statistics, Rockville, MD, 24.

of the streets whose attitudes toward a hostile world mainly reflect a mean-spirited, crude, utilitarian calculus concerned only with prices for commodities (money, ho's, and clothes) that exert an overwhelming power over others. They know the inherent dangers of what they push and their disdain translates into a scornful contempt for those who use it. Actually, they are scarcely unique in this narrow respect, in that selling what has power over people is a means to gratify desires that overpower them: gold, cars, money, clothes—whatever is the "drug" of the moment.

There is also another price paid by society for its drug subculture that deeply affects the customs, mores, and rhythms of everyday life in communities whose integrity and livability have been jeopardized. The negative dividends of drugs paid by a community are many, and not the least of them may be a measure of the solitude and oblivion everyone—drug users and abstainers—experiences. The social costs are to be seen in the physical transformations of neighborhoods that once hummed with commercial activity and are now devastated, inhospitable, and killed off by fear of crime. The inner cities, particularly the minority neighborhoods in the large megalopolises, offer a strange contrast with the community mosaic at large.

The commotions of drug dealing drain a community of its lifeblood;

with wealth gravitating into the illicit sector, social and economic life is flattened out, polarized, and diminished. The streets lose their social vibrancy and collective declarative memory—memory that inhabitants are consciously aware of; they are no longer areas in which to congregate, shop, talk, socialize or play. Instead, many have become areas of conflict and violence—domains conquered by gunfire, where a gang's stubborn occupation of some street space is defined by them as a "turf" or a "'hood." The local economy is grotesquely distorted into an export goods racket, accompanied by mutilations of everyday life that endemic crime always entails. The deficits are numerous and fall into three general, interrelated categories: drugs and crime, drugs and social dependence, and drugs and traps for children. Large proportions of those arrested for street crimes such as robbery, burglary, and larceny are drug users. The addict's need for money to finance his or her habit and the mechanism of addiction establish a link between drugs and crime (see Table 7.2).

TABLE 7.2. Drug Prevalence Among Arrestees

Arrest charge	Positive for any drug	
	Male	Female
Drug sale/possession	79%	81%
Burglary	68	58
Robbery	66	66
Larceny-theft	64	59
Stolen vehicle	60	65
Homicide	52	49
Fraud/forgery	50	55
Prostitution	49	81
Assault	48	50

Note: The urinalysis results presented in this table were gathered from 19,883 male arrestees in 23 cities and 7,947 female arrestees in 21 cities. Drugs include cocaine, opiates, PCP, marijuana, amphetamines, methadone, methaqualone, benzodiazepines, barbiturates, and propoxyphene.

Source: *National Institute of Justice 1990 Drug Use Forecasting Program*, unpublished data.

More specifically, in drug-related homicides both victims and assailants are often African-American and Hispanic males (see Table 7.3). Drug dependence is, itself, needless to say, a serious social problem. Irresponsible behaviors bring with them health-care costs to neighborhoods and involve injuries from drug-related crime, child abuse, other medical costs for drugs users, and resources absorbed in rehabilitative efforts; and then there are losses of economic productivity such as employee absenteeism; those persons incapable of, or not participating in the labor force because of incarceration for drug-related crime; lower productivity of those using or affected by someone else's use of illegal drugs, death from drug-crime victimization, or death from drug-related workplace or traffic accidents. The personal and family pain and suffering caused by illegal drug use is usually accompanied by the substantial costs to the public sector in social dependency.

TABLE 7.3. Drug-Related Homicides by Age, Sex, and Race

Sociodemographics Characteristics	Drug-related homicides in 1984 in New York City	
	Victims	Assailants
Age		
Under 21	14%	12%
21 to 30	48	31
31 to 40	24	18
Over 40	15	5
Unknown	—	35
Sex		
Male	90%	72%
Female	10	1
Unknown	—	27
Race/ethnicity		
Black	42%	37%
White	9	7
Hispanic	49	30
Other	0	0
Unknown	—	26
Total Number of Homicides	347	403

Source: Paul J. Goldstein and Henry H. Brownstein, *Drug-Related Crime Analysis—Homicide, A Report to the NIJ Drugs, Alcohol, and Crime Program*, (Washington, DC: U.S. Department of Justice, Office of Justice Programs, July 1987), 52, 54.

These predictable consequences are commonly believed to flow from the compulsive use of drugs: early deaths, elevated morbidity, the impoverishment of families, and so on. A particularly troubling aspect of drug use is the notion borne out in reality that many children who would otherwise remain on a path toward responsible citizenship are deflected by drug use. Casual experimentation—in drug-drenched communities—leads too often to frequent use which, in turn, means a reduced performance in school and forfeited life chances.

On top of health care, economic, and other social expenditures attributable to drug use are criminal justice expenditures. Significant segments of already bulging criminal justice budgets at all levels of government are encumbered because of drug enforcement, interdiction, and legal services. In 1990, the Uniform Crime Reports estimated that state and local agencies made almost 1.1 million arrests for drug-abuse violations.

Although narcotics addicts as a group extensively engage in crime, the amounts and types of crime vary considerably by individual. The criminal activity of most addicts, although rising in general, is strongly influenced by their current addiction status. Narcotics addicts commit millions of crimes per year in the United States, and many of these offenses are of a serious nature. In a very real sense, it can be said that illicit narcotics "drive" crime.

The relationships between drugs and crime are multifaceted. As Table 7.4 illustrates, drugs often act as a catalyst in two ways: (1) among desperate addicts seeking cash for purchases, and (2) among drug dealers who are concerned with sustaining their business and protecting its assets.

TABLE 7.4. The Social Costs of Illegal Drug Use

What are some of the costs of illegal drug use?

Type of cost	Millions
Public and private crime costs	
Federal drug expenditures (1991)	$10,841
All law enforcement	7,157
Interdiction	2,028
Investigations	1,288
International	640
Prosecution	584
Corrections	1,265
Intelligence	104
State and local assistance	1,016
Regulatory compliance	31
	(continued)

Type of cost	Millions
Other law enforcement	201
Drug prevention	1,483
Drug treatment	1,752
All research and development	450
State and local drug crime expenditures (1988)	$5,240
Enforcement of drug laws	2,007
Adjudication of drug law violators	123
Correction of drug law violators	3,072
State prisons	1,158
Local jails	908
Juveniles	224
Probation, pardon, and parole	677
Other corrections	122
Other criminal justice	38
Health-care costs for illegal drug users (1985)	$2,272
Short-stay hospitals	1,242
Specialty institutions	570
Office-based physicians	52
Support services	201
Other professional services	17
Medical care for drug-related AIDS cases	126
Support services for drug-related AIDS cases	64

Note: Detail may not add to total due to rounding. Costs should not be summed because the methodologies and years differ.

Sources: The federal drug expenditure data are from the White House: Office of National Drug Control Policy, *National Drug Control Strategy*, budget summary, January 1992, 212–214. The state and local justice expenditure estimates are from the Bureau of Justice Statistics, *Justice Expenditure and Employment Survey*, 1988, unpublished data. All other estimates are from Alcohol, Drug Abuse and Mental Health Administration, Dorothy P. Rice, Sander Kelman, Leonard S. Mill, and Sarah Dunmeyer, *The Economic Costs of Alcohol and Drug Abuse and Mental Illness: 1985*, 1990.

Many researchers have concluded that the prevalence and diversity of criminal involvement by narcotic addicts are high and that this involvement is primarily for the purpose of supporting the use of drugs. Furthermore, it is a consistent finding that initiation into both substance abuse and criminal activity occurs at an early age. In particular, several investigations have found that among drug-using offenders, those who reported the most crimes as adults, including the most violent crime, were characteristically precocious in their drug use and illegal activity.[23]

It is worthwhile to recall the prophetic words of the Kerner Commission Report, which spoke of racial polarization and its destructive potentials when considering the drug issue, its associated crime, and the population in American society most afflicted by it. Two societies, white and black, separate and unequal, were seen in the landmark report as inexorably evolving in separate social and economic directions. Now, white society is growing increasingly hostile to drugs. For the other population however—the poor Hispanics, African Americans, Native Americans, and possibly Asians—there is increasing susceptibility to drugs. In 1985, crack took hold in the cities. Previously, cocaine had been available as an expensive powder far beyond the reach of most ghetto residents, then crack, a cheap derivative of cocaine, arrived and many American cities, especially their slums and racial and ethnic ghettos, turned into nightmares. The horrendous experiences with drug problems that large urban complexes like Los Angeles, New York, Miami, Atlanta, Philadelphia, Houston, and Boston live with are being repeated in smaller communities, where crack strikes with swift fury.

FIGURE 7.2. Arrests for Drug Offenses: 1965–1990

Since 1965, arrests for drug offenses have made up an increasingly larger proportion of all state and local arrests

Percent of total Uniform Crime Report arrests

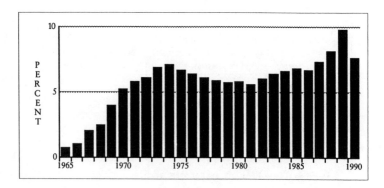

Source: FBI Uniform Crime Reports, *Crime in the United States: 1965 through 1990.* U.S. Department of Justice, Washington, DC.

From its introduction, crack became a mass-market drug, and its consumption was concentrated in poor urban neighborhoods, where its intense, pleasurable high provided a quick respite from the bleakness of the surroundings. Because crack lived up to its reputation as particularly enjoyable, many users found themselves completely immersed in it. It was not only the number of new drug abusers that was overwhelming, but also the extent of their need—largely unemployed, often homeless, uninsured, with many suffering from AIDS or other diseases related to drug use.[24]

FIGURE 7.3. Relationship of Illegal Drugs to Other Crimes

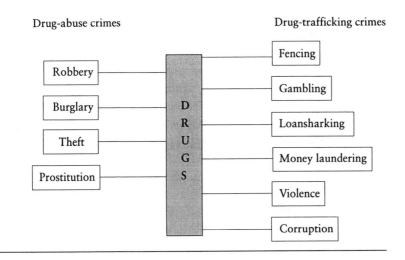

Over the past decade, America's drug problem has settled in deeply among the poor and minorities and has become an epidemic. In 1981, when Ronald Reagan became President, the nation had about three million hardcore drug users; in less than ten years the figure is reaching around six million and of these, most are poor. The "Just Say No" campaign of Nancy Reagan, despite the liberal claim that it was ineffectual, did indeed help to encourage among the middle classes a disillusionment with drugs that began to take hold in the mid-1980s. For many educated and middle-class Americans, drugs no longer seemed worth the risks.

In the inner city, however, drugs remain a palpable presence. The poor face mounting deaths and an ever bleaker future because of drug abuse. Again, since the 1980s, the surge of crack has resulted in rising deaths attributable to overdoses, and drug-related homicides have raised murder rates to record levels across the country. All of this has occurred despite an eight-fold increase in antidrug program spending.[25]

Lack of reliable knowledge about the drug menace in our cities seems most acute where the recurring problem is most urgent, and this fact weighs heavily in the debates about drug interdiction policies and treatment and prevention programs.[26] Interestingly, this relatively cheap, smokable form of cocaine still remains something of a mystery in terms of its close linkage with violence. Two ounces of cocaine hydrochloride mixed with lidocaine (a prescription anesthetic called "comeback") cooked to a boil amalgamates during the cooking process into a solid mass that can be cut into small smokable pieces that produce an immediate "rush," a pleasurable sensation of greater intensity than cocaine when ingested nasally or injected subcutaneously or intravenously. Soon dealers were peddling crack (or "pebbles") at low unit costs that were both economical and easily concealed and ingested. Its crystalline appearance conveyed an image of purity and cocaine users were quick to accept and popularize its smokable form.[27]

At first, crack was marketed in inner-city neighborhoods in or near cocaine importation points such as New York, Miami, and Los Angeles.[28] Ethnographic studies suggest that crack is often distributed in centralized locations known as "crack houses," where buyers have access to a supply and a setting.[29]

In Harlem, New York, South Central Los Angeles, and other inner-city communities around the country, poor, young and desperate street youth hunger for a piece of the fast-money action that selling crack offers. To get started it takes as little as an ounce of cocaine, an investment of about $1,000, and nerve.

Obtaining cocaine has not been much of a problem since the mid-1980s when it arrived in New York by the tons. Importation was controlled by the Cali Colombian cartel, the second largest syndicate after the Medellin groups. The chief middlemen in New York were Dominicans who got along well with the Colombians. The city (like the nation) was carved up into territories to be serviced by the drug cartels.

From the time that crack hit the streets of the most socially and economically deprived neighborhoods, its distribution was distinctively different from all other drugs, including the highly centralized heroin trade. From poppy cultivation to street sales, heroin trafficking was dominated by a single organization—the Mafia—which through ruthlessness imposed a certain order. Wars among drug groups were rare and police officers were never endangered if they had remained free from corruption. But because heroin was so tightly organized, it was vulnerable to diligent police work and it was possible to put an entire drug network out of business, which occurred in the French Connection case. With crack, a "Mom and Pop" organizational system emerged among the selling groups. Compared to the complexities of transnational heroin dealers with hierarchical manufacturing and distribution components, involving perhaps hundreds of individuals, a typical crack organization might have no more than seven or eight people—a street seller or two, a street "steerer" to direct customers, some armed guards to protect the merchandise, a police lookout, a weigher of the drugs, and a manager and a boss.[30]

Competition can be intense, with no centralized coordinated command structure imposing order. Turf wars contesting the most lucrative territories are frequent and violence permeates the entire process of manufacture and distribution. Dealers regularly rob their customers and steal from one another. Shootouts occur daily, the streets rocking with gunfire. Crack created a new breed of urban criminals, who are members of a fierce army that leaves the police badly outgunned and outnumbered.[31] By 1985, when the crack problem came to the attention of the national press, it was already deeply entrenched in New York's poor neighborhoods. Only two other cities of comparable size, Los Angeles and Miami, had similar crack problems. All three were major distribution points for cocaine, so it was not unexpected that crack would engulf them. Soon, crack moved from these gateway cities into the heartland.

In the streets of Manhattan's upper West Side, Colombian cocaine worth millions is warehoused in networks of apartments in the big prewar buildings that rise above its streets. West Harlem and Washington Heights have become the wholesale distribution depots for dealers and users in the states contiguous with New York, and the street violence associated with the mountains of cash floating throughout the minority community is further exacerbated by rampant police corruption.[32] Crack enticed into trafficking a criminal group that had previously played a major role in marijuana distribution in the United States. It did not take long for the Jamaican Posses to establish themselves as key crack traffickers in many cities around the country, according to testimony presented before government committees. Almost ten years ago, the Jamaicans were believed to control 35 percent to 40 percent of the nation's crack networks.[33] Pursuing paths of least resistance, the Posses moved shrewdly: cities known for well-organized criminal groups, such as Newark, St. Louis, and Chicago, were bypassed; in other cities, where dealers were too weak and disorganized to stand up to Posse tactics, they moved in quickly and decisively.

The question worrying drug experts is whether crack will break out like an infectious disease into middle-class populations of African Americans and whites. In some places it already has. On the West Coast, in Los Angeles, African-American street gangs are among the fastest growing group of crack purveyors in the entire country.[34] The gangs appear to have established a national network second only to the Posses. They are grouped into confederations known as the Crips and the Bloods. Fiercely territorial down to the street level, the gangs make up the two large criminal amalgamations that have heretofore concentrated on fighting one another over street corners, recreational facilities, and stretches of neighborhoods in South Central Los Angeles. But crack has changed that. Sensing the enormous profits in the drug, the Crips and the Bloods now seem to be paying less attention to one another and more attention to competing in the crack markets.

Participation in the drug economy has also meant that each gang has expanded territorially beyond the Los Angeles ghetto: More than ten thousand gang members are at work in many cities, from Seattle to Baltimore.[35] Generally, their selling techniques emulate the tactics of the Posses, infiltrating African-American communities through local contracts and avoiding warfare with the Posses or other locals. The fearful possibility is that the Crips and the Bloods—like the Colombian cartels and the old Prohibition gangs of a half century ago—are dividing up the country into sales regions, with devastating consequences for the communities caught up in the drug epidemic.[36]

The communities accommodating crack are usually run-down economically and socially with increasing impoverishment of residents, weakened social institutions, declining schools, and stagnating legitimate economic activities—all attributable to endemic crime conditions.[37]

Crack, with its low unit price, has become a choice drug, intensifying community deprivation and decay, while creating more opportunities for drug dealing and providing more economic incentives that expand the informal economy that spreads out from drug distribution.[38] The explosion of crack use has been neither unprecedented nor totally unexpected. It followed closely on the heels of cocaine use, so there existed a residual demand for cocaine products, especially less costly ones, that fueled demand for the drug.

In their study of nearly six hundred crack users in New York City, Fagan and Chin found that

> The increased involvement of young people in drug selling . . . seems to be a natural outgrowth of changes in the social and economic context of inner cities and the economies of drug distribution.

Also, the weakened neighborhood structures were unable to integrate and control the volatile drug market. Violence associated with crack resulted from several parallel processes: competition between sellers and protection of territory, regulation of employees in new selling organization . . . [and] the urge for the drug or money to buy it among habitual users.[39]

Individuals drawn into crack as users or sellers, according to Fagan and Chin, had prior histories of use and dealing. Their research shows that crack sellers were likely to be more involved in a variety of violent and nonviolent offenses than sellers of other drugs or nonsellers.[40] When the economic and social structural factors of communities are factored into the drug scene, what emerges is the latest and perhaps the most unusual in a long succession of "epidemics" that have recurred over the past two decades. The result has been expanded, but at the same time constricted, circles of drug users and sellers that mirror changes in communities whose social and economic boundaries were blurred by the destabilization of inner cities.[41] Each drug wave occurred in a context in which community norms of control that limited crime and governed drug use were fragmenting. In addition, unlike marijuana and its integration into the culture of Caribbean neighborhoods in Brooklyn, which was a peaceful affair in which profits were reinvested in the community, crack fell on neighborhoods like a match on dry tinder. Rules and norms for its use did not have enough time to develop and become institutionalized in a way that would not unhinge the community.[42]

Recent trends—the falloff in casual use, the rise in habitual use, the growing abstinence among middle-class users, the spread of addiction among the poor and unemployed—all point to the increasing importance of race and class in shaping patterns of drug abuse. Sadly, few research studies have explored these sociological factors in depth. Even advocates of legalization have tended to overlook the social settings of drug abuse. To make drugs generally available in the inner city without giving priority to the conditions prevailing there could lead to an exponential increase in consumption.

The Bush Administration (and so far, the Clinton Administration, with the exception of the Surgeon General, whose remarks on drug policy have been disavowed by the White House) steadfastly refused to consider the social setting of drug abuse.

Since 1989, the Bush Administration had nearly doubled the federal antidrug budget to more than $12.7 billion. To its credit, it had substantially increased the amount of money available for treating and preventing drug abuse, mainly through making more funds available to the states. The White House correctly identified a key component in its drug-use reduction plan: the demand side in a policy that defined supply/demand as inextricably bound together such that resources had to be properly weighted in confronting each dimension of the problem. Unfortunately, little attention was devoted to an analysis of antecedent ecological conditions that created milieux conducive to drug abuse, namely, the lack of more treatment facilities for drug problems. Better economic opportunities including the cluster of school, community, housing, health, and family supports that strengthen the social environments—however impoverished—work against the lack of opportunity and despair upon which drugs feed.

The trend toward draconian law enforcement solutions has not been limited to federal drug policies: Local and state governments have been urged to increase penalties for trafficking offenses, even to the extreme of capital punishment and life in prison without parole. The key feature of the federal government's approach is a moralistic rather than a scientific conception of the problem: The choice to use drugs (legal or illegal) is ascribed to the deficiencies of moral character in individuals. In contrast, most scientifically informed observers and a growing minority of law enforcement officials are persuaded that a social, psychological, and economic understanding of, and response to, the nation's drug problem will take us further, and at less cost to our liberties.

Fealty to the Constitution may seem no more than a platitude in view of the drug menace, but it is worth reminding ourselves of it when measures are proposed that would remove bail for drug dealers, deploy the National Guard, create nationwide curfew for teenagers, conduct street sweeps of supposed gang members, shoot down civilian planes wandering into "no fly" zones, perform random drug testing on everyone, eradicate entire crops in foreign countries, erect military-style "boot camps" that would, in the words of the strategy, "bring a sense of order and discipline to the lives of youthful, non-violent first time offenders . . ."[43] Whether such tough expedients contribute much to solving the drug problem remains to be seen. What they will do is support a climate of diluted Constitutional protections.

LAW ENFORCEMENT DILEMMAS: SOME CASE STUDIES

It is very likely that whatever deterrent value criminal laws may have for the drug gangs, these can be outweighed by the profits to be gained through expanding into market vacuums created by the imprisonment of some suppliers. One would expect otherwise—that is, as many government officials urge, confining more drug dealers would reduce the violence and other crimes related to narcotics. Washington, D.C. is a good example of just the opposite effect. Since the mid-1980s, the homicide rate in Washington, D.C.

soared, despite increased arrests of drug dealers. The homicide rate could not be attributed to police inactivity: In 1981, only 58 juveniles had been arrested for drug dealing offenses, and by 1987 that figure had reached 1,551. Adult arrests in the same period show similar rates: in 1981, adult arrests—usually of persons in their early twenties—totaled 408; by 1987, it was 5,298. Reuter's explanation of rising violence in the drug markets, despite dire criminal-justice consequences, focused on the economic dynamics of drug trafficking in a lucrative but constricted marketplace where penalties and buttressed law enforcement resources that might be thought to act as a powerful disincentive, seems almost irrelevant. For Reuter, when the number of drug dealers exceeds the demand for drugs, "[o]ne obvious way to raise earnings is to eliminate the competition through violence."[44]

In Oakland, California, the strategy endorsed by the Bush Administration of incarcerating "drug kingpins" became the centerpiece in an anti-drug war. Working with a federal strike force, the Oakland Police vice squad succeeded in convicting and imprisoning the East Bay's three leading drug dealers. With the top drug traffickers incarcerated, it was expected that street violence and other drug-related crimes would have been reduced. The result, however, was a continued increase in narcotics crimes.[45] Thus, it appears that dealer arrests tend to stimulate rather than suppress street violence and aggression where the drug market is stable and growing. Efforts to disrupt them through energetic interdiction tactics against supply systems produce at least four results none of which is particularly attractive.

First, there is the question of whether the United States can create a crust of impenetrable security against drug smugglers. According to a Rand Corporation study conducted by the Defense Department, "the U.S.-Mexican border can be crossed at many points . . . "[46] Therefore, the sheer number of people who make border crossings each year aggravate the problem of porous borders.

Second, another effect of supply reduction is that the more successful law enforcement is at cutting off supply, the more incentive drug dealers have for "hardening" drugs—that is, developing varieties that are more potent, portable, and dangerous. Law enforcement tactics may create more severe public health problems by generating demand for and production of more potent and dangerous drugs.

Third, crack is an addictive drug in a psychological sense, whatever physiological capacities it possesses. It is useful in helping people escape from reality; it makes the individual feel good by temporarily releasing them emotionally and mentally from life's grim circumstances. These feelings of despair and pessimism exist in all social groups but they are heightened by poverty, disadvantage, neglect, and joblessness. If negative feelings can be neutralized by crack, the real policy focus should be on attenuating the conditions that cause alienation and low self-esteem. The approaches to the drug problem that emphasize law enforcement and stern prescriptive measures as the best means to achieve a drug-free America ignore these fundamental elements of the problem.

The fourth consequence of drug reduction policies that are grounded in enforcement is something of a Hobson's choice in which there are apparently no policy options that offer a real alternative to drug-related crime. Increased enforcement efforts have not eliminated drug trafficking; they have shaped its conduct, altered its performance, and have been instrumental in determining the characteristics of its participants. Enforcement pressures on drug trafficking markets are designed to inhibit their performance in various ways, which means that the number of persons using drugs will be fewer and paying higher prices. In addition to making drugs impossible or difficult and expensive for consumers to buy, there is also an effort to discipline and influence the behavior and conduct of the firms and groups that constitute the industry. The objective is to reduce the size of drug-selling organizations, to make them less aggressive and less violent. But these objectives also have an effect on the organized-crime aspects of the drug industry.[47]

Whether organized-crime characteristics produce a competitive advantage or disadvantage in a drug market will depend in part on the amount of enforcement pressure on that market. A key characteristic of organized-crime groups is enforcement resistance. Their organizational routines, structures, and capabilities, including their reputation for ruthless violence against informants, reduce their vulnerability to investigation and persecution. Thus, stepped-up drug enforcement will tend to give organized-crime groups and organized-crime-like groups a relative competitive advantage, because their capacity for violence and corruption helps to protect them against ordinary enforcement actions. This might very well encourage the acquisition of organized-crime characteristics among drug-dealing organizations and groups; it is one of the potential costs of increased drug enforcement; and the discernible effect on stable markets is to make them less violent but more durable.[48] The central tension in organized crime/drug enforcement policy is that effective enforcement may be ineffective organized crime control.

Further ramifications of this analysis involve public policy goals expressed though law enforcement activities. It may seem at first obvious that if drug groups could be weakened, the overall size of the market would shrink, which is desirable. It is unclear, however, whether that result would occur. Indeed, it may very well turn out that if large drug syndicates are disrupted through seizures and arrests, there could be, in the short run, an actual increase in the overall level of drug activity for at least two reasons. First, the demand for drugs like crack is fairly stable, so there are opportunities for dealers to move in and fill the vacuums created by intensified enforcement. Second, because drugs must be moved, under circumstances of instability in distribution, the cartel suppliers may be prepared to deal with nontraditional drug-selling organizations on a consignment basis, as has happened in Los Angeles.[49]

CHANGING CONCEPTIONS AND IMAGES OF ORGANIZED CRIME

The foregoing discussion begs the question whether the drug gangs springing up on street corners in ghettos are the next generation of organized crime groups, or are they merely opportunistic criminals exploiting an illegal commodity sought by addicts? The answer depends on what we mean by an organized crime group or "firm."

The original formulation of an organized crime group (which distinguished Mafia crime families as different from organized crime enterprises) embodying a set of roles and statuses emerged from the 1967 President's Task Force on Organized Crime. The picture of an organized crime group developed there envisioned a tight structure of rank and duties and specialist roles (see chapter 2) in which the "Boss," through his lieutenants (capos), hands out criminal franchises to "soldiers" (members of the group) and their associates. Apart from a certain amount of regulation by the leaders at the top, each soldier enjoys considerable autonomy and operational independence.

Another image of an organized crime group is one that is not a group at all, but more like a "partnership" in which all that exists is a group of people involved in a criminal business. They get together and occasionally take advantage of one another's skill and capabilities. It is a fairly loose network of entrepreneurs and this may describe the street-level drug organization today. By thinking only of Mafia models of criminal organization in the area of drugs, much may be overlooked, such as loose confederation of partnerships that may in the long run form themselves—in order to operate more efficiently and safely (shielding themselves from police and competitors)—into relatively long-lasting, large-scale organizations.

What enables drug gangs to survive are assets and capacities that traditional Cosa Nostra crime families possess. The first is the potential for violence that can be used in a disciplined way. Violence is instrumental in protecting profit-generating territories and maintaining internal discipline. Drug gangs that are also youth gangs seem to be among the next generation of organized criminals who are most likely to challenge and compete with traditional organized crime.

The cluster of concepts making up the traditional notion of organized crime—hierarchial structures, operational codes, multiple criminal enterprises—do not apply with crack-selling organizations. Unlike heroin, crack, by its very nature, does not require a pyramidal structure of manufacture and distribution centralized by a transnational criminal network. Organizationally, the crack trade is looser, smaller, less given to a centralized "executive" command structure. Perhaps a reason for this is that crack does not require the capitalization that heroin or cocaine trafficking does. Crack is a "Mom and Pop" business, which means that many small-scale dealers can operate in the market and expand it rapidly and profitably.

The drug-selling organizations, although they are young, (as were the leaders of the classical Prohibition gangs), are organized, but not in the traditional sense, like Cosa Nostra crime families. There is organization in the drug trade; it is not as sophisticated, durable, powerful, flexible, multilayered, and diversified as Mafia families, but neither are Colombian cartels, outlaw motorcycle gangs, Chinese extortion gangs, or Jamaican Posses—all of which have been identified as organized crime by law enforcement authorities.

Crack, cocaine, and heroin traffickers are now deeply entrenched in the ghettos of many larger cities, and drug profits are a powerful incentive to hundreds of thousands of unemployed African-American and Hispanic teenagers. In addition, many gang members are increasingly skillful in exploiting loopholes in the law, with the result that California and New York authorities are considering new antigang legislation (see chapter 8) patterned after the federal RICO law. Such RICO statutes, similar to those in New York State, will enable prosecutors to seek longer prison terms for gang leaders.[50] Law enforcement officials in major metropolitan areas plagued with gang problems are being forced to reorganize their police departments to meet the twin threats of drugs and street gangs, which means in many places cutting back on manpower for other crimes.[51]

The indicators are that the drug/crime problem will get worse. If the analogy with Prohibition is only partly accurate, the gangs have only begun to consolidate their hold on drug trafficking. Given their growth through the 1980s and early 1990s, it seems reasonable to expect that they, like the Cosa Nostra before them, will become more skillful in evading law enforcement. The supply of smuggled drugs—Asian "China white" heroin and South American cocaine—seems almost limitless. At the same time, the federal government, which has scattered the responsibility for combating drugs among dozens of different agencies, seems to lack a coordinated national strategy.

THE CONUNDRUMS OF DRUG LEGALIZATION

The seeming intractability of the drug problem has increased support for drug legalization. In Colombia, which many see as the core region of cocaine trafficking, legalizing drugs has appeal because it promises to eliminate much of the violence and crime, but even so, the resistance to legalization remains strong because drug consumption in Colombia has risen dramatically.[52]

Since 1981, in the United States, many billions of dollars have gone into the struggle against illegal drugs. According to FBI data, this expenditure does not seem to have made much of a difference. One of every three robberies and burglaries is committed to obtain money for high-priced, illegal drugs.[53] Up to 40 percent of the homicides in major cities and 20 percent of the murders nationwide occur in the drug trade; and one of every three AIDS cases is traceable to the sharing of infected needles by drug users.[54]

There are more costs connected to the drug scourge. Gangsters are enriched in the drug trade. At least $40 billion each year goes to the criminal underworld from drug sale proceeds; police officers risk their lives enforcing the prohibition, and the enormous sums of money involved have tempted many law enforcement officers and officials, who have become accomplices of traffickers.[55]

Crack selling, which rips into communities like a cyclone, is so profitable that an "underground railroad" has formed, enabling dealers and drugs to move about across states and, when the heat is on, to virtually disappear from a jurisdiction and evade the whiplash of public sentiment. These are just a few of the costs and consequences of maintaining strict drug prohibition policies. What then should new drug policies be like?

Should the Attorney General or Surgeon General of the United States have authority over the drug problem? Seen from the perspective of a health regulatory system, if addicts could be brought into the health-care system rather than the criminal justice system, much of the underworld's involvement in drugs could be eliminated—this is the raw logic of the legalization/decriminalization argument.

A look at history is helpful in coming to terms with the polarities of the issue. During the era of Prohibition of alcohol use in the United States, emphasis was placed on eliminating the manufacture and distribution of alcohol for personal consumption. Consequently, alcoholism became less of a national problem, but organized crime flourished in its nearly exclusive role as distributor of alcoholic products.[56] The subsequent repeal of the

Volstead Act (Prohibition), although dealing a blow to the underworld that flourished and grew because of it, increased the number of alcoholics and problematic drinkers in American society.[57]

The opponents of legalization claim that its proponents are vague about the effects of their schemes on drug consumption. Jacobs describes what is at stake. His critique, put in large terms, claims,

> The drug-legalization movement is urging us to consider the transformation of American society from an alcohol culture to a poly-drug culture in which a wide range of psychoactive drugs—including heroin, cocaine and crack, marijuana, amphetamines, hallucinogens, barbiturates, and designer drugs of all sorts—would instantly be made the legal equivalents of alcohol.
>
> Advocates of . . . legalization in effect are urging the country to engage in a massive experiment. Incredibly, their hypothesis is that by legalizing all drugs and reducing their cost, the drug problem will decline if not wither away. This defies everything we know about markets, deterrence, and the propensity of people—especially Americans—to seek chemical solutions to life's real or imagined problems and challenges. Returning to prohibition after a period in which millions of consumers developed a taste for new drugs would be a daunting challenge, to say the least.[58]

It must be said that much of Jacob's scenario is pure speculation (however plausible), and that other elements of his argument are likewise very conjectural. It is doubtful for instance, that in the present era, industries will be permitted to vigorously promote intoxicating drugs—given the relentless efforts by government and private advocacy groups to restrict cigarette and alcohol advertising. However, there are basic, unresolved questions that make any position with regard to the legalization of drugs a matter of opinion at best. For example, no one knows for certain the extent to which legalization would increase the number of addicts, or whether such a policy would eventually undermine the integrity of society. Few would deny, however, that the greater availability of drugs and easier access to them would increase drug use (and addiction) beyond current levels. Whether the nation can be adequately prepared to handle the consequences of this increase is, again, a matter of conjecture. More answerable and pertinent is the question of the impact of open drug availability on crime.

To a large extent, the amount of drug-related crime is proportional to the costs of drugs, and the latter depend on supply and demand. On the supply side, there are two important considerations, both of which have to do with the effects of a vigorously enforced policy of interdiction. When it is most effective, a policy of interdiction reduces the supply of drugs and, as a consequence, raises the prices. It also increases the risks associated with drug production and distribution and thus increases the compensation demanded by drug suppliers for their services. Again, the outcome is higher drug prices. Assuming that interdiction will never entirely eliminate the supply, the ironic conclusion has to be that vigorously enforced antidrug efforts may be instrumental in increasing drug-related crime.

In view of this, some would argue that legalizing drugs would lead to substantial reduction in drug costs and a corresponding reduction in drug-related crime.[59] Such an argument assumes exclusive, trouble-free governmental regulation of the drug supply, and that may be an untenable policy. The possibility of providing a more desirable drug price, purity, unrestricted quantity, lack of restriction with regard to age, and other similar inducements could readily lead to black-market competition in drug sales and thus continue the involvement of illegal sources of supply. Also, the argument ignores the impulsivity and lack of control associated with certain drugs and the crime-linked effects of such drugs as PCP (which produces both self-destructive and assaultive behavior) and cocaine (excessive use of which is associated with violence stemming from paranoid ideation).

This leads to a consideration of the demand side of the drug equation. In view of the fact that greater demand is correlated with increased cost, the adoption of intervention strategies aimed at diminishing demand for illicit drugs appears appropriate in dealing with the issue of drugs and crime. Thus, appropriate policy recommendations would be that concerted attempts be made to dissuade individuals from becoming involved with drugs, along with persistent efforts to wean them off drugs when and if they do become involved.

Proponents of legalization face other policy problems as well. They have been rather vague about the effects of their schemes (when they are discussed at all). For example, how do they propose to contain drug manufacture and distribution within legally approved channels? By imposing a high minimum age? By limiting the number of drug dispensaries? By requiring some form of prescription? Unfortunately, the more regulations that are imposed, the more opportunities arise for an illegal market, a larger black market, and more crime and violence.

No major legalization advocate proposes a free-market model in which all presently illegal psychoactive drugs would be readily available to consumers; no one wants to treat heroin and cocaine the way we treat aspirin and other over-the-counter drugs. Of the models that have been proposed, each requires formal, regulatory controls. Essentially there are three models for regulated legalization. The first is the paradigm for cigarettes, which ostensibly cannot be bought by minors but are readily available in machines (many unregulated for minors) and stores. The second is the alcohol paradigm, which would make scheduled drugs available only in locations and establishments more heavily policed and regulated and with age restrictions enforced. The third is the prescription-drug model, in which scheduled drugs can only be obtained with a physician's prescription, and then only in carefully calibrated amounts.

The legalization argument has engendered increasing appeal in the nation because the current policies of interdiction of supply and crop eradication, however preventive they may seem, have not worked or met expectations. But legalization presently does not enjoy uniform support. The bottom-line argument of those supporting legalization is that a sober cost-benefit analysis that pays heed to the terrible consequences of current policy supports some degree of decriminalization.[60]

Suppose drugs where legalized. Their illegal status means that the bulk of the cost consists of law enforcement expenditures, (crime, corruption, courts, jails, prisons and extensive police work), welfare outlays (poorer health, lost wages attributable to drug abuse, more aid to families with dependent children, and treatment and prevention programs), and the moral costs (debased and degraded individuals). If, on the other hand, drugs were legal, the societal bill would consist primarily of the welfare and moral costs. Nonetheless, there would still be law-enforcement expenses—enforcing regulations, taxes (if any) on drugs, and the prevention of diversions should drugs be dispersed though health-care agencies. Thus, legalization without some type of regulatory apparatus does not seem possible, and the stringency of regulations as restrictions on the criteria for access to them will only raise law-enforcement costs.

With these qualification in mind, suppose once again that drugs were legalized and made accessible though the bureaucratic system of the third paradigm (the alcohol-availability model)—the most restrictive. By imagining the differential impact on a wide variety of communities, it is possible to see other dimensions and ramifications of the issue. In minority communities, the adoption of this policy would place exceptionally heavy burdens on poor communities, and since most Americans do not live in such communities, the preference for legalization perhaps cannot be justified to people who do. The testimony of those who live in the midst of the problem is unmistakably clear: they want drugs kept illegal. For them, notions that drug use is a "victimless crime" seem absurd and dangerous. Crack addicts, like heroin addicts, regularly victimize their children by neglect, their spouses by recklessly exploiting family resources, their employers by lethargy and incompetent job performance, and their co-workers by carelessness induced by drug stupors. Furthermore, the argument from consistency (that since the health and financial costs of alcohol abuse are so much higher than those of cocaine or heroin abuse, it is hypocritical to devote our efforts to preventing cocaine or drug use) is bad history and bad faith. Because we tolerate alcohol and tobacco does not bind us logically to tolerate crack in the same way. We have an entrenched social history with some drugs that we need not repeat with others. Actually, there is an interesting paradox here: What the argument illustrates is that legalized drugs and alcohol produce greater social harm (traffic fatalities, occupational injuries and lost work hours, family disruption, etc.) than illegal drugs.

If drugs are to remain illegal, society has a special obligation to prevent the vulnerable citizens of inner-city neighborhoods from being intimidated by those who seek to profit from the trade. This means initially better law enforcement—not necessarily quantitatively more police. Most police work is reactive—responding to calls for help—and that hardly serves as a deterrent for criminals. Not unexpectedly, there is little connection between levels of crime and levels of traditional police activity, but community policing may provide some relief for minority communities inundated with drug crime.[61]

This approach necessitates that police officers work together with communities to attack crime problems. Are landlords profiteering, for example, by renting to known drug dealers? Dispatching cops to arrest the dealers, which would be the traditional response, does not usually solve the problem because other dealers just move in. But to get landlords to evict the dealers and to stop renting apartment space to other dealers, then community-oriented policing might help the neighbors challenge the landlords in court, or lodge complaints with a city housing agency or fire department, or even picket the landlord's home in the suburbs.

Another problem beyond the reach of the police is the lack of opportunity in poor African-American communities, which explains, at least in part, drug dealing and the organized criminality enveloping it. There is a connection between criminal behavior and the aspiration-opportunity discrepancy that is so common in minority communities.[62]

The fact is, as we shall see in the next chapter, that some of our cities, and in particular, African-American, Hispanic, and minority communities, are being destroyed by gangs either competing for territory or engaged in meaningless violence in the streets. Controlling sources of supply is at best a holding action: How can demand be dramatically reduced? That is the question that eclipses all others.

NOTES

1. United States General Accounting Office, *Drug Control: U.S. International Narcotics Control Activities* (Washington, DC: U.S. Government Printing Office, 1993); Office of National Drug Abuse Policy, *Drugs, Crime, and the Justice System: A National Report* (Washington, DC: U.S. Government Printing Office, 1992).
2. The White House, Office of National Drug Control Policy, *National Drug Control Strategy* (Washington, DC: U.S. Government Printing Office, September 1988)
3. National Institute on Drug Abuse, *Report* (Rockville, MD: U.S. Department of Health and Human Services, 1990).
4. Ibid, 20–21.
5. Ethan A. Nadelmann, "Drug Prohibition in the United States: Costs, Consequences, and Alternatives," *Science* 245 (1 September 1989): 939–947.
6. Congressman Charles B. Rangel, "Combating Drug Abuse and Trafficking: Some New Directions," *Justice Quarterly* 1, no. 2 (June 1984): 277–287.
7. Michael E. Porter, "How Competitive Forces Shape Strategy" in Michael E. Porter and Cynthia A. Montgomery, eds. *Strategy: Seeking and Securing Competitive Advantage* (Boston: Harvard Business School Press, 1991), App. B.
8. Mark H. Moore, "Criminal Organization and the Assets They Bring to Drug Trafficking," *Organized Crime Narcotics Enforcement Symposium* (Villanova, PA: Villanova University, May 9–11, 1988).
9. Louis Kraar, "The Drug Trade," *Fortune* (20 June 1988): 27–38.
10. Peter Reuter, "On the Limits of High-Level Enforcement," *Organized Crime Narcotics Enforcement Symposium* (Villanova, PA: Villanova University: May 9–11, 1988).
11. Rensselaer W. Lee, "Colombia's Cocaine Syndicates" in Alfred W. McCoy and Alan A. Block, eds. *War on Drugs: Studies in the Failure of U.S. Narcotics Policy* (Boulder, CO: Westview Press, 1992), 93–124.
12. Phil Williams, "The International Drug Trade: An Industry Analysis," *Ridgway Viewpoints* (Pittsburgh, PA: University of Pittsburgh, Matthew B. Ridgway Center of International Security Studies, 1993), 93–96.
13. Lamond Tullis, *Handbook of Research on the Illicit Drug Traffic: Socioeconomic and Political Consequences* (Westport, CT: Greenwood Press, 1991).
14. James M. O'Kane, *The Crooked Ladder: Gangsters, Ethnicity and the American Dream* (New Brunswick, NJ: Transaction Books, 1992), 89.
15. Keith D. Harries, *Serious Violence: Patterns of Homicide and Assault in America* (Springfield, IL: Charles C. Thomas, 1990).
16. Ibid., 159.
17. James M. O'Kane, "The Crooked Ladder: *Gangsters, Ethnicity, and the American Dream,*" 104.
18. William B. Sanders, *Gangbangs and Drive-bys: Grounded Culture and Juvenile Gang Violence* (New York: Aldine De Gruyter, 1994), 141.
19. Greg Donaldson, *The Ville: Cops and Kids in Urban America* (New York: Ticknor & Fields, 1993), 102.
20. Ibid., 27.
21. Terry Williams, *The Cocaine Kids: The Inside Story of a Teenage Drug Ring* (New York: Addison-Wesley Publishers, 1991).
22. Arthur Kempton, "Native Sons," *The New York Review* (11 April 1991): 55–61, The National Crime Victimization Survey Report shows that African-American males had the highest rate of violent crime victimization with 63 victimizations

per 1,000 persons, compared with 36 per 1,000 violent victimization rates for white males. See Bureau of Justice Statistics, *Criminal Victimization in the United States, 1992,* U.S. Department of Justice, Office of Justice Programs, a National Crime Victimization Survey Report (Washington, DC: U.S. Government Printing Office, March 1994, NCJ-145125), 18.

23. David N. Nurco, Timothy W. Kinlock, and Thomas E. Hanlon, "The Drugs-Crime Connection" in James A. Inciardi, ed. *Handbook of Drug Control in the United States* (Westport, CT: Greenwood Publishing Group, 1990), 71–90.

24. Michael Massing, "The Rehabbing of America" *New York Times Book Review,* 24 January 1993, 10–12.

25. Bureau of Justice Statistics, U.S. Department of Justice, Office of Justice Programs, *Drugs, Crime and the Justice System* (Washington, DC: U.S. Government Printing Office, 1992).

26. Franklin Zimring and Gordan Hawkins, *The Search for Rational Drug Control* (New York: Cambridge University Press, 1992).

27. D. Waldorf, C. Reinarman, and S. Murphy, *Cocaine Changes: The Experience of Using and Quitting* (Philadelphia: Temple University Press, 1991).

28. James Inciardi, "Beyond Cocaine: Basuco, Crack, and Other Coca Products," *Contemporary Drug Problems* 14, no. 3 (1987): 461–492.

29. Philip Bourgeois, "In Search of Horatio Alger: Culture and Ideology in the Crack Economy," *Contemporary Drug Problems* 16, no. 4 (1989): 619–650.

30. Paul Eddy, Hugo Sabogal, and Sara Walden, *The Cocaine Wars* (New York: W. W. Norton & Co., 1989); Jeffrey Fagan, "The Social Organization of Drug Use and Drug Dealing among Urban Gangs," *Criminology* 27 (1989): 633–669; Thomas Mieczkowski, "The Detroit Crack Ethnography Project," Report to the Bureau of Justice Assistance (Washington, DC: U.S. Department of Justice, 1989).

31. Robert M. Stutman and Richard Esposito, *Dead on Delivery: Inside the Drug Wars, Straight from the Street* (New York: Warner Books, 1992).

32. Joseph B. Treaster, "In West Harlem's 30th Precinct the Cocaine Sales are Wholesale," *New York Times,* 24 April 1994, 1, 41.

33. Robert M. Stutman, "The Crack Situation in New York City," statement before the Hearings of U.S. House of Representatives, Select Committee on Narcotics Abuse and Control (New York: July 18, 1986).

34. Michael Massing, "Crack's Destructive Sprint across America," *New York Times Magazine,* 1 October 1989, 38–41, 58–62.

35. Los Angeles County Interagency Gang Task Force, *Report on the State of Los Angeles Street Gangs* (Los Angeles, CA: November 1991).

36. Erik Eckholm, "Teen-Age Gangs Are Inflicting Lethal Violence in Small Cities," *New York Times,* 31 January 1993, 1, 15–17.

37. Jeffrey Fagan and Ko-lin Chin, "Social Processes of Initiation into Crack," *The Journal of Drug Issues* 21, no. 2 (1991): 313–343; D. Massey, "American Apartheid: Racial Segregation and Formation of the Underclass," *American Journal of Sociology* 96, no. 2 (1990): 329–357.

38. S. Sassen-Koob, "New York City's Informal Economy," cited in A. Portes, M. Castello, and L.A. Benton, eds. *The Informal Economy: Studies in Advanced and Less Developed Countries* (Baltimore, MD: Johns Hopkins University Press, 1989), 220–253.

39. Fagan and Chin, "Social Processes of Initiation," 333.

40. Ibid., 324.

41. L.W. Shannon, "Ecological Effects of the Hardening of the Inner City" in R. M. Figlio, S. Halsim, and G. G. Rengert, eds. *Metropolitan Crime Patterns* (Monsey, NY: Criminal Justice Press, 1986), 27–54.

42. Ansley Hamid, "The Political Economy of Crack-Related Violence," *Contemporary Drug Problems* 17, no. 1 (1990): 31–78.

43. Ibid., 25.

44. Peter Reuter, "The D. C. Crime Surge: An Economist Looks at the Carnage," *Washington Post*, 26 March 1989, D. 7, col. 1.

45. Center for the Study of Law and Society, Courts, Probation and Street Drug Crime, *Executive Summary and Conclusions, Final Report on the Targeted Urban Crime* (Washington, DC: U.S. Narcotics Task Force, 1988), 4–5.

46. Peter Reuter, G. Crawford, and J. Cave, "Can the Borders Be Sealed?" *The Public Interest* 100 (Summer 1988): 51, 56.

47. Mark H. Moore, "Criminal Organizations and the Assets."

48. Mark A. R. Kleinman, "Organized Crime and Drug Abuse Control" in Robert J. Kelly, Ko-lin Chin, and Rufus Schatzberg, eds. *Handbook of Organized Crime in the United States*, 401–414.

49. Tom Morganthau, Michael Lerner, Richard Sandya, Monny Abbot, David Gongalez, and Patricha King, "The Drug Gangs" *Newsweek*, 28 March 1988, 20–27.

50. Kelly and Ryan, "An Analysis of RICO and OCCA," 49–100.

51. Office of the District Attorney, County of Los Angeles, *Gang Crime and Violence in Los Angeles: Findings and Proposals* (Los Angeles, California: Office of the District Attorney County of Los Angeles May 1992).

52. Michael Massing, "The War on Cocaine," *New York Review* (22 December 1988): 61–67.

53. Bureau of Justice Statistics, *Drugs, Crime and the Justice System*.

54. Ibid, 16.

55. Mark H. Moore, "Drug Trafficking," National Institute of Justice, U.S. Department of Justice (Washington, DC: U.S. Government Printing Office, 1988).

56. Mark H. Moore, "Actually, Prohibition Was a Success," *New York Times*, 16 October 1989, 21, col. 1.

57. Robert J. Kelly, "Addicts and Alcoholics as Victims," in A. Karmen and D. MacNamara, eds. *Deviants: Victims or Victimizers?* (Beverly Hills, CA: Sage Publications, 1983).

58. James B. Jacobs, "Imaging Drug Legalization," *The Public Interest* 101 (Fall 1990): 41.

59. Nadelmann, *Drug Prohibition*, 939–946.

60. James Ostrowski, "Thinking about Drug Legalization," *USA Today* 119 (July 1990): 27–30.

61. Malcolm K. Sparrow, Mark H. Moore, and David M. Kennedy, *Beyond 911: A New Era for Policing* (New York: Basic Books, 1990).

62. Cloward and Ohlin, *Delinquency and Opportunity*.

8 URBICIDE

A TALE OF THREE CITIES

There is so much bad news about American cities that it is surprising to discover that they are not shrinking but growing. According to the latest United States Census, the 23 largest cities, which have populations over 500,000, grew by 6 percent in the period between 1980 and 1990. Forty medium-sized cities with populations between 250,000 and 500,000 increased by 20 percent in the same period. In addition, the 131 cities with between 100,000 and 250,000 populations, have grown more than 15 percent, and today, for the first time in the twentieth century, they are home to more people than the great metropolises.

We propose to examine three major conurbations in the United States: Los Angeles, Chicago, and New York City, each of which has crime problems and comparatively large African-American populations. These cities are in various states of structural distress in which crime—both individual and random acts of violence and crime of the organized type, particularly street gangs—have become prominent. Our purpose is to look at the causes, structures, and consequences of the gang phenomenon on the lifestyles and integrity of communities in which they thrive.

If this urban expansion has not had much attention, it is probably because the form of these cities is both brash and ambivalent. "Impressive in scale but limited in vision, creating new opportunities but also providing massive new problems," wrote Asa Briggs.[1] He was describing Victorian cities in Britain, but he may as well have been writing about the American city of today; spread out, socially and racially fragmented, recklessly entrepreneurial, relying almost completely on the automobile, often lacking a clearly defined center, and without the trappings of urbanity that have characterized cities in the past. These trends have been accompanied by polarizations that have heightened racial fears and have increased almost as rapidly as populations. They have created an obsessive demand for security among the affluent, liberal, and conservative middle classes to such an extent that·rich neighborhoods isolate themselves behind walls guarded by gun-toting private police and state-of-the-art electronic surveillance. In the Downtowns, publicly subsidized "urban renewal" has segregated poor neighborhoods from the corporate citadels; the "siege look" of modern office buildings resembles architectural glaciers—remote and aloof from the teeming life in the contiguous working-class minority neighborhoods ringing the center.

In places such as Watts, an African-American community in greater Los Angeles that was razed to the ground during the 1965 "rebellion," one sees inner-city retail markets as recolonized around a panoptical shopping mall surrounded by metal fences and a substation of the Los Angeles Police Department in a central surveillance tower.[2]

The defense of luxury lifestyles has been translated into a proliferation of new repressions in space and movement, undergirded by the ubiquitous "armed response." This obsession with physical security has become a *zeitgeist* of urban reorganization in the major metropolitan galaxies such as New York City, Los Angeles, and Chicago. What is visible on the street level is the militarization of city life hardening the urban surface in the wake of a decade of social polarization.

This is nothing new, actually. The dire predictions of the Nixon Administration's 1969 National Commission on Violence[3] have been tragically fulfilled: We live in "fortress cities" brutally divided between "fortified cells" of affluent society and "places of terror" where the police battle the criminalized poor.

As William Whyte[4] observed of social intercourse in New York City, fear proves itself. The mere social perception of a threat becomes a function of the security mobilization itself, not crime rates. Where there is an actual rising arc of street violence, as in South Central Los Angeles or Downtown Washington, D.C., most of the carnage is self-contained within ethnic, racial, and class boundaries, which is referred to in the literature as "black-on-black" crime. Yet, white middle-class imagination, lacking any firsthand knowledge of inner-city conditions, magnifies the perceived threat through the demonized lens of racial xenophobia. The media, whose function in this arena is to bury and obscure the daily economic violence of the city, ceaselessly throw up the spectra of the criminal underclass and psychotic stalkers. Sensationalized accounts of killer youth gangs high on crack, ferment the panic that justifies the American urban equivalent of apartheid.

As a consequence, the American city is being turned inside out—or, rather, outside in. The spaces of the new malls, office plazas, and shopping zones are concentrated in the center so that streets are eliminated and public activity is constricted to areas under the gaze of security forces.

THE URBAN POLICE

How police define their relationships to the communities they are sworn to protect is best seen in their methods of patrol and law enforcement in general. After World War II, many police departments in the great cities redefined themselves as the progressive antithesis to the traditional big-city police department with its patronage armies of police officers grafting on the beat. They adopted a high-tech style modeled after elite military formations and this technology was supposed to insulate them from corruption.[5] But high-technology surveillance and response also supplanted the traditional patrolman's intimate "folk" knowledge of specific communities and neighborhoods. Thus, the police officer on foot patrol was replaced by the radio patrol car. This marked the beginning of dispersed, mechanized policing. In Los Angeles, under Chief Parker the Los Angeles Police Department (LAPD) introduced the first police helicopters for systematic aerial surveillance.[6] After the 1965 Watts rebellion, the airborne effort became the cornerstone of a policing strategy for the entire inner city. The hardware of modern, big-city police departments has metamorphosed them into a quasi-military force.[7]

As gang hysteria mounts and the war on crack continues unabated, it is very likely that police departments will expand (as will their investments in new technologies). Despite the wave of enthusiasm for a return to community policing that is being implemented, but with significant differences, the omnipresent helicopter gunships lurking overhead and the armored personnel carriers dislodging sharpshooting SWAT teams in areas in need of crowd control are an ever-present reconnaissance air force.

The conditions of city living appear to many to be increasingly uncivilized. There is no question that many urban problems are deep and structural, including the fragile economic bases, crumbling infrastructures, diminishing stocks of middle-class jobs and neighborhoods, troubled schools, deepening ethnic and racial rivalries, changing and possibly worsening social and moral habits of their populations, and crime.[8] Table 8.1 illustrates the degree to which city dwellers have adjusted their lifestyles to their perceptions and fears of street crime.

As Table 8.1 suggests, when the streets are perceived as potentially dangerous, the quality of community life suffers, and when they are dangerous enough, all who can, contemplate leaving. In the survey, the fear is more specifically a fear of teenagers.

TABLE 8.1. Crime and Its Effect on Behavior

Percentage of New Yorkers who say. . .

. . . In the last year, crime in the city has	TOTAL	WHITE	BLACK	HISPANIC
increased	32%	27%	30%	43%
stayed the same	48	49	53	42
decreased	17	19	15	13
. . . they have taken steps in the last year to protect self or family from crime	33	29	39	35
. . . because of crime, they				
avoid places they used to go	62	54	72	69
go out less at night	54	46	59	65
ride the subway less	45	38	45	59
have moved or are thinking of moving	38	25	51	52
gotten a car alarm	38	42	37	31
gotten a dog or burglar alarm	35	33	28	41
have changed the route taken between home and work or other destinations	27	22	29	33
carry a weapon such as Chemical Mace or whistle	16	15	18	19
keep a gun at home	4	6	3	3

Based on telephone interviews with 1,189 adults in all parts of New York City, conducted June 12–15, 1994.

Source: "The *New York Times*/CBS NEWS Poll; Crime and Its Effects on Behavior," *New York Times* and *WCBS-TV News*, June 19, 1994. Copyright © 1994 by The New York Times Company. Reprinted by permission.

GANG TYPOLOGIES

There is no single type of gang. They vary organizationally, demographically (by age of members), by gender (more and more female gangs are emerging),[9] by size, by ethnicity, and in terms of their crimes and goals.[10] In some cities, gangs are credited with an alarming share of violent crime, especially homicides, leading some researchers to suggest that they are now posing a more serious crime problem than in the past.[11]

Like organized crime, there is little consensus about how gangs should be defined. For law enforcement, criminal behavior is a key defining feature, whereas some social-scientific researchers view gang delinquency and criminal activity as issues whose origins must be explained.[12]

The definition of what constitutes a gang has been a topic of discussion as long as gangs have been recognized. Complicating the problem is the lack of uniform national data, and what information is collected cannot be relied upon. The debate over definitions is not trivial because definitions inevitably affect programmatic responses. As with organized criminal phenomena, definitions serve as the foundation for a community's response and influence the types and extent of resources applied.[13] But as Hagedorn observes,

> . . . the reporting of a gang problem varies with the needs for city officials to promote a respectable image of their city, for police officials to make a case for hiring more officers, for community agencies to lobby for funds for "outreach" and other reasons.[14]

Even if scientists cannot agree about a general theory of gangs, everyone recognizes that they are a problem, but how much of a problem is not clear. Many theories need to be tested and important debates continue. Few would dispute that gangs cannot be stereotyped. Some are simply a source of social support and entertainment for their members; others serve largely as economic organizations; and still others accomplish both. First, depending on the nature of the gang, members may commit a significant number of crimes, but crime is often not their primary, and certainly not their only focus. Second, adolescents and young adults are likely to join gangs in order to accomplish goals that are perceived as difficult or beyond their reach without gang support, but members may differ in terms of their specific motivations for joining and in their loyalties to gang activities. Third, research work and studies of gang actions suggest that it is rare for entire gangs to organize their activities exclusively around the sale of drugs, although increasing economic pressures may make drug selling a means of survival for more and more gang members in the future.[15] Fourth, communities with gangs differ in some respect, but in most ways they resemble each other demographically, racially, and economically. No one seems to know why some communities develop gangs while others do not, but most experts contend that community opportunity structures (for employment, family integrity and support, educational achievements, access to services) play a pivotal role in the formation and evolution of gangs.[16]

According to data from the 1991 Survey of Inmates in State Correctional Facilities the Bureau of Justice Statistics,[17] an agency of the U. S. Department of Justice reported the following: Pertaining to State prison inmates and their gang-related activities, about 6 percent of State prison inmates belonged to a gang prior to incarceration. Among the inmates who were gang members:

- 81 percent reported past drug use.
- 69 percent said they manufactured, imported, or sold drugs as a group.
- 92 percent reported that their gang fought other groups.

Of the inmates who reported belonging to a gang before entering prison, 32 percent were still members at the time of incarceration. On average, they had joined a gang at age fourteen. Half reported that their gang had sixty or more members.

Fifteen percent of students ages twelve to nineteen reported the presence of street gangs in their school, according to 1989 data from the National Crime Victimization Survey. Seventy-eight percent of students who reported gang presence at their school said drugs were available compared to 66 percent of students who reported that gangs were not present.

Students at schools with gangs were more likely to fear an attack both at school and on the way to school, and were more likely to avoid certain areas inside the school.

STREET GANGS AND ORGANIZED CRIME

In a dispassionate ethnographic study of gang activity in San Diego, California, Sanders helps to clarify gang conceptualizations that are important in our consideration of what organized criminal conduct looks like in modern African-American communities. While his work takes a perspective on how police attempt to understand gangs, his analyses also provide some ideas about the general relationship between violence and gang life that illuminates not only the essence of gang activity but also how some of these adolescent organizations may be understood as ongoing criminal enterprises, as "*proto-mafioso*" in the making.[18] This point of view is at odds with official interpretations of African-American and other street gangs that would see the analogies to mafia-type groups as profoundly misleading. Certainly street gangs and some of the larger, loosely structured gang confederations such as the Crips and the Bloods (Los Angeles) or the El Rukyns (Chicago), are not crime corporations like Mafia crime families making up La Cosa Nostra. They are not involved in labor racketeering, the infiltration of legitimate businesses, wide-scale political and law enforcement corruption, large-scale loansharking, and transnational money-laundering operations, but neither are many other groups—Colombians, Mexicans, Russians, Cubans, and Chinese—who are defined as organized-crime organizations. The key difference appears to be age—African-American street gang members are young, ranging in age from early adolescence to those in their mid-twenties (similar, incidentally, to the age range in Chinese street gangs that are defined as organized-crime entities).[19]

Many African-American street gangs that are in the drug business are small businessmen, not crime families linked together by a national crime commission. They are usually under the supervision of older dealers who, in turn, answer to a shadowy wholesale hierarchy of middlemen and drug-cartel representatives. On the other hand, the very complexity of a crack trade organized through competing gangs and small-time dealers, while it belies the demonic power that political and law enforcement agencies attribute to it, defies almost every effort by law enforcement to deliver the decisive knockout blow to eliminate it. In the ghetto itself there are innumerable crack-house franchises turning over large sums of money. If estimates, such as the Los Angeles District Attorney's report that talks of fifty thousand gang members, many of whom, it is believed, earn their livelihood from the drug trade, are anywhere near correct, then crack really is the employer of last resort. The drug trade is the equivalent of several large auto plants or several hundred fast-food stores.

Crack has given the Crips subculture and other ghetto street gangs a terrible, almost irresistible allure. This does not reduce the gang phenomenon, now or in the past, to mere economic determinism. In New York City during the 1840s, young Irish toughs invented the modern street gang.[20] These gangs operated in the Bowéry, Five Points, and Paradise Alley sections of Lower Manhattan (making the "Bowery Boys" and "Dead Rabbits" just as dreaded as the Crips and the Bloods are today). These early street gangs developed families for the forgotten, a total solitary collective, closing out other personal empathic relationships and transmitting self-hatred into a tribal rage directed outward indiscriminately toward social institutions and all others outside the group.[21]

There is little reason to believe that the crack economy or the street gang subculture will stop growing, whatever the scale of law enforcement suppression. Nor will they stay confined to the ghettos, although the epicenters remain in the ghetto zones of hard-core unemployment—like Watts,

South Central Los Angeles, Harlem, Brownsville, Bedford-Stuyvesant in New York, and the South Side of Chicago.

Some African-American gangs have accommodated the aspirations of the new immigrants by integrating Latino members and by licensing crack-dealing franchises. With the economic gangplanks pulled up and compassion becoming strictly rationed because of the federal deficit and new welfare reform proposals, where school budgets operate on austerity criteria, where demagogues demand the death penalty for drug dealers and three-time offenders, is it any wonder that poor youths are hallucinating on their own desperado, "original gangster" power trips? In Los Angeles, Chicago, and New York City, to mention just three large cities, gangs are multiplying. Police and citizens are more fearful and have even developed a taste for lynch-mob tactics.

At the same time, gang criminologists struggle to define delinquency and street gangs. This has meant debates over methodologies and classifications. For our purposes, gangs are different from adolescent groups in that gangs use violence to accomplish criminal ends.

As Sanders puts it:

> . . . a better definition of gangs would include criminal and violent behavior as major activities. The violence is connected to . . . territoriality. If a group is going to claim territory *seriously,* [Sanders' italics] it is going to have to be willing to use violence to defend it. Otherwise, it has no way to sustain claims over the public domain. It is virtually contradictory to say that a gang is territorial and not violent.[22]

And like organized-crime groups, exceedingly little time, it turns out, is devoted to violence. It is the willingness and reputation for violence that makes a gang a gang and an organized-crime group an organized-crime group. Many gangs closely resemble organized-crime groups if not in terms of structure per se, then at least in terms of the criminogenic assets at their disposal. No one expects daily "drive-by" shootings, just as crime families are not engaged in weekly murders and contract killings. What is most important is the knowledge within the community among citizens, law enforcement agencies, and gang rivals that a group will use violence when it deems it necessary. This is what sets gangs apart from other juvenile groupings.

Concerning gang structures, the Los Angeles District Attorney's office reassures its citizens that despite the power and threat of the Crips they are not an organized crime group:

An apparently imposing group like the Crips is in fact a loose association of more than 200 gangs many of which are at war with one another, and none of whom recognized—or pretends to exert—any kind of central authority. Apart from a shared name, the color blue, a commitment to the gang life-style (Crippin'), and their hatred of Bloods, Crips have no shared purpose and virtually nothing in common. Even the acceptance of other Crips as "cuzzies" (cousins), holds only within the limits of bloody local rivalries.[23]

The report goes on in this vein, suggesting that the Crips are not a "black Mafia," that their leadership is weak, situational, nonhierarchical, and not centralized.

When one examines studies of mafia phenomena, they are not defined simply as associations with the aim of committing crimes. It is a dangerous illusion to consider the Mafia a single, monolithic association with a stable organizational structure like that of a commercial enterprise.[24] When the FBI assembled its strategies to confront La Cosa Nostra, the American Mafia, by focusing its efforts on crime-family bosses, it was believed that by taking down the leadership, the crime families would fragment. That did not happen.[25] Crime families are flexibly organized, composed of semiautonomous "crews" and associates that function, in reality, with or without bosses. Most important, Cosa Nostra crime families are intertwined with the legitimate worlds of business, commerce, labor, government, and entertainment. To dislodge them, to crush their power and influence, is a problem that goes beyond law enforcement capacities. It is an issue of the structure of the social system, with its class stratification system and the intrinsic obstacles associated with social mobility for minorities. In short, the conditions that give rise to mafia are not unlike the conditions that spawn African-American gangs.

The African-American street gangs (as well as some other minority adolescent groups) are primarily focused on making money. In Jankowski's study, he creates a business–recreational continuum on which African-American gangs fall solidly in the business category.[26] A major motivation for joining a gang is that it offers a means of making money and acquiring some local prestige. This does not mean that gangs are held together tightly by a code of "brotherhood" in the way that mafiosi are and even this is doubtful today. What solidarity exists tends to be localized and governed by the need to maintain a gang structure to pursue moneymaking activities as well as other prerequisites.

While they are not training grounds for organized crime syndicates as such, African-American street gangs function as distribution systems for organized crime entities. As Jankowski says, "It would be more accurate to view today's gangs as independent components of the broad structure by which contemporary crime has been organized."[27]

We saw earlier that several African-American career criminals in the period post–World War II through the 1970s sought to emulate Mafia crime family structure in order to create autonomous organizations. Many of these, including Leroy Barnes and Frank Lucas, had ties with the crime families in the narcotics business. Others operated within the ghettos independent of Mafia affiliation, remaining comparatively small scale, but entrenched within the local communities. The modern phenomenon of African-American street gangs is yet another manifestation of criminal activity that is "organized" in the broad sense of the concept—not in terms of Mafia crime families that developed and matured in specific social, economic, and cultural circumstances, but in response to conditions in their communities and socioeconomic environments.

For example, in New York City, white working-class communities infested with Mafia organizations serve as slum nurseries for the underworld, training grounds and apprenticeships in crime, where skills are sharpened and knowledge of criminal techniques is acquired. Many career criminals who later achieved major leadership roles in the Cosa Nostra were former street-gang members. In fact, the gangs were more like appendages to crime families, with the fledgling gangsters playing subordinate roles in a variety of street-crime activities—as runners and strong-arm goons in gambling operations; as drivers and accomplices in loansharking and cargo-theft schemes; and as distributors of stolen goods and other vice products. Eventually, those who proved themselves, who demonstrated the capacities for violence and cunning, could be formally inducted into an adult crime organization.[28]

The example of the "Jungle Boys," a former African-American New Haven, Connecticut gang, illustrates the trend toward entrepreneurial, organized criminality occurring within some youth gangs.

Formed in 1984, they were linked early on with drug trafficking in New Haven.[29] The gang established a command hierarchy resembling, and possibly emulating, the power structure of a Cosa Nostra crime family, with a boss, underboss, lieutenants, and soldiers. Before they were dismantled, the Jungle Boys had virtually taken over a housing complex and intimidated the local neighborhood residents and businesses for more than five years.

In 1992, a law enforcement task force composed of Federal Bureau of Investigation, Drug Enforcement Administration, Alcohol, Tobacco, and Firearms (Department of Treasury), and State and local police, raided gang locales, arrested the leadership, charged them with drug offenses under RICO statutes and destroyed the gangs.

In this case, the traditional characteristics of street gangs—defense of territory, recreational use of illegal substances, and petty crime—were not the defining features of the gang's identity: The Jungle Boys did not mobilize to protect their geographical locales—although based in a metropolitan area. In fact, many of the members lived outside the city and engaged in the purchase and sale of real estate for investment purposes. The gang's durability and strength (it required a Task Force of federal, state and municipal law enforcement agencies to mount a meaningful response to it) depended not solely on its reputation for violence and coercion but on its capacity to integrate itself into the legitimate segments of the local community by defining itself publicly as a "cultural organization," by sponsoring "community meetings," with local business professionals, by applying for city grants and redevelopment money while engaging in extortion and gun play with other gang rivals. In all of this it was frightfully effective.[30]

As the Jungle Boys and other groups demonstrate, gang recruitment processes are not limited to street and neighborhood assessments of prospective members, but are facilitated through the large and dangerous prison system. Strong ties formed in street gangs are sustained even in prison,[31] and rather than suppress gang activity, prisons tend to perpetuate it, and because the gangs are so influential in the prisons, as they are in many neighborhoods, inmates feel compelled to affiliate with one gang or another to survive the incarceration experience.

Outside, in the communities and neighborhoods, gangs such as the Jungle Boys and its Hispanic equivalent, the powerful Latin Kings, spread across the archipelago of impoverished neighborhoods, transforming them, redefining their social geography into "sets," gang terrains, that are defended because they function as criminal markets for the gangster/businessman.

Even more than a commitment, the obsession with money is tremendously important. However, there is more to the attractiveness of gang life than power through violence and the prestige that money confers. There seems to be barely a corner of ghetto life left untouched by the facts of gang imperialism; the gang economies are hungry for markets and members and thus become more absorbed with the defense of their turfs, which often means a resort to ferocious violence. Thus, many of the identifying traits that define entrepreneurial gangs are dynamic forces that operate pragmatically to maintain a gang's sovereignty as much as they define its boundaries and edges. "Monster" Kody Scott's autobiographical account of his gang life in South Central Los Angeles is chilling testimony about how one becomes totally immersed in the gang élan, its mystiques, tribulations, and preoccupations. It is not about money per se or destructive zeal, but about precarious, ephemeral glory. The typical adolescent anxieties about sex and self-identity are exacerbated in the aggressive gang's surroundings. The gang member and gang apprentice are constantly being tested in the unforgiving, smoldering streets by and through rituals and rites of passage, an acceptance that must seem gratuitously cruel to outsiders.[32] What strikes the reader of Kody Scott's life is the cold detachment and indifference to suffering expected of a gang "homey."

It is a sobering experience to read accounts of gang life by participants. Those not in the ghetto often see and feel it as a "colony" of the oppressed—as an exotic geography and people. The disturbing eruption of angry voices from within the embattled communities can be disconcerting, an awful din of strife in a world crowded with the discontented and rejected; but these horror stories also reveal active points of energy of an emerging self-assurance and trust, even within the crime and violence when read closely and sympathetically.

From the perspective of the police, social researcher, and social worker one might see gangs as epitomizing and reenforcing pathological traits. On the other hand, for the "insider," callousness, violence, and self-destructive behavior may be examples of raw courage in the willingness to run the risks of humiliation and death on a daily basis. Indifference may be a tactical accommodation to the randomness and unpredictability of street action, a combination of intelligence, shrewd judgement, and lightning calculations of success and failure. Thus a "cool" demeanor is visible evidence of "balls and brains." Langston Hughes' evocative phrase captures this less crudely: ". . . the wind imprisoned in the flesh."

The field of inquiry then, how one measures and pictures the realities of African-American street gangs and their environments, is constituted by the questions we ask and the perspectives we take. The street-gang scene emerges as a consequence of our interpretive activities—not the opposite, where the ghetto reality stands ready to be explicated, described, and analyzed as if it were a fixed, static phenomenon ready to yield its intrinsic truths to any interrogator.

THE STREET GANG AS A CHRYSALIS

African-American gangs are not just subgroups subordinated to larger, more professional, bureaucratized crime syndicates but are in themselves organized entities engaged in violence and varying types of criminal conduct. Those gangs with a vertical/hierarchical organizational structure would seem more able to effectively maximize profits from criminal activities than those more loosely put together, who are preoccupied with the conventional interests of ghetto youth: turf defense. In order to expand their customer base, more territory needs to be conquered, and in order to accommodate a broader domain, a larger recruitment pool of members is required, necessitating a stronger, centralized leadership to manage a larger, more expansive gang. Otherwise, the gang could be worn away at its edges by competitors.

Jankowski points out that in New York, African-American gangs were impressed by the success of Mafia crime families and by other gangs that were highly organized, where survival was equated with being well organized. "Well organized" meant adopting a structure of authority and rank not unlike Mafia families.[33] Thus, contingencies of the criminal market and environment coupled with gang goals constitute significant inputs in the kind of structure they develop and articulate.

In Chicago, Keiser found the Vice Lords, a gang in existence more than two decades ago, to be highly organized and divided into branches much like the contemporary Crips and Bloods "sets."[34] Within each branch the gang was divided by age, and each age group had a hierarchy of officers. The structure also included cliques or "running partners" within each branch. Each branch warlord or president made decisions about fighting, and, if all of the groups making up the Vice Lords decided go to war, then the president of all the branches would make a decision. After the gang reorganized itself, further structural refinements included a board (not unlike the "Commission" of La Cosa Nostra) made up of representatives from each of the gang's branches that advised the general leadership. The advantages in collective, committee-like decision making reflect a degree of sophistication in which responsibility for decisions that might lead to a gang member or gang enemy's death is diffused so that no one could be held personally accountable for a decision involving a serious criminal offense.

Whether gangs are loosely organized or tightly structured in ranks and varying degrees of authority and responsibility, the basic unit of reference reflected in the term "homeboy" is the local neighborhood—much like Mafia crime families, whose foundational structure is the "crew," the small clique of associates and members orbiting around a "soldier."

Criminal justice agencies often underestimate the subtleties of gang structure by depicting it exclusively as a traditional pyramid with leaders at the top and subordinates, recruits, and "wannabes" at the bottom. By using this model, law enforcement has often missed the variety and complexity of gang organization, its dynamical changes, and may mistakenly expect that targeting leaders will disrupt an entire gang. In fact, gangs are quite varied and flexible, with a variety of organizational structures and multiple leaders and cliques, each with slightly different interests and responsibilities. What is clear both to law enforcement agencies and social researchers is that modern gangs, including African-American groups, are more violent than their counterparts of twenty or even ten years ago. The reasons are not difficult to discern. First, more weapons are available and they are more sophisticated and lethal. Second, "drive-bys"—hit and run tactics using automobiles—are common gang-war tactics because of the availability of cars. Finally, gang membership generally may have grown.[35]

Weapons are everywhere on the streets of American cities, not just among gang members. National crime data illustrate the widespread availability of weapons. As Table 8.2 shows, one major finding from the National Crime Surveys is that offenders were more likely to have weapons in violent crimes committed against African Americans than in those against whites. The percentage of violent crimes against African Americans in which the offender had a gun was nearly twice the percentage of violent crimes in which whites were the victims.

TABLE 8.2. Presence of Weapons in Violent Crimes: 1979–1986

| Type of weapon used by offender | Type of Crime and Race of Victim | | | | | |
| | Crimes of violence* | | Robbery | | Aggravated assault | |
	White	Black	White	Black	White	Black
Total	100%	100%	100%	100%	100%	100%
No Weapon	60	42	43	30	6	3
Weapon	33	48	46	57	94	97
Gun	11	20	17	29	29	36
Knife	9	14	16	16	22	27
Other	12	13	11	10	38	30
Type not ascertained	2	2	2	2	4	3
Don't know	7	10	11	12	—	1**

Note: Percentages may not total 100% because of rounding. If the offender had more than one weapon, the crime is classified by the most serious weapon present.

— Less than 0.5%.

* Includes data on simple assaults, which by definition cannot be committed by an armed offender, and rape.

** Estimate is based on 10 or fewer sample cases.

Source: Bureau of Justice Statistics, Special Report, *Black Victims* (April 1990). U.S. Department of Justice, Office of Justice Programs, Washington, DC.

A point that deserves to be reiterated is the marginalization of social groups that produce street gangs. Street-gang members live in social environments that seem antiseptically quarantined from the larger world. The isolation and economic disadvantage do not mechanically determine gang criminal behavior, or for that matter, the formation of gangs as compensatory structures for what is lacking in conventional everyday familial and institutional supports, but African-American, Latino, Asian, and white youth live very much in social worlds that are constricted and parochial economically, and the subworlds of neighborhood and community are shaping and are shaped by that reality and those social experiences.

Fortress L.A.: The Crips and the Bloods

L.A. today is like the Balkans, rich with blood feuds that outsiders can scarcely understand. In the bleaker African-American and Hispanic sections, there are turfs, each "territory" inviolate, divided between gangs ready to defend against any incursion, and to retaliate with heavy firepower in "drive-by" commando strikes against trespassers.

A gang's turf is usually only one or two blocks square and walking to a 7-Eleven or a minimarket a block away, but in another gang's territory, is an invitation to mayhem. Even going to school can be an adventure, a trek through a half-dozen city-states controlled by competing gangs with short fuses.

Today it is conservatively estimated that there are 50,000 gang members throughout the city. In 1926, the Los Angeles population of 1.3 million was 90 percent white, of Western European stock, and with the exception of a strong Jewish community of between 50,000 and 100,000 people, there were no significant pockets of Eastern or Southern Europeans. The other 10 percent of the city comprised 45,000 Hispanics, 33,000 African Americans, and 30,000 Asians.

The population of the city has since exploded to 3.4 million, not including the surrounding county and its satellite cities and urban frontier sites on the fringes of the core, which would add 5.5 million more. L.A. has become less "Anglo," less amendable to white elites. Over eighty languages are spoken in the city's schools, and 39 percent of these pupils come from homes where English is not the primary language. In 1990, at the University of California at Los Angeles (UCLA), the largest single racial group is Asian. Today L.A. has the largest Japanese, Iranian, Thai, and Filipino communities in the country. According to the 1990 preliminary census, 40 percent of the city was Hispanic, 37 percent Anglo, 13 percent African-American, and 10 percent Asian, Pacific Islanders and others. And in the Anglo neighborhoods the sound is Spanish.[36]

FIGURE 8.1. Southern California Crips Sets: Los Angeles and San Diego

52 Hoover	Neighborhood Crips	98 Main Streets	Ghost Town Crips	East Coast 118
59 Hoover	Broadway 112	Broadway 52	Playboy Style	East Coast 97
74 Hoover	Ruthless Posse Crips	West Coast Crips	Grape Street Crips	East Coast 89
83 Hoover	5-Deuce Crips	Front Street	102 Budlong Gangsters	East Coast 69
92 Hoover	Pocket Hood	Back Street	99 Mafia	East Coast 62
107 Hoover	Bahala Na-Barkada	Raymond Crips	Lantana Block	83 Main Streets
112 Hoover	Linda Vista Crips	Shotgun Crips	Gear Gang Crips	94 Main Street
Rollin' 30	Santana Blocks Rollin' 90's	Rollin' 20 Crips	105 Underground Crips	Water Gate
Rollin' 40	Venice Shoreling Gangsters	Front Hood	106 Playboy Style	Marvin Crips
Rollin' 60	Playboy Gangsters	P.J. Watts	Insanes	94 Hoover
Nutty Blocks	Watts Baby Coc Crips	Kelly Park Crips	Kitchen Crips	8-Tray Gangsters
East Coast 1	East Coast 190	Schoolyard Cs	Inglewood Village Crips	357
East Coast 59	Schoolyard Crips	Compton Crips	Tiny Oriental Crips	

Note: Street names are usually pronounced not as numbers but as separate words (e.g., Five-Deuce Hoover, Eight-Tray Gangsters, Broadway One-Twelve, East Coast Six-Deuce, and so forth). The rolling numbers are pronounced as seen: Rollin' Sixties.

Source: Compiled from: Leon Bing, Do or Die (New York: Harper-Collins, 1991); William B. Sanders, Gangbangs and Drive-bys (New York: Aldine De Gruyter, 1994); District Attorney's Office, Gangs, Crime and Violence in Los Angeles (Los Angeles: Office of the District Attorney, May, 1992); Kody Scott, Monster: The Autobiography of an L.A. Gang Member Sanyika Shakur, A.K.A. Monster Kody Scott (New York: The Atlantic Monthly Press, 1993); and personal interviews.

The chief Los Angeles gangs are the Crips (approximately 30,000 strong now) and the Bloods (about 9,000) composed of Latinos and African Americans. Their expansion to other parts of the country took off in 1986. The Crips gang migrated into Seattle and Oklahoma City in 1988,[37] and in 1991, the Justice Department placed the Crips and the Bloods in 32 states and 113 cities. Some experts think that the Los Angeles–based gangs now control up to 30 percent of the crack trade.[38] Neither gang is rigidly hierarchical, and both are broken into loosely affiliated neighborhood groups called "sets," each with 30 to 100 members. Many gang members initially left Southern California to evade police. Others simply moved as the crack epidemic spread, by setting up branch operations in places where friends or family were located.

FIGURE 8.2. Southern California Bloods Sets: Los Angeles and San Diego

Athens Park	Black P Stones	Bounty Hunters
8–9 Families	Inglewood Families	Swans
West Side Pirus	Ludas Park Pirus	Rolling Twenties
Outlaw Twenties	Miller Gangsters	B-Bop Watts
Treetop Pirus	Holly-Hood Pirus	Denver Lanes
Pablos	Five-Deuce Villains	Pasadena Devil Lanes
Fruit Town	Lime Hood	*Kompton Fruit Town
Van Ness Gangsters	Skottsdale Pirus	Ujima Village Bloods
* Karson Pirus	* Kabbage Patch Pirus	Six-Deuce Brims
Nine-Deuce Bishops	Sirkle Sity Pirus	Five-Nine Brims
Pomona Island Pirus	Mid-Sity Gangsters	*Senter Park Pirus
Compton Pirus	Northside Blood	Skyline Pirus
Lincoln Park Pirus	Little Africa Pirus	Eastside Pirus
Bell Haven	Sirkle Sity	Thirty-Seventh Street
Bounty Hunters	Bounty Hunters	Fruit Town
Neighborhood Pirus	Avenue Pirus	Krenshaw Mafia
5/9 Brim Pirus		

*Note that the capital letter C has been changed to letter S or K

Source: Compiled from: Leon Bing, *Do or Die* (New York: Harper-Collins, 1991); William B. Sanders, *Gangbangs and Drive-bys* (New York: Aldine De Gruyter, 1994); District Attorney's Office, *Gangs, Crime and Violence in Los Angeles* (Los Angeles: Office of the District Attorney, May, 1992); Kody Scott, *Monster: The Autobiography of an L.A. Gang Member Sanyika Shakur, A.K.A. Monster Kody Scott* (New York: The Atlantic Monthly Press, 1993); and personal interviews.

Compared with Los Angeles, other cities to which Crips and Bloods have branched out have been easy pickings, especially for "rollers" or "Ogs" (Original Gangsters) and others in their twenties, with a thirst for more serious cash, who have established connections with Colombian suppliers, made in their L.A. drug operations. Crips and Bloods are reflections of a demographic bulge in which members tend to be in the most criminally prone age cohorts—adolescence to adulthood. And when the demographic factor is coupled with the high unemployment rate among young African-American males (36 percent), the conditions for the rapid growth of crime and violent activity by gang members, individually or collectively, are present and are not unusual.

It cannot be gainsaid that in economically depressed communities crime is often seen as an attractive alternative, if not the only one, to prolonged deprivation. Generally, illicitly earned income among gang members, primarily drug money, is not recirculated in the community, banked, invested in commercial enterprises, or used to capitalize commercial activities that benefit the community as a whole. Instead, income is usually used for personal luxury items or reabsorbed by the drug economy, whose infrastructure lies outside the community of the users it exploits. Unlike the policy rackets, illicitly generated drug monies flow out of the community and are drained off by large non-community-based syndicates.

The first generation of African-American street gangs emerged as a defensive response to white confrontations in the schools and streets during the late 1940s.[39] Until the 1970s, these gangs tended to be defined mainly by school-based turf rather than by microscopically drawn neighborhood territories. Besides defending African Americans and offering a protective shield to teenagers from racist attacks, these early gangs were also the architects of social space in new and hostile settings.

The decimation of the Black Panthers led directly to a recrudescence of gangs two decades ago. "Crippin," the most extraordinary gang phenomenon, was a bastard offspring of the Panther's former charisma, which filled the void when the Panthers were crushed by law enforcement groups across the country.[40] The legends about the Crips agree on certain particulars: The first "set" incubated in the social wasteland resulting from the clearance for the Century Freeway, which removed housing and destroyed neighborhood ties in Los Angeles. One legend has it that *Crips* stands for "Continuous Revolution in Progress." However apocryphal this may be, it best describes the phenomenal spread of Crips sets across the ghetto between 1970 and 1972. Under incessant pressure from the Crips, independent gangs federated as the Red-Handkerchief Bloods. The Bloods have been primarily a defensive reaction-formation to the aggressive emergence of the Crips.

This was not merely a gang revival, but instead a radical permutation of African-American gang culture. The Crips inherited the Panther aura of fearlessness and transmitted the ideology of armed vanguardism. "Crippin" often represents an escalation of intraghetto violence to "Clockwork Orange" levels (murder as a status symbol). They blend a penchant for ultraviolence with an overweening ambition to dominate the entire ghetto. The Crips achieved, like the El Rukns in Chicago, a "managerial revolution" in gang existence. If they began as a teenage substitute for the fallen Panthers, they evolved through the 1970s into a hybrid of teen cult and proto-mafia.

In 1972 at the height of Crips hysteria, a conference gave a platform to the gangs, which produced a document of their grievances. To the astonishment of officials, the "mad dogs" outlined an eloquent and coherent set of demands: jobs, housing, better schools, recreational facilities, and community control of local institutions. It was a bravura demonstration that gang youth, however trapped in their own delusionary spirals of vendetta and self-destruction, clearly understood that they were the children of deferred dreams and defeated ambitions. Young African Americans have seen their labor-market options virtually collapse as the factory and truck-driving jobs that gave their fathers and older brothers a modicum of dignity, were replaced by imports or relocated to white areas far out of the Los Angeles megalopolis. The deteriorating labor market for these young males is a major reason the countereconomy of drug dealing and youth crime has burgeoned.

With minimum outcry from elected officials, the tacit expendability of African-American and Latino youths can be directly measured by the steady drainage of resources from the programs that served their most urgent needs. Job alternatives for gang members have been almost nonexistent, despite widespread recognition that jobs are the most potent deterrents to youth crime. The educational system has been in steep decline; between 1980 and 1989 (the last ten-year analysis) there has been a steady decline of students completing eight years of elementary schooling.[41]

The specific "genius" of the Crips has been their ability to insert themselves into a leading circuit of the international drug trade. Through "crack" they have discovered a vocation for the ghetto in the ghetto's new world-city economies. Peddling the imported, high-profit rock to a bipolar market of final consumers, including rich whites and poor street people, the Crips have become as much lumpen capitalists as outlaw proletarians.[42]

In an age of narcoimperialism, they have become modern analogues to the "gunpowder states" of West Africa, those selfish, rogue chieftains who were middlemen in the eighteenth-century slave trade, prospering while the rest of Africa bled. The contemporary cocaine or crack trade is a stunning example of what some economists call "flexible accumulation." The rules of the game are to combine maximum financial control with interchangeable deployment of producers and sellers across variable markets.

The appearance of crack has given the Crips subculture a terrible, almost irresistible allure. There is little reason to believe that the crack economy of the new gang culture will stop growing, whatever the scales of repression, or stay confined to African-American ghettos.[43]

Almost two years after the burning and looting that swept Los Angeles, much of the gutted areas most heavily impacted remain blighted.[44] The conclusion seems obvious: South Central Los Angeles has been betrayed by local and state governments. There is a deafening public silence about youth unemployment; the schools are asphyxiated—they are underfunded, overcrowded, and mismanaged—leaving thousands of impoverished youth with few alternatives but to enlist in the Crips/Bloods employment programs operated by the distantly elusive cocaine cartels.

Economic recovery programs have been shunted aside in favor of a politics of social control in which a siege mentality grips the imagination of the city's political warlords. The "new" Los Angeles Police Department, preoccupied with careerism and distracted by the cacophony of police and fire sirens and sporadic gunfire, brandishes its weapons with promises that it will be ready for the next outbreak.[45] A collective psychosis has enveloped Los Angeles as the riot anniversary and sensational trials around the Rodney King incident come and go. What has happened, in retrospect, is that neighborhoods are fragmented and divided in a multiracial city because the root causes of the unrest and violence have not been addressed. Meanwhile, the phobias of the middle class, living in a collective state of denial, and the poor, have traumatized the affluent and threaten to criminalize the have-nots. In both communities, families seem close to panic or vigilantism.

It is unlikely that Los Angeles will fold up and disappear or be swallowed up in an earthquake. It may learn to get along with its fear and psychic (as well as geological) trembling and its panzer-like police force, just as a third world city like Mexico does with its twenty million people living in the country's largest metropolitan complex that has no functioning public school system, a city government that cannot by any standards be taken seriously, an unemployment rate twice that of Los Angeles, substandard housing everywhere, and like Palermo, Sicily, upscale communities festooned with razor wire and private armed guards protecting against the street violence and mayhem.

Required throughout eternity to roll a huge stone to the top of a hill, only to have it plunge back down just as it reaches the crest, was the fate of Sisyphus. He angered the gods and was punished with a meaningless task. The myth symbolizes futility and for many in Chicago's neighborhoods, the fate of Sisyphus may aptly describe their lives.

Throughout the 1980s, El Rukns was the major African-American crime group in Chicago. It began as a coalition of street gangs formed by Jeff Fort, whose extraordinary career is neither unexceptional nor unusual. Fort's career fits into the traditional pathway of an organized crime leader, similar to that of Barnes and Lucas, and ending (momentarily) with incarceration. Fort was born in 1947 in Mississippi and arrived with his mother in Chicago in 1955, settling in the Woodlawn area of the city. Leaving school after the fourth grade, Fort was semiliterate and destined to a street life. As a teenager he began his criminal leadership as the head of Woodlawn's Blackstone Rangers in a long and bloody war of survival against rival groups.

Fort grew up in a ghetto where the only stable businesses were those dispersing drugs, alcohol, junk food, and cheap entertainment. The contrast in the meaning of this blight in Chicago's African-American communities could not be more startling. The Honorable Elijah Muhammad, the powerful leader of the Nation of Islam through the three decades since World War II, owned a stately mansion on Chicago's South Side that served as his headquarters for the Nation. It was the Nation of Islam's movement, now led by the fiery spellbinder, Minister Louis Farrakhan, that raised the taboo subject of violent self-defense among African Americans, pointing out that in the United States, violence and heroism have been made somewhat synonymous except when it comes to African Americans.

Things were as bad as the Muslims and Malcolm X said they were and Jeff Fort personified the worst fears, not of the Muslims, but of the minority segments of society who wondered out loud with Muslim encouragement why they should be patient, forbearing, and more farseeing than whites. The intensity of Elijah Muhammad and Malcolm X in those early days of the 1960s were matched by the bitter isolation of the disaffected young men in the streets of Chicago's South Side. Both shared a single-mindedness and were candid about their hatred of the conditions in which they found themselves. The Muslims treated with scorn the doltish and servile African Americans who insisted upon integration as a way of putting an end to a society that had spelled out with brutal clarity, and in as many ways as possible, what it thought of African Americans.

By the time he was eighteen, Jeff Fort transformed the Blackstone Rangers into the Black P Stone Nation, a coalition of twenty-one gangs ruled by a commission of gang leaders known as the "Main 21" with Fort at its head.[46]

His criminal career from the start was marked by a flair for the melodramatic. His original gang nucleus, the Blackstone Rangers, was identifiable by the red berets they wore in 1962—a defiant act that challenged the police and other gangs. In each of the succeeding years through 1965, when the great gang consolidation came together, Fort's Stones tripled its membership through ingenious and forcible recruitment tactics: In the Woodlawn streets one became a Stone or else.[47] The gang spread across the city of Chicago and impressed other gangs with its size and power. By 1966, Fort's control and influence over African-American street gangs in large sections of Chicago had been achieved. According to Seibel and Pincomb, by 1968 the Black P Stone Nation began to evolve into an organized crime entity:

> Segments of the Stones operated throughout Black communities, in the infamous Cabrini–Green Housing Projects on the near-north side and all the way to the southern-most portion of the city.
>
> Fort's first effort at putting his power to work was by charging people attending school; a quarter a day in grammar schools and a dollar in high schools.[48]

From schoolyard shakedowns, the gang proceeded to extort money from the street prostitution trade. The cost of doing business was $50 a day per hooker. To make it unmistakably clear that they fully intended to exercise control over street prostitution as "protectors" in 1971, a prostitute who refused to pay was viciously murdered.

In the early and middle phases of his criminal career, Fort did not consider himself the spiritual property of the people who produced him. He did not consider himself to be their savior, he was far too modest and self-centered for that lofty role, nor was he willing to consider himself a servant of the people. He was not a racist, not even if he thought he was. His intelligence was more complex than that and if he had been a racist, few would have thought him dangerous. He would have sounded familiar and even comforting; his rage would have simply confirmed the reality of white power. What made him dangerous and unfamiliar was not his hatred of whites but his appetites for wealth and power attained at any costs. Fort reflected social impulses white society feared in that he unhesitatingly and ruthlessly acted in ways grudgingly respected in society at large: He grasped at what he wanted and pushed aside all obstacles in his way.

In the same period, Fort cleverly linked himself with social activists and community organizations and went so far as to apply for a federal grant designed to train gang members in marketable, legitimate job skills. Under the auspices of the Woodlawn Organization, the Black P Stone Nation received federal funding from the Office of Economic Opportunity in the amount of $1 million. The rationale for the grant made sense; some white clergymen and community activists were interested in channeling gang violence into constructive learning programs. But the Mayor of Chicago was outraged by what he believed was the coddling of gangsters, so by 1969, a U.S. Senate investigation was convened at which Fort, who was subpoenaed, appeared before the Senate Permanent Subcommittee on Investigations, introduced himself, and walked out. He was imprisoned for contempt of Congress and the embezzlement of $7,500 in federal funds. The embezzlement bore the hallmarks of a racketeering scheme: Lower level leaders of the Stones were hired as program instructors and recruited adolescents to enroll as students, for which they received weekly stipends to participate in the program. When checks were disbursed, they were endorsed over to Fort's lieutenants, with each enrollee receiving a nominal compensatory amount. After serving two years of a five-year sentence, Fort was paroled and his organization came to dominate large areas of Chicago's South Side African-American community.

With his strength solidified through murder and intimidation, Fort moved beyond extortion activities into prostitution and local neighborhood businesses. By 1971, the Black P Stone Nation took on narcotics dealers and made them pay a "street tax." These events precipitated a warning from the "Outfit," Chicago's La Cosa Nostra, which played a major role in the organization of local drug dealing. La Cosa Nostra in Chicago was not involved in the street distribution and wholesaling of drugs but offered its protection for a price. When the Stones imposed their extortion fees on bags of dope, the Outfit sent a warning but Fort was not impressed. Two associates of the Outfit were found slain in front of its headquarters shortly after Fort had participated in a "sit-down" with Cosa Nostra bosses.

Chicago's Cosa Nostra, the Outfit, by this time was no longer actively participating in the street crime but retained the streets as protection markets over which they ruled by reputation and tradition. The Stones challenged the hegemony of the Outfit, and realistically, the odds favored Fort's forces. At full strength the Outfit could muster several hundred members and associates. They were feared because of the mystique the Mafia had engendered in Chicago and across the United States. But with elderly leaders and middle-aged soldiers safety ensconced in their rackets and legitimate businesses, were they any match for the young, hungry, fearless Stones?

The murder of Outfit associates was an act of defiance that persuaded Chicago's Cosa Nostra to back off. By 1972, the Stones had broadened their criminal activities to include large drug conspiracies, while other members preyed upon community businesses for protection money amounting to $250,000 a year.[49]

By 1982, Fort had been convicted on federal drug conspiracies charges. While in prison the El Rukns was born. Fort identified himself thereafter as Prince Malik and the Black P Stone Nation became El Rukns, with its headquarters rechristened (if that is the word) as the Grand Major Temple.

The new incarnation was not a prison experience conversion; Seibel and Pincomb offer an interesting speculation about Fort's motives. Along with other organized criminal enterprises, Fort's Black P Stone Nation was heavily invested in real estate properties on Chicago's South Side. Although most properties were held in blind trusts, federal authorities would have little difficulty in establishing true ownership in order to seize criminally generated assets for tax evasion and RICO violations. Thus, to avoid that possibility, Fort could acquire tax-exempt status for himself and his gang if it was a religious organization.

The charade succeeded for a time. In 1983, Prince Malik of the El Rukns Sunni Muslims, through their temple Masjid Al Malik, played an active role in the mayoral race. Rather cynically, the Jane Cook County Democrat campaign organization paid an estimated $10,000 to El Rukns to support her candidacy in the African-American wards and to serve as poll watchers. In the 1920s, the Capone crime cartel performed similar services for its candidate, "Big Bill" Thompson. And in 1984, El Rukns achieved national recognition when Reverend Jesse Jackson publicly praised them for their role in a voter registration drive on behalf of his presidential campaign.[50]

In 1987, Fort was convicted of a terrorist plot hatched from a federal penitentiary in Texas. The El Rukns were tied to Moammar Gadhafi of Libya in a scheme involving bomb placements and gunrunning. For this, Fort was sentenced to eighty years. A year later, in 1988, while in prison, another conviction followed—a murder conspiracy which put Fort away for life. This 1988 conviction was the result of Fort and three other El Rukns in 1981 murdering a rival gang member (Willie Bibbs). Bibbs, a member of the Titannic Stones, was murdered because he had failed to heed the El Rukns warning to share the proceeds of his drug dealings.

Names in the Street: The New Custodians of Crime

The end of the El Rukns and Jeff Fort can hardly be claimed a victory for

Chicago, its police, or its citizens. A study of street-gang crime in Chicago since the transformation of El Rukns reveals that more than forty gangs are active in the city and four of them account for 69 percent of all street-gang motivated crime.[51]

Figure 8.3 shows the configuration of criminal activities of Chicago's gangs with a focus on the four most powerful "Folk" and "People" alliance groups. The data indicate that most of the drug incidents occurred among the Vice Lords or the Black Gangster Disciples Nation. The Vice Lords were heavily involved in heroin trafficking—more than all the other street gangs.

FIGURE 8.3. Street-Gang Incidents by Offense Type—Four Largest and Other Gangs: 1987–1990

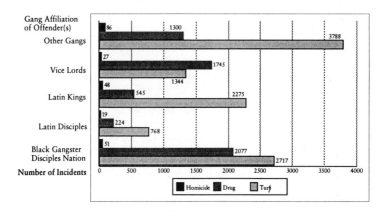

Source: Carolyn R. Block and Richard Block, "Street Gang Crime in Chicago," see note 51.

The Black Gangster Disciples Nation (BGDN), the original nemesis of the El Rukns, has reemerged, fierce and determined, and since 1991 become the strongest street gang in Chicago's South Side. The political lessons of Prince Malik on organizing alliances as a survival strategy have not been lost on the new gangs. In the mid-1980s, the BGDN and the Latin Kings—the largest Latino street gang in Chicago, active in the growing Mexican neighborhoods—joined with the Vice Lords, a predominantly African-American gang, to form the "People Alliance." The confederation activities of the African-American gangs in particular may reflect an act of desperation, given the fact that the African-American population of Chicago is declining, whereas the Latino population is growing.

The increases in the violence among street gangs and within the alliances indicate that the relative stability of the "treaties" began to unravel dramatically in the late 1980s and early 1990s (see Figure 8.4).

The social and ethnic ghettos of Chicago are more dangerous in the 1990s than they were during the height of El Rukns influence. The risk of homicide, according to C. Block and R. Block, was higher for African Americans and Latinos than for whites, regardless of age or gender. Part of the explanation has to do with the proliferation of guns, especially automatic weapons known as "street sweepers." The proportion of automatic weapons increased almost 10 percent from 1987 to 1990. This increase in automatic weapons could account for the increase in the number of street-gang motivated homicides.

FIGURE 8.4. Street-Gang Motivated Homicides: 1987–1990

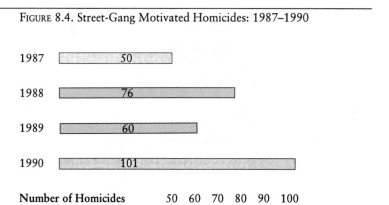

Year	Number of Homicides
1987	50
1988	76
1989	60
1990	101

Number of Homicides   50   60   70   80   90   100

Source: Carolyn R. Block and Richard Block, "Street Gang Crime in Chicago," see note 51.

The persistence of street-gang crime, whether turf defense or drug trafficking, in Chicago, as in other cities, must be understood in the context of race discrimination, joblessness, weapons availability, and not least, drugs as the vital, lethal commodity that transforms adolescent street gangs into organized-crime enterprises.

New York: The Open City

New York City was and remains the seedbed for invention, change, and humanism. Garibaldi hatched the Risorgimento on Mulberry Street; Franklin Delano Roosevelt invented the New Deal on Wall Street; Melville wrote

Moby Dick in his home near Canal Street; Bartok composed his Concerto for Percussions on evening walks in Central Park; Meyer Lansky befriended Lucky Luciano in the Five Points section of Lower Manhattan; James Baldwin poured out his heart and soul into *Go Tell It on a Mountain* in Harlem; and the Rockefellers manipulated the currencies of the world from their Fifth Avenue corporate cockpits.

For the inhabitants themselves, New York is a stern mistress. Each believes himself or herself an expert on the urban reality. New York's silhouette of social and ethnic groups is global and orchestrated like a sociological minuet. A visitor will find familiar distillations of San Juan, Rome, Athens, Dublin, Hong Kong, Tokyo, Tel Aviv, Odessa, Manila, Kingston, Istanbul, Paris, Naples, Saigon, Damascus, Budapest, and many more. But the ethnic villages and enclaves do not live in perfect harmony; they are often frazzled with tensions and violence.

New York has been the home of the five most powerful Cosa Nostra crime families in the United States for more than a half century. Interestingly, until the 1930s, African-American communities were left alone, more or less, with their own types of crime—mainly numbers gambling, prostitution, relatively small-scale theft, fencing, and narcotics. Their organized crime was contained, unique to Harlem. Then, as the underworld flexed its muscles during Prohibition, white syndicates overwhelmed the African-American rackets, either destroying them outright with their firepower and political power or absorbing them into their networks. Those African-American gangs that survived intact, unfettered to the Italian underworld, were generally small-scale operations. A celebrated African-American gangster in New York City, Ellsworth Raymond "Bumpy" Johnson, who acted as a middleman for the Italian syndicates from the 1940s through the 1960s (an account of Johnson is reported in chapter 6) is an example of Cosa Nostra utilizing African-American middlemen to exploit independent African-American criminal enterprises.

CRIMINAL NETWORKS IN NEW YORK

Since the collapse of the Barnes and Lucas drug syndicates in the 1970s, the history of African-American organized crime has reverted to its loose organizational style of the 1920s, when numbers banks operated as small fiefdoms with no centralized pattern of control. The very lack of centralization was a key feature that enabled the policy rackets to survive as long as they did before coming to the attention of the white syndicates and the political machines.

Ianni's work, which was conducted in the 1970s in Harlem, found no pattern of organizational behavior similar to contemporary La Cosa Nostra families. Instead, he observed clusters of African-American criminal "networks" in which individuals were knitted together in criminal activities, exchanging and sharing resources. The participants in these operations were being recruited from adolescent street gangs, correctional facilities, and known neighborhood criminals. The criminal cliques in Harlem that Ianni described may be thought of as formative organized crime groups—if our notion of organized crime is a Mafia crime family—or, more plausibly, as organized crime in its birth pangs, in its incipient state. A very interesting aspect of the crime scene is that much of the criminal conduct is directed toward the needs of other ghetto dwellers. The networks are part of the community and could barely survive without community support in the marketing of illicit or licit goods and services.

Gangs were everywhere in New York City in the 1950s. In white, African-American, Latino, and Asian communities throughout the five boroughs, some gangs were quite large and very violent. The Flatbush Tigers (Brooklyn), a white, ethnically mixed fighting gang, or the Bishops (Brooklyn), also a sizable African-American fighting gang, were active in turf wars and some petty crime. Others, such as the Gremlins and Garfield Boys, were also involved in petty crime, but these gangs served as recruiting centers for Mafia crime families in Brooklyn. In the Bronx, the Fordham Baldies, a white street gang that frequented the Italian enclave of 187th Street, were used to recruit members into the Genovese crime family that made their headquarters in the area. Another Latino/African-American street gang with members throughout the Bronx during the period were the Savage Skulls, resembling present-day Crips and Bloods in that almost every section of the Bronx had independent gangs claiming the identity of the Savage Skulls with no centralized leadership existing among or between the gangs.

It is apparent that many of the poor, working-class communities of New York City functioned as incubators for organized crime enterprises— if we understand the concept to mean crime committed through entrepreneurial organizations in which men and women work together for mutual profit in some illegal operation, just as they might in a legitimate small business. Before the present-day drug scourge, the gang members who went beyond adolescent pranks, petty vandalism, and meaningless street fighting would be considered candidates for careers in organized crime.

SOCIAL BANDITRY IN NEW YORK'S METROPOLITAN GHETTOS
Barnes and Lucas were destroyed by a combination of law enforcement and conflicts within their organizations, but it would be a mistake to think that

this ended either the viability of African-American syndicates modeled along the structures they invented and developed, or dampened the persistence of others to create organizations anew. Given their activities, public disapproval of their product, drugs, and the knowledge and skills of law enforcement acquired in combating Cosa Nostra crime, Barnes and Lucas's organizations were successful though short-lived.

In fact, the success of criminal enterprise can no longer be measured in terms of its leadership's durability. Ever since law enforcement agencies acquired anticrime tools such as RICO, electronic surveillance, wiretaps, undercover operations, task forces, and witness security programs, the length of a Mafia boss's reign over a family has been drastically diminished. No modern Cosa Nostra chief enjoys the immunity from arrest, prosecution, and constant surveillance his predecessors did.

If drugs serve African-American criminals as Prohibition did Italian-American bootleggers and other ethnics as a building resource and increment of power in crime, what emerges in terms of organization is not much more than an organizing motif. The failure of Barnes and Lucas is testimony to this. The driving force that could mold African-American organized crime into something substantive and as durable as La Cosa Nostra is militancy— a sense of solidarity, a "we consciousness," that transcends any particular criminal (or noncriminal) endeavor. Certainly, the social system is oppressive enough, and attempts at social and political mobility have been resisted at every step. Thus, as African-American power in its political, social, economic, and psychological manifestations grows as an opportunistic force, solidarity may actually nurture the beginnings of mafia-type organized criminal enterprises.[52] This futuristic scenario has some theoretical plausibility in that the incentives needed to elaborate criminal organizational power are in place. The main source of energy would be in the impoverished African-American communities themselves, which see the community crime activist, who may or may not be involved in drug trafficking, as both victim and victimizer. Within the community, the struggle against crime appears to focus on drugs and the violence and mayhem they engender.[53] Drugs destroy not only people but also communities by draining off resources and creating fearful images in the society at large as threats to the social order.

The Continuum of Organized Crime: Illicit Enterprise

On the other hand, beneath or alongside the drug-selling groups are more traditional criminal enterprises—gambling, boosting and fencing, loansharking, and prostitution—that are not considered socially harmful by many ghetto dwellers. It is the drug dealer that is universally detested in the ghetto.

Let us allow that the tolerance of nondrug crime is expedient, provisional, and ambiguous. The question is why should ghetto dwellers be sympathetic to, and even envious of, those who have achieved some success in organized crime? For many of the same reasons that other ethnic groups put up with organized criminal activities in their communities: Crime is perceived by many as one end of the American business continuum and is seen more as an admittedly sordid business venture than a destructive social evil. Although organized crime is crime, it follows many of the small rules and conventions of the business system. Of course, distinction can be made between criminal and noncriminal behavior, but these are often blurred in the climate of poverty and discrimination where sharp business practices, favoritism, and prejudice by police and a corrupted political system function with relative impunity. Organized criminal activities do not quite fit the stereotypical conceptions of crime. They are, in many aspects, an extension of legitimate market activities into areas normally proscribed. Often they take place beyond the existing limits of the law—for profit and responses to illicit demands.

Putting up with it, to the extent that the violence and mayhem is muted and contained, may be understood as a function of the shifting horizons of legality. For example, for decades numbers operated as an illegal activity until the New York State Legislature decided to legalize it. A previously criminal enterprise that entailed the commitment of significant resources, arrests, convictions, and violence was redefined by decisions that reflected economic calculations as much as moral assessments of the impact of numbers gambling. It is important to remember that "legal" and "legitimate" are social constructs sensitive to economic criteria. Figure 8.5 illustrates a taxonomic tree in which the spectrum of business activity from legal to illegal is illustrated.

Although conventional theories of organized crime were never generalized beyond a specific organization, Cosa Nostra, it is possible to reconstruct the process along a different set of parameters that emphasize the linkages between the legitimate and illegitimate sectors of the society.

Ghetto dwellers envy and criticize organized criminal activists to the extent that they intuitively grasp that the line between many business practices and crime is thin indeed, so thin that it can scarcely be distinguished by most people. The psychological conflicts over right and wrong in an economic environment that is malleable and confusing constitute one dimension of the problem. The ability to distinguish between legitimate and illegitimate business behavior is subject to cultural pressures and is rendered more morally and ethically difficult in a consumer society in which the values of "achievement" and "material success" are promoted indiscriminately yet affect all racial and ethnic groups and classes. Some groups are cut off from legitimate ways of obtaining these goals and, at the same time, have less emotional security. Those with financial security, stable families living in decent communities, have little reason to consider crime as a vocational possibility.

FIGURE 8.5. A Taxonomy of All Economic Activity

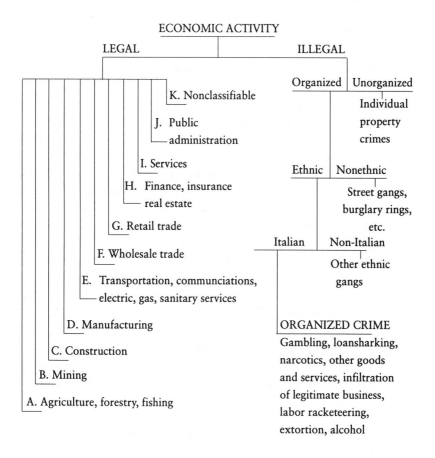

ECONOMIC ACTIVITY

LEGAL | ILLEGAL

K. Nonclassifiable

J. Public administration

I. Services

H. Finance, insurance real estate

G. Retail trade

F. Wholesale trade

E. Transportation, communciations, electric, gas, sanitary services

D. Manufacturing

C. Construction

B. Mining

A. Agriculture, forestry, fishing

Organized | Unorganized

Individual property crimes

Ethnic | Nonethnic

Street gangs, burglary rings, etc.

Italian | Non-Italian

Other ethnic gangs

ORGANIZED CRIME
Gambling, loansharking, narcotics, other goods and services, infiltration of legitimate business, labor racketeering, extortion, alcohol

Source: Adapted from Dwight Smith, "Organized Crime and Entrepreneurship," *International Journal of Criminology & Penology*, May 1978, p. 169. Distribution of legal activity based on Bureau of the Budget, Standard Industrial Classification Manual. Listing of organized crime activity based on President's Commission. *Challenge of Crime in a Free Society*, 188–194.

Twenty years ago, Ianni argued that political militancy might serve as the bonding factor and source of solidarity needed to weld disparate criminal groups together into some sort of mafia. That has not happened, in spite of the fact that the very conditions he and others specify as prerequisites for mafia were prevalent.

Hobsbawn described mafia in Sicily and elsewhere as a form of social banditry that seeks to overcome oppression and poverty through collective rebellion that in time evolves into a shadow government and system of law unto itself.[54] In its peasant Sicilian setting, mafia is at first a form of social protest that degenerated into racketeering and pure criminal conduct. Mafia-type criminal groups emerged in impoverished African-American urban environments when they developed in at least three capacities.

1. A collective hostile attitude toward the law and criminal justice system, which means substituting ones own code of rules to regulate relationships. In this way a network of gangs held together by a common code becomes a mafia.

2. A shared ideology of oppression holding together a coalition of political activists and criminals around a sociopolitical reform movement.

3. A harnessing of political energy and criminal aspirations whereby better access to political power would be possible, and at the least, the ability to corrupt the political structure is feasible.

What is possible in New York may apply equally in other cities. However, these elements did not come together in any substantive way in New York, Chicago, or Los Angeles.[55]

The social history of various American ethnic groups suggests that as these groups attain political power, the organized criminal activities associated with the particular ethnic group prosper, further suggesting that the two forms of mobility are often intertwined. What is less evident is that in the case of African Americans, it is not at all clear that these connections have materialized in any measurable way.

It is widely taken for granted that corruption of public officials and law enforcement is a key prerequisite for organized criminal activities. Political bosses and leaders of political machines, to be successful, must be able to guarantee some protection to those who provide illicit goods and services in demand. In other respects, the head of a political machine must be able to arrange variances and liquor licenses for the right people. And he or she must be willing to close their eyes to all kinds of infractions and illegalities if they wish to survive politically.

Although the avenues of corruption have been cultivated by whites, the growing political and economic autonomy of the African-American community suggests that rackets and political organization are, or will be, major continuing elements of slum life. Although African-American criminals may find it difficult to ingratiate themselves into the kinds of social relationships with white politicians that offer protection, it is not far-fetched to imagine the temptations that African-American politicians operating from machines may experience to provide services and favors for those on the periphery between the legal and the illegal.

There are parallels in the economic roles of "legitimate" and "illegitimate" businesses in the ghetto. Both forms are concerned with the provision of goods and services for which there is an economic demand. The relevant difference between the provision of licit and illicit goods and services is small, as shown in gambling and trafficking in consumer goods. In terms of social status, the legitimate business groups and the criminal groups in the ghetto are poles apart. Yet, status does not fully determine behavior and the interrelationships between groups. Functions modify these relationships in social settings in which the informal economy is as large as the formal economy.

"Just as the political machine performs services for legitimate business, so it operates to perform not dissimilar services for illegitimate business: vice, crime and rackets."[56] Minority politicians asserting themselves in the ghetto are likely to organize in terms of their perceptions of their functions and their own survival needs. For both the legitimate and illegitimate sectors within the ghetto, the political machine has a similar function. Above all, it must satisfy the needs of its clientele and constituencies for an operating environment that enables the criminal and noncriminal alike, in some cases, to meet economic demands without due interference from the government. Whether a political machine turns a blind eye to crime or vigorously attacks it depends on the relative economic and political strengths of the client or the protagonist. Finally, as far as market demands for goods and services are inadequately met by the legitimate sector, an alternative illegal sector will emerge and persist to fulfill them.

IN THE OUTER METROPOLIS: GANG SUPPRESSION STRATEGIES

The appearance of crack in the drug scene has created another criminal phenomenon, another stratum of "organized" crime that has not been integrated into the stable, low-profile, African-American syndicates operating in the ghettos. The dealers are volatile, scheming, and constantly engaged in violence against competition, customers, and law enforcement. Violence has always been a feature of drug trafficking, but the current levels associated with crack gangs seems unprecedented. The *New York Times* summarized what many law enforcement specialists in narcotics, social workers in communities afflicted by the trafficking, and social scientists sense about the new drug menace and how it affects not only users but purveyors:

> Older drug rings, wary of drawing police attention, generally avoided conspicuous violence. New York's new gangs, like similar groups in Los Angeles and Washington, are composed mainly of undisciplined teenagers and youths in their early twenties. They engage in gun battles on the street and have been known to execute customers for not leaving a crack den quickly enough.[57]

Since the mid-1980s, other smaller cities and towns have seen devastating increases in assaults and killings, led by a doubling in the murder rate among juveniles. Most of the victimizers and victims are young African-American men. Where they operate, the gangs are held responsible for significant increases in homicide rates, and their use of violence is new in that, unlike other criminal enterprises, they have begun to intimidate individual citizens and groups of citizens who resist gang intrusions into their neighborhoods. What has happened in Little Rock, Arkansas seems indicative of general trends nationwide.

Little Rock, with a population of almost 200,000, is experiencing a big-city epidemic of gangs, guns, crack, and murder. In 1992, it had a record 62 murders, up from 52 in 1991, and an average of 37 over the five years preceding that. In 1992–1993, Little Rock's murder rate in relation to it population has equaled that of New York or Los Angeles.

The African-American neighborhoods of Little Rock are emblazoned with the Crips and the Bloods, Vice Lords, and Folks gang graffiti—names appropriated from Los Angeles and Chicago gangs with which some local groups are also loosely affiliated.[58] In some instances, street-gang specialists from the Los Angeles Police Department were asked to consult with police departments in cities in Oklahoma, Nevada, and Arkansas in order to "decode" the graffiti.[59] Many gang "totems" are peculiar to California: "187," for example, discovered in Little Rock, refers to the Californian penal code number for homicide; another is a pitchfork signifying the Folk Nation, a super-gang alliance in Chicago.

The organized gangs in Little Rock did come to the notice of then Governor Clinton, who called community leaders and law enforcement officials together and implemented youth programs. However, the gangs were already well entrenched. As with their counterparts in the big cities, gang members in places like Little Rock are young and well armed. About half identify with the Crips and the Bloods and the others with the Folk Nation or Vice Lords of Chicago. These larger, older gangs appear to have formed alliances and use the smaller city and town gangs as distributors of crack.

Exactly how the police in large or small cities can best deal with the gangs remains uncertain. One approach is to ignore the fact that many street gangs are also drug gangs and to use the same strategies that proved effective in the past.[60] This strategy was designed primarily to reduce intergang violence, to prevent neighborhood extortion from merchants by the gangs, and to minimize the seriousness of their crimes. It was not designed to eliminate the gangs, although some efforts were made to turn them toward constructive activities. The key assumption underlying the strategy was that by establishing communication with gangs, law enforcement expectations could be made known. It was also hoped that vigorous policing would discourage gang activities.

However, this strategy does not seem suitable in dealing with drug gangs. The fighting gangs of earlier periods were only mildly dangerous to society when compared with the new drug gangs. The street gangs of the 1950s and 1960s were principally engaged in violence toward one another and were not involved in large-scale drug dealings as modern ghetto gangs are. Accommodations negotiated by street-gang units of the police were possible with the early gang leaders. Gangs could remain intact so long as they refrained from violence, and, with few exceptions, the gangs were not engaged heavily in entrepreneurial criminal activities. Such accommodations do not seem possible or appropriate with the drug gangs, whose dealing typically involves the systematic use of fear and violence to establish their trafficking operations. Sterner responses seem called for.

Another approach is to define the street drug gangs as organized criminal enterprises and to utilize all of the techniques that have been developed to deal with traditional organized crime. These would include developing informants through criminal prosecutions, payments, and witness security programs; reliance on electronic surveillance and long-term undercover investigations; and the use of special statutes, such as RICO and its state equivalents that create criminal liabilities for conspiracy, extortion, or racketeering.

Such tactics work in destroying organized crime enterprises but they are time-consuming and expensive. Perhaps the elaborate apparatus of organized-crime control is not required to contain drug trafficking groups—

merely undercover operations and persistent small-scale police actions. An important point in neighborhood crackdowns is that the leverage of resources should depend on the willingness of the local communities to join police in resisting drug use that drives drug trafficking. Neither the police nor citizens can deal with these situations by themselves. Citizens need law and law enforcement to oppose drug dealers. Likewise, there are only a limited number of police officers that can be committed to neighborhood enforcement activities. Thus, a suppression strategy that uses police to break the hold of drug dealing in communities is the initial step which, if followed by community action prepared to assume responsibility for holding onto gains, may very well work.[61]

These victories and successes, however, are not irreversible and must be regarded as provisional and temporary. Bold initiatives, such as "Operation Pressure Point" in New York, can be undone by inadequate planning. In New York, police simply made more arrests than prosecutors could prosecute, than the courts could adjudicate, and the prisons hold.[62] With these experiences in mind, deliberate planning approaches involving coordinated police intervention and prevention, coupled with efforts to improve the quality of life in communities where drug gangs operate, may just work. In this regard, witnesses from Texas and Illinois, who testified during 1991 as part of the National Field Study on Gangs and Gang Violence, recommended the implementation of comprehensive, community-defined, community-based strategies for controlling crime, intervening in the lives of youths and young adults at high risk for involvement in gangs, drug use, and drug trafficking, and preventing future criminal activity.[63]

Expert opinion from law enforcement and scientific research suggests that in order to be effectively controlled, the organized criminal behavior associated with drugs in African-American and minority communities must be attended to. Police strategies developed strictly for the control of street crime are not likely to be successful in themselves because they are oriented toward criminal acts rather than transactive groups processes. In organized crime, it is the combination of money, coercion, illicit demand, and corruption that produces results. The implications of the research reviewed here are that an understanding of the community, its social, political, and economic structures must be the initial step in developing adequate responses to a form of crime that threatens to undermine community life as a whole.

Our focus has been on the three large cities of the African-American migration to the Northeast, North Central, and Western sections of the United States. Why, it could reasonably be asked, have there been no significant organized criminal trends in the old cities of the South, where the

African-American population was heavily settled initially and which many who moved north and west still consider home? In a review of a recent book about Huey Newton, the founder of the Black Panther Party, Blauner makes a point with relevance to this issue:

> Black communities in the North and West lacked the church-based organizational solidarity of Southern areas, and without an institutional structure of legalized segregation to protest, they also lacked clear targets for their even more widespread anger and alienation, especially among the youth.[64]

The idea that the church in the African-American community exercised a powerful influence on its communicants by channeling pent-up anguish into nondestructive modes of action and expression may help to explain why Northern and Western communities experience the street-gang phenomenon and the violence associated with the vice industries operating in the ghettos. The Southern church served as a complementary socializing agency, just as the Catholic Church, during the great transatlantic migrations in the nineteenth and early twentieth centuries, went beyond its mission and provided a social home and moral center for the Catholic immigrant community.

The church in the African-American Southern communities, more than a belief-affirming institution, was also oriented to goal attainment. The goals were to prepare and assist the young and dissolute in acquiring social skills, respectability, and above all, assimilation into the African-American community with traditions of family stability and respectability. The Muslims today seem to share this mission. They, like the Baptist congregations in the South, are the dominant force in the lives of their members. Their schools and social mechanisms educate, acculturate, and in general, structure young lives, insulating them and at the same time prudently exposing them to the larger non-Muslim community.

In Chicago, Los Angeles, and New York City, massive, anonymous urban centers with large immigrant populations of white ethnics, Latinos, and African Americans, the effectiveness of the Baptist Church could be minimal at best—affecting comparatively small, stable communities. On the other hand, one would think that the nightmare of everyday survival, the fears induced by the bureaucratic machinery of big government, the plurality of strongly different social and religious attitudes would have bewildered the migrants from the small towns and cities of the rural South, and the absence of opportunity for social participation in a racially brittle environment would have driven the migrants to recall the only form of social/religious experience they had known in their communities, the Church. However, the small, fragmented ghettos functioned within an urban context and its religious–moral idiom was not always amenable to the cultural traditions of newly arrived Southerners who could not easily identify the urban ministries as agents of solace and benefaction. In this respect, African-American migrants were not unlike Italian immigrants confronting an Irish Catholic clergy in America.[65]

It was this process of change in the midst of colliding values, perspectives, and needs that may have produced an ambivalence toward religious institutions among many migrant African Americans. In any case, research work on the transformation of African-American religious institutions in the context of demographic change and displacement regionally and structurally in terms of a rural–urban continuum might shed light on such issues as social coherence and fragmentation and their outcomes in the everyday life of people.

NOTES

1. Asa Briggs, *Victorian Cities* (Berkeley, CA: University of California Press, 1993).

2. Spiro Kostof, *The City Assembled: The Elements of Urban Form through History* (Boston: Bullfinch Press/Little, Brown, 1993).

3. National Commission on the Causes and Prevention of Violence, *To Establish Justice, To Ensure Domestic Tranquility Final Report* (Washington, DC: U.S. Government Printing Office, 1969).

4. William Whyte, *The Social Life of Small Spaces* (New York: Harper & Row, 1985).

5. Thomas A. Reppetto, *The Blue Parade* (New York: Free Press, 1978).

6. Mike Davis, *City of Quartz: Excavating the Future in Los Angeles* (New York: Verso Press, 1990).

7. John Sturner, Sheldon F. Greenberg, and Deborah Y. Faulkner, "Equipment and Facilities" in William A. Geller, ed. *Local Government Police Management*, 3rd ed., (Washington, DC: International City Management Association, Municipal Management Series, 1991).

8. Michael C. MacDonald, *America's Cities* (New York: Simon & Schuster, 1984); Wesley Skogan, "Fear of Crime and Neighborhood Change" in Albert J. Reiss Jr., and Michael Tonry, eds. *Communities in Crime* 1986, vol. 8 of *Crime and Justice: An Annual Review of Research*. (Chicago: University of Chicago Press, 1986) (203–229), and Richard M. McGahey, "Economic Conditions, Neighborhood Organization and Urban Crime" in Albert J. Reiss and Michael Tonry, eds. *Crime and Justice: A Review of Research*, vol. 8, (Chicago: University of Chicago Press, 1986), 231–270; James K Stewart, "The Urban Strangler: How Crime Causes Poverty in the Inner City," *Policy Review* 37 (Summer 1986): 2–6.

9. J. Hagedorn and P. Macon, *People and Folks: Gangs, Crime, and the Underclass in a Rustbelt City* (Chicago: Lake View Press, 1988); C. Taylor, *Girls, Gangs, Women and Drugs* (East Lansing: Michigan State University Press, 1993).

10. Irving Spergel, "Youth Gangs: Continuity and Change" in Norval Morris and Michael Tonry, eds. *Crime and Justice: An Annual Review of Research*, vol. 12,

(Chicago: University of Chicago Press, 1990): 173–197.

11. Carl S. Taylor, "Gang Imperialism" in C. Ronald Huff, ed. *Gangs in America* (Newbury Park, CA: Sage Publications, 1990): 103–115.

12. James F. Short, "New Wine in Old Bottles? Change and Continuity in American Gangs" in Huff, *Gangs in America*, 223–239.

13. Catherine H. Conly, Patricia Kelly, Paul Mahanna, and Lynn Warner, *Street Gangs: Current Knowledge and Strategies*, National Institute of Justice, Issues and Practices, U.S. Department of Justice, (Washington, DC: U.S. Government Printing Office, August 1993).

14. John Hagedorn, "Back in the Field Again: Gang Research in the Nineties" in Huff, *Gangs in America*, 246.

15. Office of the District Attorney, *Gangs, Crime and Violence in Los Angeles*.

16. Frederick M. Thrasher, *The Gang: A Study of 1,313 Gangs in Chicago*, abridged, (Chicago, University of Chicago Press, 1963); Martin S. Jankowski, *Islands in the Street, Gangs and American Urban Society* (Berkeley, CA: University of California Press, 1991); Mercer L. Sullivan, *Getting Paid: Youth Crime and Work in the Inner City* (Ithaca, NY: Cornell University Press, 1989); Robert J. Kelly, Ko-lin Chin, and Jeffrey Fagan, "The Structure, Activity and Control of Chinese Gangs: Law Enforcement Perspectives," *Journal of Contemporary Criminal Justice* 3, no. 3 (August 1993): 221–239.

17. U.S. Department of Justice, *Drugs and Crime Facts, 1993* (Rockville, MD: Drugs and Crime Data Center and Clearinghouse, 1993), 27.

18. William B. Sanders, *Gangbangs,* 4–5.

19. Ko-lin Chin, Jeffrey Fagan, and Robert J. Kelly, "Patterns of Chinese Gang Extortion," *Justice Quarterly*, 9, no. 4, (December 1992): 625–646.

20. Herbert Asbury, *Gangs of New York: An Informal History of the New York Underworld* (New York: Capricorn Books, 1928).

21. Robert J. Kelly, "Organized Crime: Past, Present and Future," *USA Today Magazine* 120 (May 1992): 78–80.

22. Sanders, *Gangbangs,* 11.

23. Los Angeles District Attorney, *Gangs, Crime and Violence*, 36.

24. Raimondo Castanzaro, *Men of Respect*.

25. U.S. Senate, Committee on Governmental Affairs, *Organized Crime: Twenty-five Years after Valachi* 100th Cong., 2nd sess., (Washington, DC: U.S. Government Printing Office, 1990).

26. Jankowski, *Islands in the Street*, 80–81.

27. Ibid., 132.

28. John Davis, *Mafia Dynasty: The Rise and Fall of the Gambino Crime Family* (New York: HarperCollins Publishers, 1993).

29. Pablo Oters, *Gang Violence in Connecticut* (Fairfield, CT: Connecticut State Police, 1993).

30. George F. Kain, "New England Entrepreneurs: The Nature of Gang Activity in Connecticut" (unpublished paper, Graduate School, The City University of New York, 1994).

31. J. Skolnick, T. Correl, C. Navarro, and R. Rabb, *The Social Structure of Street Gang Dealing* (Sacramento, CA: Office of the Attorney General, State of California, 1988).

32. Kody Scott, *Monster: The Autobiography of an L.A. Gang Member Sanyika Shakur, A.K.A. Monster Kody Scott* (New York: The Atlantic Monthly Press, 1993).

33. Jankowski, *Islands in the Street,* 69–70.

34. Lincoln R. Keiser, *The Vice Lords: Warriors of the Streets* (New York: Holt, Rinehart & Winston, 1969), 12–19.

35. Irving Spergel, "Youth Gangs: Continuity and Change," 177–179.

36. Report of the Independent Commission of the Los Angeles Police Department (Los Angeles, California: County of Los Angeles, 1991), 228.

37. Gorden Witkin with Muadi Mukenge, Monika Guttman, Anne Moncreiff Arrarte, Kukula Glastris, Barbara Burgower, and Aimee L. Stern, "The Men Who Created Crack," U.S. *News and World Report*, 19 August 1991, 44–53.

38. Ron Curran, "Malign Neglect: The Roots of an Urban War Zone," *L.A. Weekly*, 30 December to 5 January 1989.

39. C. Ronald Huff, ed., *Gangs in America*, Sanders, *Gangbangs* 116. The author reports that this practice of extorting money from school students is a reason to join a gang: to avoid being victimized.

40. Leon Bing, *Do or Die* (New York: HarperCollins Publishers, 1991).

41. Bureau of Census, *Statistical Abstract of the United States 1991*, 111th ed. (Washington, DC: U.S. Government Printing Office, 1991).

42. Mike Davis, *City of Quartz*, esp. chap. 5.

43. John Gregory Dunne, "Law and Disorder in Los Angeles," parts 1 and 2, *New York Review*, 10 October 1991, 23–29; 24 October 1991, 62–70.

44. Robert Reinbold, "Six Months after Riots, Los Angeles Still Bleeds," *New York Times*, 1 November 1992, 1.

45. Marc Cooper, "Falling Down," *The Village Voice*, 23 March 1993, 24–29.

46. Abadinsky, *Organized Crime*, chap. 5.

47. George Seibel and Ronald A. Pincomb, "From the Black P Stone Nation to the El Rukns: Reflections of a Chicago Street Cop," *Criminal Organizations* 8, nos. 3 & 4 (1994), 3–9.

48. Ibid., 4.

49. Ibid., 8.

50. E. R. Shipp, "Chicago Gang Sues to Be Recognized as Religion," *New York Times*, 27 December 1985, 8.

51. Carolyn R. Block and Richard Block, "Street Gang Crime in Chicago," *National Institute of Justice: Research in Brief*, Office of Justice Programs, U.S. Department of Justice (Washington, DC: U.S. Government Printing Office, December 1993), 1–11.

52. Robert J. Kelly and Rufus Schatzberg, "Types of Minority Organized Crime," Rufus Schatzberg, *Black Organized Crime*.

53. Seth Mydans, "Gangs Go Public in New Fight for Respect," *New York Times*, 2 May 1993, 1, L 38.

54. Eric J. Hobsbawn, *Primitive Rebels* (New York: Norton, 1959).

55. William Robbins, "Armed, Sophisticated and Violent, Two Drug Gangs Blanket Nation" *New York Times*, 25 November 1988, A 1, B 14.

56. Jerome Krase and Charles La Cerra, *Ethnicity and Machine Politics* (Lanborn, New York: University Press of America, 1991), 9.

57. Selwyn Raab, "The Ruthless Young Crack Dealers," *New York Times*, 20 March 1988, 1, B 6.

58. Erik Eckholm, "Teen-Age Gangs are Inflicting Lethal Violence on Small Cities," *New York Times*, 31 January 1993, B 1, 7–8.

59. Los Angeles District Attorney's Office, "Gangs, Crime and Violence," 36.

60. Cloward and Ohlin, *Delinquency and Opportunity*.

61. Craig D. Uchida, Brian Forst, and Sampson O. Aunon, "Controlling Street-Level Drug Trafficking: Evidence from Oakland and Birmingham," *National Institute of Justice*, U.S. Department of Justice (Washington, DC: U.S. Government Printing Office, June 1992).

62. Lynn Zimmer, "Operation Pressure Point: The Disruption of the Street-level Drug Trade on New York's Lower East Side" Occasional Paper, *Center for Research in Crime and Justice* (New York: New York University School of Law, 1987).

63. Catherine H. Conly, *Hearing Summary of the National Field Study on*

Gangs and Gang Violence, Dallas, Texas, U. S. Department of Justice, National Institute of Justice (Washington, DC: U.S. Government Printing Office, December 1991)

64. Bob Blauner, "The Outlaw Huey Newton," *New York Times Book Review,* 10 July 1994, 3, 22–23.

65. Robert J. Kelly, "Power and Piety: Early Experiences of Italian Immigrants in American Catholic Pastoral Life, 1880–1920" (paper presented to the University Seminar on Religion and Civil Society, City University of New York, 1980).

9 SUMMARY AND CONCLUSIONS

Three major historical trends are apparent in the evolution of organized crime in African-American communities throughout the twentieth century. From its beginnings in the urban enclaves of the 1920s, policy gaming (the numbers game based on clearing house bank totals that was first observed in Harlem) attracted a medley of players and providers, including legitimate business people, professionals, workers, and career criminals. Early African-American policy was well organized but hardly perceived as a "criminal" activity in the Harlem community. Its reputation for generating sizable profits brought the policy racket to the attention of formidable white crime syndicates that managed through collusion with corrupt politicians and police to wrest it away from its African-American originators and operators. Policy gambling was structured around banks, and an elaborate network of runners, collectors, and other organized-crime–like characteristics; in its early form under African-American dominance it did not harm the community in ways usually associated with such criminal conduct.

In the early decades of the twentieth century in Harlem and in other communities, numbers and policy were viewed as a highly public form of recreation and economic activity—part of the community's life. Numbers gambling was widespread and its operators enjoyed a degree of public esteem and respect. The influence of policy from a criminal standpoint was benign, and the crime correlative with it was small. When, however, it was absorbed into the orbits of white criminal syndicates, policy was transformed: It lost its communal quality, its symbiotic integration into the informal economics of the community, upon which so many residents relied.

In other African-American communities, enterprises that functioned illegally attracted career criminals within the community and could resist co-optation into powerful white syndicates. What Harlem's early policy syndicates lacked were the components of systemic violence—enough gunmen, gangsters, and street hoodlums who could mount defenses against competitors and predators, and political influence that could harness political protection.

The early "Kings and Queens" of policy never took up arms against the white mobs and the result was that the conventional vice industries in Harlem were yoked to the white underworld for the next forty years. In all cases, the lack of political influence worked against African-American criminal groups; their political marginality meant that in a showdown they were inconsequential.

In subsequent decades leading up and through World War II, African-American criminal enterprises in vice industries and drugs were satellite organizations dependent upon Cosa Nostra families and other organized crime groups. But as political and social power accumulated within African-American communities, the bonds of subordination loosened: The former clients of La Cosa Nostra asserted their independence and began to develop their own markets and sources—principally in drugs—and replace white groups.

Perhaps because there is no African-American equivalent of a Cosa Nostra crime family, the 1986 President's Commission on Organized Crime paid scant attention to criminal activity in African-American communities. The Commission's Report fleetingly refers to radical prison groups, active in the 1980s, as possible incubators for future syndicates. Yet, testimony presented at Commission hearings suggested that large-scale and low-level drug trafficking networks managed by African Americans could be found in every major community in the United States. Witnesses discussed levels of organization that were both highly structured and crude.

The Commission also ignored the important body of work by social scientists who have examined the linkages between organized crime and ethnic minorities and found that mainstream institutions had not been able to provide adequate service levels in poor communities. The vacuum is filled with informal, illegal entrepreneurs. The idea that an association exists between ethnic minorities and illegal enterprises in terms of structural blockages and opportunities has been well established, yet the Commission apparently chose not to wonder about what kinds of criminal behavior existed and were emerging in one of the most oppressed minorities in the United States.

The problem was not unique to the President's Commission. In an overview at a symposium on organized-crime control, the FBI Assistant Director of Investigations referred to "nontraditional" organized-crime groups, including "the outlaw motorcycle gangs, Mexican and Colombian narcotics' cartels, and Oriental organized crime gangs." Incredibly, there was no mention of African-American organized crime.

Despite the meltdown of the Mafia throughout the United States, brought on by vigorous prosecutions and mounting evidence that organized crime is not limited to the operation of La Cosa Nostra and its crime families, the latter still seems to dominate official and public thinking. The concession the President's Commission Final Report made concerning non-Italian organized crime was its recognition that Asian and Central and South American groups were playing significant roles in drug trafficking and minor extortion rackets in their ethnic communities. This is especially interesting in that official agencies have for some time abandoned alien conspiracy theories and embraced the view that organized crime is an integral part of the social system. Still, the fixation with the Mafia—a legacy perhaps from the Kefauver days and the emphasis placed on it by many official and academic studies—persists.

But why suppose that organized crime that does not fit the pattern of a mafia is not "organized"? The structure of African-American organized criminality may indeed vary from its white counterparts and its scale may be modest by Cosa Nostra standards; these aspects in themselves are suggestive of a continuum of organized criminality ranging along several axes of size, division of labor, normative operating procedures, and power to influence the external constraints likely to impinge upon their activities.

Because the Cosa Nostra/Mafia model may not apply neatly to African-American organized crime does not mean that it did not or does not exist. African Americans involved in ghetto criminal networks are driven by aims similar to those that motivated Irish, Jewish, and Italian criminals who preceded them: assimilation into, and accommodation by, the larger American society. Apart from pervasive, cruel poverty, the cultural and structural forces that shaped the growth and evolution of white, ethnic organized criminality may not yet be present among African Americans and Hispanics. There does not appear to be a cultural ethos coupled with a kinship system among African Americans that could produce a high degree of organizational development in criminal syndicates characteristic of Italians. Certainly, African-American criminal networks would be expected to respond to their own subcultural imperatives. And they may substitute in place of kinship and extended-family solidarity, peer relationships formed in street gangs and ties forged in prison. Also, strengthened by a common sense of victimization in a racist society, that process itself may form the catalyst necessary to produce and sustain enduring criminal enterprises among African-American criminals.

The rise of African-American organized-crime groups in the post–World War II era seems to have run alongside the rise of African-American political consciousness, with the awakening of social militancy. Major African-American traffickers in drugs surfaced at approximately the same time, the early and mid-1960s, when militant pressures were mounted for jobs, educational reform, fair housing, and a greater share of political power. Apparently, a combination of factors coalesced, some with unanticipated consequences, that produced legitimate and illegitimate opportunity structures. In the wake of sweeping reforms, African Americans gained greater control over their communities; and as their political strength grew, criminal elements were able to take advantage of the declines of white power and influence within the ghetto crime scene. Thus, they seemed poised more than at any other time to wrest the ghetto from bondage to white syndicates and emerged not only free of La Cosa Nostra political and police clout but also able to independently bargain with whites who were no longer able to exploit the ghettos.

As the ghettos developed their newfound strength and accumulated political punch, the political agent, the operator, the machine functionary, not unfamiliar in white communities, with connections in the "administration" or City Hall, appeared on the scene. And as the African-American ghettos became more politically assertive and economically more viable, a host of new actors arose. The "minority middlemen," the ghetto power brokers, were equally comfortable in the official world of government and business and in the ghetto shadows of opportunism and crime, where favors are arranged, deals are made, and prominent roles are assumed in social, economic, and political affairs.

The ghetto underworld is not a homogeneous, monolithic structure of power and influence wielded only by African Americans. Since the late 1960s in New York City, New Jersey, Baltimore, Washington, D.C., cities in Florida, California, and in Toronto, Canada, the Rastafarians have engaged principally in marijuana and cocaine smuggling on a comparatively large scale.

It is probable that, as with other ghetto-bound criminal groups, a system of patron/client relations exists that is more viable as an operational strategy in such a setting. What they do utilize are the two instruments that all durable criminal enterprises must possess: a capability and reputation for violence and criminogenic assets, including resources to corrupt and neutralize law enforcement control agencies.

Research on the ethnic and social organization of the minority vice industries suggests that sociocultural characteristics of provider subgroups are important factors affecting the manner in which responses are structured to meet consumer demands. Today, in major African-American communities where a large underclass exists, where unemployment is high and despair deep, crack/cocaine is the currency of the informal economy. To an extent unknown among the more traditional vice rackets, the crack gangs reflect the local dynamics of the emergent trafficking systems infecting communities. In these respects, modern minority criminal groups have little structural resemblance to La Cosa Nostra crime families. Still, these groups are no less dangerous, nor are they likely to be short-lived or only drug-dependent because the gangs may continue beyond the demand for crack and transform themselves to meet the illegal market conditions of other commodities in demand. Crack enables minority criminal groups to generate essential criminogenic assets (the use of violence and the availability and distributions of illegal commodities). Once established, these groups can explore other criminal opportunities in much the same way that the white criminal groups did in meeting the demand for illicit alcohol.

During the spread of minority gangs in the mid-1980s the United States was caught in a pincer movement: The Los Angeles street gangs moved east, and the Jamaican posses moved west, and between them, by the end of the decade, they had introduced much of the country to crack.

Compared with Los Angeles, other cities have been easy pickings, especially for "rollers" or "Ogs" (Original Gangsters) and others in their twenties, with a thirst for more serious cash, who have established a connection with Colombian suppliers. Crips and Bloods are reflections of a demographic bulge whose members tend to be in the most criminally prone age cohorts—adolescence to adulthood. Coupled with the high unemployment rate among young males (36 percent) the conditions for the rapid expansion of minority crime are present.

In communities where economic depression is severe, crime is often seen as an attractive alternative, if not the only one, to prolonged deprivation. The crime that emerges, however, is not in the least beneficial to these communities. Generally, illicitly earned income among gang members, primarily drug money, is not recirculated in the community, banked, invested in commercial enterprises, or used to capitalize commercial activities that benefit the community as a whole. Instead, income is usually used for personal luxury items or is reabsorbed by the drug economy, whose infrastructure lies outside the community of the users it exploits. Unlike the policy rackets, illicitly generated drug monies flow out and are drained off by large non-community-based syndicates.

Although the study of street gangs is emerging now as a vast cottage industry, little has been written about Los Angeles's sociologically destructive gang culture. This was not merely a gang revival but was instead a radical permutation of gang culture. The Crips inherited the Panther aura of fearlessness and transmitted the ideology of armed vanguardism; and "Crippin" often represents an escalation of intraghetto violence to "Clockwork Orange" levels (murder as a status symbol). The Crips have also blended a penchant for ultraviolence with an overweening ambition to dominate the entire ghetto. The Crips achieved, like the El Rukns in Chicago, a "managerial revolution" in gang existence. If they began as a teenage substitute for the fallen Panthers, they evolved through the 1970s into a hybrid of teen cult and proto-mafia.

Several factors affect the development and persistence of organized crime. Corruption of public and law enforcement officials is a primary prerequisite for traditional organized criminal activities. The level of corruption implemented by African Americans may not be as widespread, intricate, or exist on a scale as large as that of white organized crime. Among African Americans, corruption may still be rudimentary and minor compared to white activities. Several factors—some historical, others structural—may account for their putative absence in large-scale corruption. With ghetto-bound vice activities, corruption may be limited to small street payoffs. Scattered and independent, certain vice activities can flourish, but when they arouse public attention because of their profitability (as numbers gambling did fifty years ago), the pressures from police have increased to such an extent that they reorganized and eventually were subsumed into more powerful white crime syndicates against which they were helpless. Where criminal activities were capable of expanding beyond the confines of the ghetto community and extraghetto illicit profits were realizable, as with drugs, compromises and coordination with non-African-American crime activists occurred. Similarly, when white and other criminals infiltrate the African-American ghetto, they seem to require the permission of African Americans.

Ironically, law enforcement pressures on drug activities and markets appear to have spawned organized-crime-like characteristics among ghetto drug traffickers. One defining feature of organized crime is its resistance to law enforcement through corruption and violence that intimidates its victims and clients in order to reduce its vulnerability to investigations and prosecution.

As Kleiman points out, if the consequences of antidrug efforts at all levels of government are assessed, then some paradoxical outcomes are possible: (1) if the levels of drug enforcement losses incident to working in a drug market are relatively low, the disadvantages of heavily armored organization in terms of day-to-day dealings will outweigh their advantages in terms of keeping out the clutches of the law; (2) organizations with high-level capacities for violence have costs: customers, suppliers, and employees may understandably avoid such groups with reputations for mayhem and murder. On the other hand, with intensified enforcement, including more agents, arrests and seizures, prosecution, and incarceration, the losses incurred by free-lance dealers and those who lack the resources to frighten associates into silence and corrupt police, the losses incurred will make greater investments into enforcement resistance seem worthwhile. Tightened drug enforcement across the board will tend to give organized-crime groups and organized-crime-like groups relative competitive advantage, because their capacities for violence and corruption helps to shield them against ordinary enforcement actions.[1] Thus, drug dealers may be encouraged by determined street enforcement strategies to acquire organized-crime characteristics.

Drugs, especially heroin and, it seems, crack/cocaine, constitute what economists call a relatively inelastic demand product market.[2] Unlike markets in which product demand is elastic—where consumers respond to price increases by cutting back consumption or vice versa—with heroin and cocaine, changes in price and the availability of drugs have minor effects on consumption patterns. The side effects of price and product fluctuation are, however, considerable. As prices rise, street crimes are likely to increase, for example. If this is so, the drift of drug enforcement policy toward vigorous street enforcement is not desirable from an organized-crime-control perspective, although it may help reduce drug consumption. The key tension in organized crime and drug enforcement concerns the policy conundrum that effective drug enforcement may be badly organized crime control.

A Theory of African-American Organized Crime

Much of the theoretical work in organized crime research has been fraught with controversies over competing paradigms of Cosa Nostra organization and activities, and even whether an entity such as the "Mafia" actually exists.[3] Using the data discussed previously, we propose a theory of organized crime. A general theory of organized crime is desirable but at this stage in the field's development of data and sophistication, none seems plausible. As Reuter points out, theories of organized crime tend to be talking about different phenomena.[4] Reuter's point seems well taken: Cressey, a sociologist, builds a structural model that relates the interactional lives of power, authority, position, the division of criminal labor, and the various statuses within a crime family; Ianni, on the other hand, examines organized crime as a cultural response to particular social, economic, and political conditions that minorities confront in everyday life. In contrast to these orientations, Reuter, Schelling, and other economists think about organized crime in terms of illegal transaction of goods and services and the structure of illegal markets. Thus, different and often disparate pictures of organized crime confuse the law enforcement and scientific communities as well as the general public.

As we observed previously, the phenomenon is complex and lends itself to different analyses of its many features and constitutive elements, all of which seem equally plausible, but this often blinds us to the interplay of social, cultural, and economic factors in communities where crime is viable as a supplement to, or substitute for, legitimate opportunities and institutional supports.

We begin with exclusions. Organized crime in African-American communities cannot be reasonably thought of as an "alien conspiracy," as with ethnic immigrant groups who, it is alleged, brought their forms of organized crime into the United States. Proponents of conspiracy theories, and this usually means believers in a Mafia conspiracy, contend that a secret organization originating elsewhere, not indigenous to the United States, made its way here during a period of massive immigration.[5] With the exception of Jamaican Posses, the manifestations of organized criminality among African Americans seem to have emerged out of the social conditions of their communities and lives. It is, of course, psychologically convenient and reassuring to posit immigrant groups as the purveyors of crime; it serves as a *diabolus ex machina*, a foreign evil force, that if purged will mean the restoration of safe, crime-free communities, no matter how poor or oppressed. It is arrogant and a distortion of the facts to attribute organized crime to some immigrant, foreign groups. Jamaicans and Nigerians are engaged in drug trafficking and smuggling, but they are not the dominant criminal forces in African-American or any other communities. More to the point, early chroniclers of organized crime wrote of community environments, of the social and economic aspects of big-city life as the incubators of crime.[6]

The bureaucratic model proposed that organized crime is structurally similar to corporations. This was popularized by the 1967 Task Force Report[7] that described Cosa Nostra crime families as virtually no different than the bureaucratic skeleton of any large-scale business corporation. What the Cressey model described was a crime bureaucracy—a group of criminals rationally deployed in specific positions in a power hierarchy whose purpose is the efficient achievement of goals. The model has been challenged as too rigid and has not been tested or confirmed by empirical studies.

Other approaches to organized crime depict it not as a transplanted foreign import or as a formal organization, but as an integral part of our socioeconomic system, following in the tradition of earlier scholars who saw the community as the environment that bred crime. The chief exponent of this line of argument has been Francis A. J. Ianni.[8] For Ianni, the issue of origins in the acrimonious debate that raged as to whether organized crime in the United States was controlled by twenty-four Mafia crime families is cast aside as irrelevant. Recognizing the presence and formidable power of Italian-American syndicates is one thing; what needs examination is how, if at all, the socioeconomic status of ethnic and racial communities in urban areas is a potential breeding ground for organized crime as official reports describe it.

Ethnic succession refers to the process whereby ethnic, racial, and religious groups—usually immigrants or minorities—use organized crime as a means of social mobility. The interesting question arising from this perspective concerns the variations in the ethnic and racial composition of the American underworld and what this tells us about social stratification, economic opportunity, and social mobility in society at large.

Broadly conceived, the historical evidence suggests a sequence of ethnic groups dominating certain types of crime in cities where they permanently settle, with control eventually passing from one to another slowly or rapidly, violently or sometimes relatively peacefully, and not immediately noticeable. Ethnic succession also suggests that organized crime groups do not spring to life fully matured but develop through stages of increasing sophistication to the point where they may merge into the legitimate sectors of the society. Above all, if they have any continuity and durability they must be sensitive to local social and economic conditions. Their expansion or contraction is usually a consequence of several factors: markets for illegal goods and services, criminal competition, law enforcement pressures, and above all, community reactions.

In the case of African Americans, organized crime has always had a presence. Not as large or powerful as Cosa Nostra families, and often forced to submit to them, it takes numerous forms in response to community conditions and demands, from policy rackets and gambling enterprises to drug trafficking in modern inner-city communities. The structure and form also vary in terms of the nature of the products and services offered: the size and wealth of the consumer markets; the strength of criminal competition; law enforcement zeal in control, its corruption, neutrality and indifference; and the general response of the community at large through its institutional infrastructures. If some community institutions possess community influence, such as the African-American religious organizations, this may check the spread and contagion of crime.

Ethnic succession does not seem to apply to African-American communities in the way it has worked among Jews, for instance. During the great immigration period at the beginning of the twentieth century, the Jewish underworld expanded, keeping pace with the influx of Eastern and Southern European Jews. Jewish crime—at least, the type associated with street vice and rackets—was a transient phenomenon, destined to virtually disappear as the immigrants Americanized and became more surefooted in their new homeland. Organized crime within the Jewish ghettos and enclaves could be seen in part as a consequence of the immigration experience and the economic marginality it engendered. Anti-Semitism also further stigmatized and isolated Jews, which slowed their social mobility considerably, but crime itself was not an outcome of some collective defect or cultural flaw. As Jews assimilated and acculturated, in spite of all the obstacles they encountered, the underworld that had developed and thrived in their ghettos slowly faded. And those Jews who continued to pursue criminal careers tended to do so in enterprises and circumstance divorced from Jewish contexts.[9]

For purposes of this discussion, characteristics identified by Hagan and Maltz are appropriate for creating a classification schema that may be applied to African-American groups of criminals.[10] Organized crime, according to these writers, means criminal enterprises. In addition, there are other distinctive, defining characteristics: corruption, violence, continuity, and involvement in multiple criminal enterprises. These attributes are thought to be features of all organized-crime groups. Corruption, for example, is a mechanism used to nullify and to immunize groups from law enforcement, and to gain an edge (as we saw with Schultz and Salerno and other white gangsters in Harlem in the 1930s and 1950s), in the competition for markets and contracts. The potential for violence, or its threat, also appears to be omnipresent in organized-crime groups. Because they lack legitimate access to the legal system, it is through the use or threat of violence that organized criminal groups keep both competition and internal rebellion suppressed. Continuity is an attribute that means a group is self-perpetuating. It continues beyond the life or participation of any particular individuals.

Then there are the characteristics of *structure* and *involvement* in legitimate business. *Structure* refers to a criminal division of labor elaborated into roles and positions. Some organized-crime groups, primarily Italian–American crime families, appear to have a fairly well-structured hierarchy with leaders, bosses, and subordinates in a rank order of authority; and each position calls for varied jobs and responsibilities. This is, at least, the traditional description of organized-crime groups. One further feature deserves mention. It is characteristic of many members of Cosa Nostra and is thought by many scholars to reflect the dynamic organizational logic of criminal organization: Almost all organized-crime members own, share partnerships in (secret or overt), or work in legitimate businesses as well as in their illegitimate enterprises.

In addition to enterprise, the two other dimensions that distinguish organized crime—at least historically—are ethnicity and conspiracy. Ethnicity has been a defining element of organized crime among Italian, Chinese, Cuban, Japanese, Nigerian, Jamaican, Irish, German, Polish, Vietnamese, and other groups, and continues to be so. There are a number of factors associated with ethnicity that create an environment out of which crime in general and organized crime in particular can grow. Some of these are tied to the link that often exists between ethnicity and being an immigrant. Ethnicity-related factors include a greater sense of trust and kinship among fellow members, which makes it easier to operate because they share so many tacit cultural understandings. Besides its social-bonding, cultural facets of language and customs, ethnicity has some disadvantages for potential victims: It describes, especially for immigrants, a target population of special vulnerability; fellow ethnics are usually best positioned to exploit those who have difficulties in finding legitimate occupational opportunities, who are ignorant about the social expectations and customs, and lack language facility. They can be exploited as victims or recruited into crime.

Substituting "race" for "ethnicity" in the case of African Americans suggests analogously that whereas ethnicity has operated in American society to create the thresholds for participation in organized crime, so too does race. Racial discrimination, as has ethnic immigrant status, may function as a mechanism prompting many African Americans into crime through an alternative set of opportunities—a "queer ladder of social mobility."

We have seen that criminal enterprises have emerged in African-American communities. These possessed varying degrees of sophistication, structure, durability, and continuity. In the 1920s and 1930s, enterprises were communally oriented gambling operations linked closely to the neighborhoods and not generally perceived as threatening. Other criminal activities included prostitution and narcotics, which were entrepreneurial, individualistic, and not organized on a broad scale. And where political influence was lacking—that is, where the capacity to corrupt was modest at best—African-American criminal enterprises were easily crushed by more politically powerful criminal competitors.

Throughout the 1940s and into the 1960s and 1970s, African-American organized criminal groups were yoked to Mafia crime families either through coercion or voluntarily for supplies of illicit goods and services to meet the demand. Efforts to develop autonomy did not succeed until drugs entered the picture. And even then it was not until the 1970s that independent African-American groups began to reclaim their racial territories as their criminal "markets."

Drugs provided significant opportunities for criminal conspiracies. *Conspiracy* addresses the issue of how a particular criminal activity is planned. It is the operating strategy; it accounts for the methodical, systematic, and secretive action of sophisticated criminal groups. In the 1980s and 1990s, cocaine became the product that enabled many African-American criminal groups to amass wealth and develop the potential for racketeering and infiltration of legitimate businesses. This process is unfolding and developing. In comparison with La Cosa Nostra, drug gangs with a growing diversified criminal portfolio may best be described as a "proto-mafia"— as a Mafia in the making.

Over time, assuming that social and economic conditions do not change radically, it seems likely that African-American criminal organizations will broaden their scope and go beyond satisfying the need of local drug markets (although this is a formidable and lucrative enterprise in itself) and operate vigorously as their political influence increases in many illicit sectors previously closed to them.

There are indicators that African Americans demonstrate in incipient form many of the characteristics—with certain qualifications for ethnicity and race—that have been historically associated with the growth and development of organized crime in America.

Clearly, what groups do exist are not homogeneous. Some are sophisticated, employ violence, have some degree of structure, and may shrewdly corrupt law enforcement agents and public officials. What is not known is the degree of continuity of various groups; nor is much known about their size, their internal structures, how members become members, the kinds of internal discipline exercised, or whether there are codes of secrecy and behavior.

A key component identified as a necessary condition ensuring the viability of criminal organizations is corruption. It is a uniquely powerful instrument. The dismal record of major urban areas with respect to organized crime corresponds with long histories of machine control of such cities where the social and political exclusion of African Americans was obvious. The focus on local political authority is, of course, arguable. Perhaps the emergence of recent ethnic groups, the Chinese, for example, demonstrates that the corruption of political authority is not necessary for the initial acquisition of durable power. However, the formation and maintenance of criminal enterprises among the Chinese have been limited to the confines of the ethnic ghetto. To the extent that illegal market opportunities provide attractive alternatives, groups of individuals will move to provide goods and services. In addition, the persistence of depressed economic conditions and inadequate institutional infrastructures (schools, police, health and human service organizations, churches) that loosen ties to the dominant political/ social culture provide a breeding ground for recruits into organized criminality. Corruption comes into play as a tool for sustaining and expanding criminal enterprise. The susceptibility of local political authority to corruption in the near future should profoundly affect the maintenance, continuity, and growth potential of African-American organized-crime groups.

The traditional perspective on organized crime in America may be understood in a three-stage model with some variations allowing for institutional control and containment responses from official agencies. The conditions favorable to organized crime in general and for specific African-American versions of it are as follows:

1. Continued discrimination in the society at large that impedes economic development
2. The existence of a criminal-underworld structure in the United States that encourages entry and participation in crime
3. A perception that law enforcement and criminal justice are weak and therefore not deserving of fear and respect.

African-American criminal groups demonstrate in incipient form many of the characteristics that have historically been associated with the growth and development of organized crime in America. If the conditions listed previously persist, a coalescence of disparate and competing groups may develop—much like the formation of large syndicates during Prohibition, when previously warring gangs merged in the interests of survival and profits. Drugs may be the bonding mechanism bringing together African-American criminal organizations.

In terms of the traditional models, the end of Prohibition and the internal struggles among Italian factions (The Castellammarese War) provoked two milestones in the American underworld: (1) the collapse of the Prohibition syndicate alliances and (2) the emergence and eventual dominance of La Cosa Nostra as the most formidable criminal organization. Its power and predominance, however, precipitated governmental responses that have decapitated the leadership of the crime families and set in motion internal gang warfare and succession crises. Whether the law enforcement apparatus of RICO prosecutions, undercover work, electronic surveillance, and other anticrime strategies permanently weakens La Cosa Nostra remains to be seen.

In the case of African-American groups, however, should the process of coalescence materialize, and this is problematic, the possibilities of their expansion beyond the ghettos into racketeering and symbiotic merging with the legitimate sector will depend upon their capacities to exercise a key criminogenic asset: corruption. If La Cosa Nostra is any guide to historical experience, it is clear that its growth and influence depended upon the characteristics of ethnic solidarity and the deft employment of corruption and violence. Many African-American groups have demonstrated their ability to use violence, but whether they can corrupt law enforcement agencies and political officials to facilitate their survival and growth awaits history.

Finally, it is necessary to remind ourselves that the discussions and analyses focus on particular segments of the African-American community. The constant harping on Mafia threatens to produce a stereotypical, one-dimensional vision of Italian-American life as intrinsically criminal. Likewise, there is the danger that one segment of the African-American community might be seen as representing the whole, and it is not difficult to see how this can happen. First, because impoverished African Americans are the most sensitive to the ups and downs of the economy, are more vulnerable to crime and injustice, and because, until the last few decades, the bulk of the population was located on the lower rungs of the economic ladder, the political agenda emphasized measures that called for jobs, social services, training, and education focused on the poor and near poor. And while affirmative-action measures compelled an otherwise recalcitrant white society to open the doors of opportunity for the African-American middle-class, the social-welfare programs targeted at the lower class have shown few positive results.

According to the 1990 Census, over a twenty-year period the number of African-American families with incomes under $15,000 rose to 37 percent of the population at the same time those with incomes of more than $50,000 rose from approximately 10 percent to 15 percent of the African-American population. The gap between the haves and have-nots has grown considerably, and as the underclass image is reinforced in the media, refractory impoverishment—which is real and unnerving—sustains the crime statistics. Another reason why the underclass image threatens to generate lasting impressions of African-American life and culture in general, and why a more balanced picture does not emerge, has to do with political expediencies of both white and African-American political leaders. Even the mass media embraces the African-American subcultural world as one of downtrodden families (usually female-headed), living in communities replete with drug dealers, users, and gun-toting adolescents. The focus on poverty made sense because this was and is a serious threat to social and economic mobility. Unfortunately, it distorts the picture of the community at large and may only add to the fear within the white society of the African-American young male, who is often depicted in the popular imagination as a dangerous predator. The spectacle of more policing, more arrests, and simultaneous reductions in social-reform programs adds fuel to the fire of racial apprehensions and casts doubt about future social and economic prospects that would enhance hope and opportunity.

Our last point is simply made. If organized criminal behavior is conceived as an outcome of racism in its many manifestations and actualities (as we do), then affirmative-action, social-welfare programs, and educational reforms just short of revolutionary are the antidote to virulent racism. If one considers racism analogous to a virus, an invasion of the social body's equilibrium, so should the remedial antibody of socially sensitive reform policies "invade" the body politic. Why we do not equate the two and decline to fight the disease because the medicine we employ may be temporarily disruptive of normal functioning is the great moral issue that, if undecided, will continue to express itself in the ways described here. Strong illness, strong remedy—the formula is as appropriate to the health of the body politic as it is to the body proper.

NOTES

1. Mark A. R. Kleiman, "Organized Crime and Drug Abuse Control," 401–414.

2. Peter Reuter and Mark A. R. Kleiman, "Risks and Prices: The Economics of Drug Enforcement" in Michael H. Tonry and Norval Morris, eds. *Crime and Justice: An Annual Review of Research* (Chicago: University of Chicago Press, 1986): 115–135.

3. Robert J. Kelly, "The Nature of Organized Crime and Its Operations," 5–50.

4. Peter Reuter, "Research on American Organized Crime" in Robert J. Kelly, Rufus Schatzberg, and Ko-lin Chin, eds. *A Handbook on Organized Crime in the United States*, 91–120.

5. Joseph Albini, *The American Mafia: Genesis*, 91–120.

6. John Landesco, "Organized Crime in Chicago," part 2, *Illinois Crime Survey* (Chicago: Illinois Association for Criminal Justice, 1929); Frederick Thrasher, *The Gang* (Chicago: University of Chicago Press, 1963).

7. Task Force on Organized Crime, *1967 Task Force Report: Organized Crime*. (Washington, DC: U.S. Government Printing Office).

8. Francis A. J. Ianni, *Ethnic Succession in Organized Crime: A Summary Report*, Law Enforcement Assistance Administration, U.S. Department of Justice

(Washington, DC: U.S. Government Printing Office, 1973); Ianni, *Black Mafia.*

9. Jenna W. Joselet, *Jewish Crime and the New York Jewish Community, 1900–1940* (Bloomington: Indiana University Press, 1983).

10. Michael D. Maltz, "Defining Organized Crime" in Robert J. Kelly, Ko-lin Chin, and Rufus Schatzberg, eds., *Handbook on Organized Crime in the United States,* 21–38; Frank Hagan, "The Organized Crime Continuum: A Further Specification of a New Conceptional Model," *Criminal Justice Review* 8 (1983): 52–57.

EPILOGUE

AN EXCURSUS ON THE CRIMINAL TOPOGRAPHY OF THE AFRICAN-AMERICAN
SOCIAL EXPERIENCE

The history contained in this book deals with events, clear and obscure, and with ideas and emotions. Particularly in matters of crime and criminal justice, students find themselves overwhelmed by the heterogeneity of the data. Materials are, for the most part, only slightly measurable, and are not, except to a limited extent, empirically comparable. They are of all types and levels of sophistication: from the shoddiest journalism to gracefully written and cogent accounts of serious sociological investigations; from personal memoirs to full-scale biographies. Under these circumstances, the first and major temptation to be avoided is the urge to be encyclopedic. The desire, laudable in itself, to "cover" material adequately—to write some sort of "definitive" study—when applied to the field of crime verges on a dangerous illusion.

Another lure that must be resisted are the enticements to see a clear design, or to impose a neat pattern on recalcitrant data. The prominence of the La Cosa Nostra model so widely and, in our view, recklessly employed by both law enforcement practitioners and scholars, has distorted the realities of African-American crime, because the employment of explanatory models developed out of databases assembled from Cosa Nostra criminal behavior does violence to the integrity of material of non-mafia phenomena. We have not hesitated to structure our data using modern theories and perspectives, nor have we shied away from the obvious variations on those models that the African-American experience demonstrate.

Naturally, social scientists specializing in African-American life have been consulted throughout the course of this study, whatever their area of speciality. Inevitably, these are references to deviant behavior and criminal conduct in works concerned with poverty, family life, delinquency, racial discrimination, education, community, social-class mobility, politics and economics of minority businesses, and so on.

One of the *dramatis personae* in early African-American studies is the towering figure of W. E. B. Du Bois—a man of enormous intellectual power and versatility, whose influence was exercised and still resonates across several intellectual disciplines. Perhaps next we should mention E. Franklin Frazier and Oliver Cox, social scientists whose work on race and class issues was without parallel in the pre–civil rights movement period. On the importance of these figures, along with St. Clair Drake, Horace Cayton, and Kenneth Clark, there is little serious doubt. Modern scholars following these traditions include, among others, John Hope Franklin, William Julius Wilson, Orlando Patterson, Hyland Lewis, Eugene Genovese, and Martin Bernal.

The idea of consulting a number of imaginative writers may appear somewhat questionable in a social-scientific monograph. Although we have not written literary history, in our century we think it is apparent that more than ever before, literary artists have come to play a serious and self-conscious role in the enunciation of values and the presentation of issues, more than was the case in the last century, with the obvious exception of Frederick Douglass. The novel, theatrical drama, and film have developed the task of making concrete and thereby more readily approachable the insights and findings of the philosophers and social scientists. Imaginative African-American literature in our time has reached a stage of sophistication and aesthetic beauty that is, in terms of its quantity and quality, unprecedented. One might say that we are in the midst of a second "Renaissance." African-American literature in the twentieth century has done much more than popularize the work of scholars, it has surrounded its depiction of society with a penumbra of symbol and suggestion and has not only borrowed from academic scholarship but also fed its own discoveries and ideas back into social theory in a dense interplay of reciprocal influence.

Much of the literature that does treat crime and the criminal justice system is personally redemptive and salvational, rendered with great skill from the inside and from the vantage point of the victim. *The Autobiography of Malcolm X* by Malcolm Little, *Soul on Ice* by Eldridge Cleaver, *Soledad Brother* by George Jackson and, more recently, *Monster: The Autobiography of an L.A. Gang Member Sanyika Shakur, A.K.A. Monster Kody Scott* by Kody Scott, break the silence of the inner city and do much more: They render the despair and decay of the ghetto and also palpably provide the voices that Toni Morrison believes are essential in any genuine effort to start again. Morrison thinks of radical emergence as a rupture of the beleaguered "us" and the "other" and she does so in criminal justice terms:

Silence from and about the subject was the order of the day. Some of the silences were broken, and some were maintained by authors who lived with and within the policing strategies. What I am in interested in are the strategies for breaking it.[1]

In our analysis of organized criminality as a social phenomenon that involves the role of "policing strategies," we are also especially concerned with showing appropriation of the Mafia metaphor—itself a denigrating description of Italian-American culture—and its licensing as an analytical tool explaining the alien, conspiratorial nature of crime. A theoretical version of this ethnic provenance is a model of origins and development that describes organized crime in psychological, economic, and sociological terms. One hears of "predators," "parasitic" and ultimately "symbiotic" relationships and liaisons as emblematic and definitive of ethnic organized crime groups.[2] The Cosa Nostra/Mafia model obliterates history and becomes the paradigm of research, scholarship, and law enforcement practice. These are matters not simply of academic speculation but of urgent political moment. The predominance of the mafia stereotype testifies to the invalidity of much mainstream criminological scholarship to confront the challenge of its own domain supposition; some daring professional self-reflexivity would reveal many of the biases and prejudices embedded in this area of scholarship. For example, as Reed asks provocatively but pointedly about media coverage of violence among African Americans: Why is it, he wonders, that such violence is portrayed as pathological whereas violence among whites can be explained away? And why, Mr. Reed writes, "while Asian Americans are promoted as a model minority by an establishment media, their tangle of pathologies being virtually ignored, Latinos are all but invisible?"[3]

Were one to turn the pages of Shakur's (aka, Monster Kody Scott) account of his life as a Los Angeles street-gang member without an informed frame of reference of violent criminal behavior among impoverished minorities, the impression left would be that of a massive psychosis hanging over the ghetto. Put in perspective, however, the African-American story against crime and violence is one of triumph instead of failure. Violence is not the sole province of African Americans. The racial and ethnic history of the United States of 130 years ago is ripe with the prefiguring of modern ethnic and racial conflicts in cities such as Chicago, Boston, Philadelphia, Los Angeles, and New York. In New York, the clashes between immigrant Irish and African Americans during the draft riots of 1864 bear an uncanny resemblance to contemporary struggles for power in the Jewish/African-American tensions in the Crown Heights section of Brooklyn and in the abrasive exchanges between the Nation of Islam and Jewish organizations around the country.

At the height of the Civil War, the worst of poverty and prejudice bedeviled African Americans fleeing from the slave-bound South and hordes of Irish immigrants escaping from Ireland's horrific potato famine and infamous British Corn Laws. Scrambling for sanctuary, both groups clustered as rival outcasts in the teeming slums of New York. Across the decades, both groups secured "footholds" in construction through the mechanisms of church faith and shrewd city politics; and they rose up, sometimes through the expediencies of crime, from slums where their frictions exploded in a chilling bit of history.

The draft riots, which cost 119 lives, surely rank as the worst in American urban history—more bloody and savage than the racial–labor confrontations in St. Louis and Kansas City. The riots pitted the Irish against government forced military mobilization policies but victimized African Americans. For the upper classes who witnessed this grisly episode, it was a shot across the privileged bow; sooner or later it would occur to the combatants that they were being duped and used as cannon fodder in a struggle whose ultimate beneficiaries would be the affluent middle and upper classes, whose nativist antagonisms exploited both immigrant and former slave. An outcome of the rioting impelled by those fearsome disorders was city housing, sanitation, and public safety reforms. But so was the enduring accusation that the Irish "underclass" was largely responsible for creating its problems.

By the middle of the nineteenth century, African Americans were already a generation deep into American history when they lost their menial and skilled jobs to the immigrant population. Although there was some honest intermingling in the racial conflict, the Irish appropriated the American advantage of being white to struggle out of the entanglements of poverty and abuse.

Other parallels with modern African-American experience stand out. In 1863, the Irish had "Dagger John" Archbishop John Hughes, a tough, raucous defender and spiritual shepherd, an Irish clan chieftain, who because of his bare-knuckle style never fully enjoyed the confidence of the Vatican bureaucracy of the Roman Catholic Church and was never admitted into its inner sanctum as a cardinal. The Archbishop was the voice of the beleaguered immigrants who were mocked, denigrated, and resented for their cholera-ridden shantytowns, their lack of education, their homelessness and child neglect, and their drug addiction (alcoholism). Today, there is a bewildered and angry public that is too often quick to lay the ravages of drugs, crime, AIDS, school dropouts, and family disintegration in the laps of African Americans; and there is a tradition of advocacy by spiritual leaders in the community, whose political activism is reminiscent of Bishop Hughes. African-American ministers follow in the footsteps of Rev. Martin Luther King and Rev. Adam Clayton Powell, who serve as spiritual shepherds and "clan chieftains."

Following through on the possibilities in our search for continuities that history is revelatory, it is reasonable to suppose that the policy rackets in the ghetto and communities in the pre–World War II period were examples of organized crime in its infancy and that as conditions changed, so would the structure and composition of organized criminal behavior. Instead, we discovered discontinuities, radical departures from both the style of crime, the behavior of participants, and, significantly, the types of individuals drawn into it. For instance, many standard accounts begin with the influx of drugs in the ghettos, seeing these as the bases of incipient growth and criminal coalescence. Our research uncovered data showing that policy, gambling, and prostitution rackets were the incubators of subsequent traditions. Thus, the drug-oriented crime groups merely amalgamated and transformed earlier organizational and criminal cultural styles of earlier practice. The evidence, however, forced a new understanding of our fundamental assumptions.

African-American organized crime is a kaleidoscope of activities, embracing the familiar traditional vices and new forms of syndicate crime. The sheer diversity of groups, their structural variations, and participants defies the predictability and control strategies that emerged in historical periods in which the community was less porous, more likely to reflect the class complexities and heterogenous lifestyles of African Americans. Today, the racial ghetto as contrasted with the African-American community is an economic dead end. Its inhabitants tend to be increasingly "underclass" people with few opportunities and little hope. Thus, it is violent because it is full of despair; those who can, leave; those who cannot, find themselves in "hoods"—well-armed gang-defined territories, where police venture cautiously and only occasionally.

In these impoverished communities in particular, there is much freelance crime and also organized crime, but not of the Cosa Nostra variety. There are no "vice areas" to speak of that surround or are part of African-American neighborhoods, as was true decades earlier in Cleveland and in New York, with its tenderloin district, in Columbus, Ohio, with its "Badlands," in Detroit and its "Heights," catering to disreputable clientele. Racism was at high tide and it may still be. In the years immediately after World War I, law enforcement officials and political authorities were actively engaged in African-American community life, not as servants of the people, but as manipulators and exploiters. Morrison's diagnoses about "policing strategies" that inflict harm and foster crime are borne out by historical analysis. African-American communities were ravaged by red-light districts catering to vices—all tolerated and encouraged by police and white politicians.[4]

It seems clear that organized crime in African-American communities is not just a mutation on the dominant Cosa Nostra theme. Take as a specific instance of this issue, the theoretical projections and impositions, the so-called "Black Mafia" motif, which appears in much of the government literature and in reports and conference proceedings. In these documents, there is the *topos* of minority crime compared with the vaunted La Cosa Nostra with emphasis on its control, hegemony, and authority. Ianni's research[5] in Harlem, after his groundbreaking ethnography of a Mafia family,[6] attempted to verify his hypotheses on ethnic succession by describing the organization processes and beginnings of what he called a "Black Mafia." Instead, he found hybrid versions of "networks"—small-time hoodlums involved in a number of petty criminal activities lacking those bonding mechanisms of Italian mafia cliques that confer power and durability.

The literature and evidence from the ghettos and communities themselves in terms of Italian crime-family models offer a more complex picture of crime: Some of it is a feeble attempt to replicate Italian–American crime families; other accounts are nothing more, or less, than descriptions of satellite criminal groups yoked to white gangsters for protection, supply of illicit products, and sundry other resources.

If we think of mafia as a generic criminal culture rather than as an organizational entity, then the evidence suggests that the incipient elements are in place and the crucial ingredients present for criminal behavior geared to the illicit demands and appetites of the African-American communities.

In the wake of the civil rights movement, which awakened the county to the intrinsic immorality of racism, a resistance developed among the victims, accompanied by a polemical literature that sought to revitalize communities by eradicating their immediate evils; crime, especially drug trafficking and vices, were defined as importations into the African-American communities, as instances of the colonization and imperialism enveloping the ghetto. Through literature and street action, through community organization and low-level electoral politics, and the vigorous proselytizing of clergy—Christian and Muslim—a disenchantment set in, unleashing on oppositional culture, sometimes expressed in violence (the Black Liberation Army), and sometimes in separatist ideology promising racial liberation (the

Nation of Islam). The latter two groups seem to be expressions of an immense cultural shift in certain segments of the African-American communities away from the terrain of the ghetto and its dispiriting sensibilities to the theoretical domains of liberation and equality. For the Nation of Islam, freedom from the ghetto wasteland of crime, oppression, drugs, and degradation requires, according to Minister Louis Farrakhan, an act of political will and a deep psychological, introspective conversation with oneself; for others, violence against the agencies of oppression—the police, schools, courts, and prisons—will loosen the grip of enslavement. Popular expressions of this culturally inaugurated thinking are found in some militant rap music and "gangsta" rap, which is how many ghetto youth see their worlds; when arrested, they speak of being "captured" by "Amerikans," and refer to their friends and associates as "Afrikans"—those alert to the constrictions of inequity and hostility prevalent in a society dominated by racists.

Fanon, who puts the issue of racism more dramatically and decisively than anyone, although expressing his concern in the context of international imperialism, provides us with a collective, inclusive conception of remediation and reanimation when he urges Europeans to repudiate the impulses toward domination and debasement and to "stop playing the stupid fawn of the Sleeping Beauty."[7]

For Fanon, violence is a method that enables the oppressed to overcome the divisions between racially diverse groups and he infers that, in some ways, violence and crime also serve similar psychological purposes in African-American ghettos. Organized crime is clearly opportunistic and instrumental, but the abundant violence associated with so much of it seems simply gratuitous—a way of striking out, even against one's own, against the emotional destruction and impotence one feels.

CHALLENGING THEORETICAL ORTHODOXY AND AUTHORITY

The relevance of modern social–scientific and criminological theories that focus extensively on African-American crime is being debated within the disciplines.[8] The claim is that a paradigmatic asymmetry afflicts contemporary criminological work attributable to a lack of sufficient numbers of African-American criminologists and the absence of a subfield concerned with the exploration of a body of research that may be termed "black criminology." We have seen that various models of organized crime are indeed partial and even biased because of their data sources and unreflexive ethnocentric conceits. In general, they lack a sensitivity to social–ecological variables involved in criminal behavior and do not give serious, detailed attention to race as a key variable; and, in what seems characteristic of mainstream criminological research, the theoretical approaches fail to differentiate the diversity of racial ethnicity, such that racial identity is confused with ethnic homogeneity. Thus, the picture of African-American crime is incomplete because it is crude and undifferentiated. We might add that, with few exceptions, the body of mainstream criminological theory is stunningly silent on racist-oriented theory. The silence might generously be construed as a oversight or as a deliberate abstention in the interest of more generalizable, race-blind science.

Racism did not end, did not suddenly become the past when the civil rights movement helped to dismantle the vestiges of Jim Crow segregation. A legacy of connections still binds communities throughout the United States in what Georges-Abeyie tellingly refers to as "petit-apartheid."[9] Race and its social ramifications are still without question a most powerful force in everyday life in the United States, and, although poverty, race, and crime constitute a well-known triad in the public's view, nevertheless, the cultural implications of such realities are often screened out of criminological and deviance theorizing.

A look at some influential theories of deviance and crime will illustrate the points we have been making. What are called "control," "strain," and "cultural deviance" theories represent three of the most dominant perspectives in American criminology since the 1950s. Strain and cultural deviance theories seek to explain why individuals and groups engage in delinquency and crime, whereas control theories reverse the causal order by examining the question as to why more individuals and groups do not engage in more crime.[10] The major statements of these theories were developed more than three decades ago and nurtured several research streams and specialities in street-gang theory and community studies. The current focus on gangs incorporates ethnic and racial variables in their descriptive narratives with attention to the empirical testing of these well-established criminological theories.[11]

Russell's point that African-American youth crime is disastrously high cannot be disputed, but the links between race and crime are not clear. Surely, she does not mean to suggest that there is some genetic and biological difference that will explain it; nor, in view of recent research developments over the past fifteen years, can one claim persuasively that low-income levels alone in inner-city communities are connected causally with criminal behavior. This has been the popular thinking that no longer is widely supported in the social science literature.

What Russell must mean by her emphasis on race and crime is that traditional theories about crime, ethnicity, poverty, and education, among other variables including race, are not satisfactory. Indeed, the theoretical complications in the field have led back to theories based on individual psychology and biology.[12] These "biologically" oriented approaches tend to see criminals as fundamentally different from other people—less bound by cultural restraints and less rational in behavior.[13] Crime is portrayed as the product of individuals of low intelligence or with defective personalities. Furthermore, high crime rates in certain localities are explained as the result of the movement of already deviant individuals and families into these impoverished neighborhoods rather than as an analysis of criminal behavior linked to a cluster of economic and social disadvantages affecting particular groups and communities.

Rather than "race" itself as a solo variable, the social and economic legacies of race ought to be a key issue in national research agendas. The ethnographic data contained in field surveys and especially in memoirs distinctly indicate the relevance of economic aspects of criminal behavior in African-American communities. In these documents there is a steady emphasis on economic motivation, problems in family life, inadequate schools, and perceptions of a social structure and larger culture that deliberately restrict opportunity.[14]

Crime and Delinquency Theories and Explanation

Theories of crime and delinquency have passed successively though biological, psychological, sociological, and economic modes of explanation. The earliest theories portrayed criminals, as individuals physically and psychologically different from noncriminals.[15] These were scientifically discredited later, to be replaced by psychodynamic explanations that usually and typically traced criminality to family problems. Theories of this sort have a long, durable, and complex history.[16] During the 1930s, sociologists refocused attention away from psychological factors toward the brute facts of urban life by documenting the high concentration of arrests among poor males in the inner cities.[17] Some theorists stressed the cultural aspects rather than the ecology of the inner-city communities, portraying delinquency and crime—irrespective of race—as learned behavior transmitted within the local neighborhoods, while others emphasized social inequality as the driving force for all types of criminal conduct.[18] The influential study by Cloward and Ohlin synthesized most of the elements of previous theories and research by positing a close relation between criminal subculture and specific local structures of economic opportunity.

However, these explanatory theories began to unravel as questions arose about the weight assigned to the concepts of culture and subculture.[19] It was pointed out that poor residents of slums and ghettos were themselves the most frequent victims of crimes and, more to the point, most were law-abiding citizens who did not condone crime. Furthermore, it was observed that the declining rates of crime associated with age, irrespective of race and ethnicity, were difficult to explain solely in terms of culture. The critiques of cultural causality generated research that produced new data that cast doubt on the notion of crime as specific to poor, inner-city neighborhoods.[20]

Later studies examining the relationship between social class, employment, and crime also proved unsatisfactory, because the correlation between aggregate crime and employment rates did not hold up as expected: as in the 1930s when unemployment rates were high but crime rates were low despite the growth of organized crime; and in the late 1960s, when employment rates and crime rates rose together. Quantitative studies using individual-level data have failed to demonstrate strong, correlative relationships between unemployment and criminality. For example, inner-city teenagers, including African-American youth with serious economic problems, who would seem prone to criminal activities, do not necessarily commit crimes less often during periods when they are employed.[21]

A great methodological chasm separates various perspectives investigating crime causation and its precipitating factors. The issue of the skewed rise in African-American crime, especially among young males, naturally arouses concern and calls for a scientific inspection of the relevant factors likely to affect the crime rates.

By the 1990s, the stage was set for a rejection of both sociocultural and economic explanations of crime for a number of reasons: The link between economic opportunity and criminality is much more complex than previously thought; and purely cultural perspectives failed to explain the widespread distribution of crime and delinquency throughout the class structure.[22]

The earlier sociologically oriented work relied heavily on qualitative studies that charted the development and unfolding of criminal careers in specific social environments of ghettos and slums. More recent economic and sociological studies with a quantitative bent are not particularly sensitive to the nuances of local-level processes. Although not based on random sampling techniques that would make them precisely comparable to one another, or to purely quantitative studies, some ethnographic researches of life in poor, inner-city communities attempt to show how criminal careers develop in specific environments and how crime is both generated and controlled within these environments. The important research work led by Whyte,[23] using ethnographic methodologies and observation strategies characteristic of anthropological field work, enabled him and later researchers to get inside and convey a sense of the community and its interplay of economics, politics, family life, street life, education, and culture. The approach dispelled the myth of social chaos in poverty-ridden communities lacking behavioral norms. Moreover, these field studies redirect attention to the importance of physical ecology in analyzing the social organization of urban neighborhoods.

In terms of the scope of studies on crime, race, ethnicity, and environment, methodological reconciliation and eclecticism may help to overcome research obstacles that have stymied the effort to settle some questions. Methodological purity has not seemed to work as well as anticipated: Small-scale studies are not readily generalizable to larger populations, nor can they measure individual variations in subjects along any matrix of activities or effects. On the other hand, when they do look at the individual, large-scale surveys tend to look at the person divorced from his or her living environment and miss a great deal in terms of exogenous factors that impinge on the individual. Some combination of qualitative, ethnographic techniques, and survey-type quantitative research assessing both individuals and their groups simultaneously seems called for. And this would apply across racial groups.[24]

What shape would such a research perspective take? It would be a medley of data-gathering strategies and fieldwork orientations designed to develop comprehensive pictures of crime in African-American communities—or in any communities composed of diverse ethnic groups, races, or classes.

Community Research: Resurrecting a Tradition

An emphasis on the local community as the basic unit of analysis, which would entail in-depth descriptions of the social, political, economic, and cultural environments, would provide a perspective on the crucial issue of the relationship, the interactional effects between individual decisions and the system of structural constraints in which the individual lives and makes decisions about jobs, school, family life, and crime. There is an interactionist tradition already established for research involving the African-American experience that can be revivified along these lines: The early, pioneering work of Du Bois, St. Clair Drake, and Cayton, and more recently, William Julius Wilson, stretches across the twentieth century and represents a way out of the theoretical difficulties described earlier.

In terms of organized crime, this approach can yield rich data about how individuals get into crime; the types of crime they engage in; the victims; those likely to be victims, and how police responses may be mobilized.[25] Here, the community is seen as the locus of interaction, where values are learned, ideas and knowledge are generated and tested, and choices of conduct are made. In its complexity the community is not only the matrix embedding values, beliefs, and choices, it is also the locale and social habitat where the constraints and opportunities of the larger society are narrowed to practical laws, norms, customs, and commercial realities within which individuals make choices.

The culture of the community is another master variable in a research strategy that describes and defines *community* as an evaluative screen where the worth of specific choices and options are determined. Thus, the inputs of the community in terms of its institutional systems, its culture, the structure of both legitimate and illegitimate opportunities, constitute the setting in which the individual decides or chooses to go to school, to work, and/or to engage in criminal activities. Selecting the community as the research unit avoids the problem associated with "displaced" individuals who, when torn loose from specific contexts, lack identities as inhabitants of socioeconomic and cultural locales that frame and inform their lives. By portraying individuals as communally situated, more detailed pictures of criminal dynamics are possible. Demographic statistics alone, wrenched out of social environments, tell us little and may actually distort the realities of crime and criminal careers in neighborhoods.

Interpreting crime as a decisional process that fluctuates as circumstances change in the life of the individual, we can see the criminal and noncriminal as making choices in socially bounded spheres of interaction. How well local communities articulate with different sectors of the labor market, and what differential associational ties individuals establish with criminal groups in their communities will affect transitions from noncriminal to criminal activity and back again into noncriminal roles. The approach allows the researcher to ask not just whether different individuals choose to invest in education and training or whether they decide to move into crime or legitimate employment, but also how such choices are conditioned by the social environments of the neighborhoods in which they live and by the overlapping relationships of those communities to such institutions as the schools, churches, commercial sector, and the criminal justice system.

Family Factors

As the crucible of personality, the family influences the formative psychological stages in at least two important ways: through resource provision and socialization. Regarding the first, the resources provided by the family can make a profound difference in a child's success in school and in making a favorable entry into the labor market.[26] Using the same logic, in contrast to affluent families, impoverished families may be nurturing and loving and yet unable to provide the advantages necessary for a career that will allow a child to escape poverty. We recognize that middle-class families may possess such resources and still produce violent and antisocial children, but their problems are more likely related to emotional and psychological disturbances and not precipitated by the anxieties associated with the social status of grinding poverty and alienation.

Furthermore, the fact that poverty, joblessness, and the structure of welfare separates husbands and fathers from their families in poor neighborhoods has important consequences for children raised in those environments. Even with respect to family background, it is difficult to separate individuals from structural factors.[27] Sullivan's study showed that families with high levels of resources allow their sons to avoid or move quickly out of exploratory criminal involvements and into employment.[28] The research also suggested that the absence of fathers and adult men from families contributed to a weakened social control environment. The link between the high proportion of female-headed households and high crime rates results in patterns of weakened socialization within the household and weakened social control within neighborhoods. No doubt, such environments would tend to enhance the conditions for criminal activity.

Andrew Billingsley's survey of African-American family life in light of sociological field research suggests some disturbing trends.[29] For example, in 1890, according the United States Census studies, 80 percent of all African-American families with children were headed by married couples. In 1960 the proportion was 78 percent. But after 1960, it declined steeply: 1970, 64 percent; 1980, 48 percent; and by 1990, it had plummeted to 39 percent. By contrast, in 1990, the corresponding figure for whites had fallen only to 81 percent.

Drawing from other research work on the African-American family, Billingsley argued that the decline of marriage is largely due to the impact of job loss experienced by African-American men, especially in the working class. Between 1955 and 1980, employment for African-American men aged twenty to twenty-four declined from 78 percent to 55 percent. For Billingsley, this decline is a major reason for the downturn in their marriage rates and in the upturn in unmarried parenthood.

Economic trends affecting family stability are important, perhaps even necessary, foundational factors in any explanation of the roots of crime (excluding white-collar crime), but they are in themselves scarcely sufficient.

For example, the African-American two-parent family declined in the 1970s and early 1980s, when the economy was in recession. But it did not decline during the Great Depression of the 1930s. Moreover, marriage rates fell in the 1960s, when the economy was expanding and African-American income and college enrollments were rising. Billingsley argued that African-American men who lost jobs in the 1970s and 1980s often broke up their marriages, but so did African-American men with jobs, to a lesser degree, but also at a rising rate. Economic and occupational matters are important but they are not the whole story, nor can they function as reliable predictors of crime rates. The racial and cultural context and social environment fit in very importantly not only as destabilization factors but also in affecting lifestyles and supports for behavior patterns that may be deviant.

What Billingsley wanted to say (and we agree) is that employment conditions have a strong effect on both family structure and low-level social control. And given this, it would be invalid to cite family factors alone as more important than employment conditions in explaining high rates of crime. What is empirically clear is that the two are interwoven, that together with the high proportions of female-headed households in inner-city neighborhoods where employment prospects are discouraging, crime rates are high.[30] Neighborhoods and their socializing environments would appear to play important roles affecting young male criminal activities and propensities. Attempting to ascertain the separate effects of employment, neighborhood social control, and family socialization is methodologically difficult and probably not informative about cause-and-effect mechanisms. Rather, it seems that the combination of factors—female-headed households, poverty, local institutional supports (schools, churches, police, etc.), and the cultural context of neighborhood environments—contribute to low or high rates of criminal activity and a disposition among young men to find criminal activity plausible.

Economic Factors

The fact should not be obscured that sociocultural and economic processes are intricately linked together, both generally and especially in criminal activities. Individuals do not decide to engage or not to engage in crimes merely on the basis of the projected risks and benefits relative to other possible investments of time, energy, and resources. Perspectives that define involvement in criminal activities as no more than or no different from individual choices to participate in legitimate work predicated on differential investments in education and training, combined with native abilities that culminate in varied degrees of success in the labor market, ignore the interpenetration of the social and economic realities of specific communities.

For minority youths, the effects of labor market access are particularly severe. What impacts harshly and relentlessly on ghetto residents, especially the young, is the failure of traditional conventions wherein families provide support while youth prepare educationally for future employment. This institutional bulwark is compromised in many of the social situations of inner-city minority youth: Their parents are simply too poor and suffer too frequently from joblessness themselves to build up a financial resource for their children. In addition, the schools in these communities are in such disarray that they cannot substitute for the lack of accessible decent employment opportunities by providing marketable skills useful in the mainstream sectors.

This failure of the schools is deeply implicated in the concentration of organized street crime and its most intractable manifestation: drug trafficking. Ideally, schools serve as supplementary socializing agents and as the supplier of marketable occupational skills. Most schools in inner-city African-American communities, however, are inadequate for both of these functions.

The point cannot be made emphatically enough that the link between unemployment (and even underemployment) and high rates of street crime is pervasive. It is not just a matter of joblessness and crime—that abstract formulation is too crude; rather, they are especially pernicious in communities where joblessness and communal poverty are concentrated and persistent. The results are greater levels of individual and collective stress, weakened social controls, and higher levels of crime.

To examine organized criminal behavior divorced from its structural context of a neighborhood in crisis is to see it as irrational, as possibly the product of a deranged personality or cognitively deficient individual. Such a perspective seriously misrepresents it.

One important theoretical attempt to understand how these structural and dynamical social and economic forces mix and produce a sort of shared understanding among those in like circumstances—in effect, a subculture—may be found in Albert Cohen's discussion and formulations of a "delinquent subculture."[31] Unlike other theorists who adopt a rather rigid concept of culture, Cohen's ideas operate within an interactionist perspective that situates the criminal behavior of the individual from a working-class background in the encounter with a school culture that has a distressing tendency to denigrate the youth's system of values. The emergent subculture of delinquency that Cohen inscribes evolves out of, not prior to, criminal conduct.

Following these theoretical leads, organized crime may be accounted for in situational terms that are community-specific with reference to the context in which it unfolds and takes on substance as a social practice. The other advantage in not seeing it as an "alien conspiracy" but more as a consequence of antecedent social and economic conditions is that such a formulation has the capacity to incorporate empirical variations and amplifications into a broad theory that is neither rigid nor abstract. The approach is to conceive of organized crime as dynamic, as sensitive to, and responding to community-specific structures of opportunity. To discover the cultural meanings of crime in the interactionist perspective requires that attention be paid to data specific to each community, including locally specific ways in which work, school, family, occupational opportunities, and access to commercial goods and services constitute interrelated categories that create a community's social ecology that may or may not be poised to incorporate crime as a substitute strategy for failed or nonexistent institutional supports.

Themes of the Resistance and Opposition Culture: Gangsta Rap

Our analysis would be incomplete were we not to mention another important element that figures into the popular perception of organized crime. To dismiss the effects that the image-making of the electronic media coverage and portrayal of African-American crime has on popular attitudes would be irresponsible.

For the most part, what is reported is compressed into thirty-second items, "sound bytes," that suggest what is or is not anti-American, racist, or criminal. A good example of this phenomenon is rap music.

Congressional Hearings before Senate and House Committees amounted to trials on the subgenre of hip-hop music now catalogued as "Gangsta Rap." Some officials, African-American representatives such as Congressperson Maxine Waters, acknowledged the offensiveness of the foul, insulting language, but chose to focus on other dimensions of the lyrical content that speak of painful experiences of rejection and failure. Snoop Doggy Dog, Ice Cube, Ice-T, and Queen Latifah are the artists of the underclass who reflect real problems. For Congressperson Waters, reality itself gives birth to rap music.

On the other hand, others see rap music differently; their minds are made up that rap induces and glorifies crime, and, because it is obscenely suggestive of criminal attitudes in ghetto life, government is obliged to silence it.

If Waters is correct, then an honest assessment of the conditions that create rap music is warranted. Hip-hop singers are not politicians or professional social theorists or policy makers or, for that matter, social and political prophets. Yet, they find ways to use the mechanism of their music to elaborate on the already existing structure of attitudes, feelings, and beliefs in underclass segments of the African-American community.

A great deal of gangster rap is directed at the criminal justice system and the white power structure. African-American hatred exists—that fact is certain; the sooner it is recognized and the search begins for its reasons, the better. We can agree partially with Stallworth's conclusions of gangster rap:

> It (gangsta rap) reflects elements of the black community as a whole with an emphasis on the subculture of gangs. It reflects the morals and ideals of black gang culture. It is a record of the thoughts, desires, emotions and actions of a select group of people coping with the realities of their existence. For future generations, it will provide a glimpse into a brief strand of time on the social evolutionary scale of inner city America. Censorship, banning it from the lives of the young, is not the answer towards eliminating the influential aspect of "gangsta rap."[32]

To interpret the roots of gangster rap as a musical style of rebellion among postindustrial minority youth, whose bleak future prefigures a nihilist version of reality, is likely to be greeted by its critics as nonsense. Many would see violent music as a cause of violent behavior. Assuming that the critics of gangster rap define it as pathological rather than as an art form, however distasteful, this criticism that rap is so dangerous that children need to be protected against it testifies to its power. Indeed, if its roots are in the ghettoized underclass, then it is a voice of those locked into dead-end life styles. And outlawing gangster rap would only deepen the isolation of those victimized by the inability of government to develop meaningful (hope-giving) urban and economic policies. Is it really in the interest of government to make expressions of the ills of the underclass even easier to ignore?

To call gangster rap dangerous pathology, simpleminded, or assaultive is mistaken, we think. In a new way, the music (a system of communication) cannot be dismissed or silenced because it is integral to a political movement that has mutated into a vastly more complex ideational system than its original beginnings in the civil rights movement. To become aware of oneself as oppressed is the founding insight that has spawned a host of different expressive genres—gangster rap among them.

In summary, the struggle for emancipation is a very complex battle over the course of different political destinies, different personal histories and circumstances, and it is replete with works of the imagination whose expression is equally varied. We see gangster rap in the modern context of mass media as a vital, invigorating counterpoint to the cultural machinery of the larger society that relentlessly defines and codifies everything about minorities and does it thoroughly, leaving few items untouched or unstudied. As base and degrading as rap imagery is, it is a symbolic call to arms, an effort at insights that provide some resistance, and therefore refuge, from the turbulence of the immediate experiences of violence, oppression, and alienation that lay hold of the ghetto.

One cannot fail to notice the politics in which gangster rap is embedded. It bears repeating that no matter how apparently dominant the mainstream media in the society, there are always going to be parts of the social experience that it does not cover and control. From these peripheries has emerged opposition and rebellion that is typically self-conscious. This is not as complicated as it sounds. Opposition to a dominant structure of power arises out of a perceived, perhaps even militant awareness, on the part of individuals and groups outside and inside the mainstream's feelings that certain of its policies are wrong. Rap music is a manifestation of internal criticism; a reaction of the victims in their own idiom, recounting their experiences. Consequently, the extraordinary defensive reaction to rap is understandable. This music on its merit is only apparently dependent (and by no means parasitic) on mainstream, white styles; the results of its originality and creativity have been more than a shock—it has transformed the very terrain of the popular mass culture musical idiom. No longer do musical style and idiom dwell within the dominant culture, if they ever did; the media power structures, the record companies, cannot ignore the audience and so they face a dilemma: To produce gangster rap engenders a hail of criticism from mainstream critics, politicians, and even some African-American social activists; to boycott the work of these artists will not crush it and may only magnify its popularity.

Lodged at its lyrical, narrative heart, so to speak, and through its often tawdry and obscene language (which matches the speech of everyday life) is a complex of hope, betrayal, and bitter disappointment. The result conveyed is of an unfulfilled life and culture in a crisis, expressing itself in a fragmented language of torment, angry insistence, and often uncritical condemnation of outside enemies (usually the police). Gangster rap is also more a signal than a symptom of wrongs and problems. It can convey something essentially hopeful; the old invented histories of America and its great iconic heroes are giving way to newer contestatory accounts of what is so intense and discrepant in the contemporary moment.

These hybrid counterenergies are at work in many fields among many individuals; these moments provide a community of incipient cultural formation made up of numerous antisystemic hints and practices for living not based on a felt sense of domination or coercion. They fueled the uprisings in the 1980s and 1990s.

It is possible to see gangster rap as the bearer of a cultural energy whose lyrics, in particular, may be seen as a reaction to the continuing grip of society's hand on the throat of the ghetto. Is it a celebration of violence? The answer is yes, but with important qualifications. To note this, however, is not to demand of the gangster rap musician, or any African-American artist at this time, an impossible delicacy, subtlety, and poise, but to remind ourselves that more than one passion, however crass by conventional standards, animates their work.

The themes of gangster rap are turbulent but there are (perhaps surprisingly) some generous and hospitable sentiments. More interestingly, rap is a socially and politically sensitive narrative that is thereby a representation of power. It is not that the powerless do not have stories, and it is not that they do not get to tell their stories, it is that they are scarcely perceived as capable of having stories; their stories of who they are, what they desire, how they live, are not so much refused as ruled out, seen as unimaginable as pieces of recognizable history. With no acceptable narrative to rely on, with no permission, as it were, to tell, the rappers reject the silence and express themselves vociferously and volubly.

We might think of gangster rap with its obscenities, refusals, and reversals as a counternarrative, an act of recovery that parodies and caricatures the acceptable modes of artistic expression. The rapper's lives constitute the grist of their "epics" that can turn into simple, murderous versions, but they live inside their stories and perspectives and reject the representation of themselves by others who construct a myth of their reality.

A careful examination of gangster rap lyrics would show that they emphatically repudiate the system of ideas and descriptions by which the dominant white society has mapped out the African-American society—especially the underclass and ghetto segments of it. Rap reflects the lives, histories, and maze of rituals and customs of those who actually live in ghettos and inner cities. Actually, the differences between gangster rap accounts of impoverished African-American life and those of mainstream social description and commentary are only slightly different. There is much to be learned from rap.

The fact that it chooses an organized crime term, *gangster,* to define itself is also instructive. In the ghetto, it is the gangster, the outlaw, who defines the oppressive forces and manages to survive without groveling in the dust and submitting to racism.

NOTES

1. Toni Morrison, *Playing in the Dark: Whiteness and the Literary Imagination* (Cambridge, MA: Harvard University Press, 1992).

2. Edwin H. Stier, and Peter R. Richards, "Strategic Decision Making in Organized Crime Control: The Need for a Broadened Perspective." (Langley, VA: The National Institute of Justice, 1987), 65–80.

3. Ishmael Reed, *Airing Dirty Laundry* (Reading, MA: Addison-Wesley Publishing, 1994), 72.

4. Kenneth L. Kushner, *A Ghetto Takes Shape: Black Cleveland, 1870–1930* (Urbana, IL: University of Illinois Press, 1976).

5. Francis A. J. Ianni, *Black Mafia.*

6. Francis A. J. Ianni and Elizabeth Reuss-Ianni, *A Family Business: Kinship and Social Control in Organized Crime* (New York: Russell Sage Foundation, 1972).

7. Frantz Fanon, *The Wretched of the Earth* (New York: Grove Press, 1967), 106.

8. Katheryn K. Russell, "Development of a Black Criminology and the Role of the Black Criminologist," *Justice Quarterly* 9, no. 4 (December 1992): 667–683.

9. D. Georges-Abeyie, "The Myth of a Racist Criminal Justice System" in B. MacLean and D. Milovanic, eds., *Racism, Empiricism and Criminal Justice* (Vancouver: Collective Press, 1990): 92–120.

10. Some of the best known and most widely cited control theories in criminology that have set the standards are Travis Hirschi, *Causes of Delinquency* (Los Angeles: University of California Press, 1969) 16–34; G. Sykes and D. Matza, "Techniques of Neutralization," *American Sociological Review* 22, (1957): 664–670; Walter Reckless, "A New Theory of Delinquency and Crime," *Federal Probation* 25 (1961): 42–51. The major Strain and Cultural Deviance include Albert Cohen, *Delinquent Boys* (New York: Free Press, 1955); Cloward and Ohlin, *Delinquency and Opportunity*; Marvin Wolfgang and Franco Ferracuti, "The Subculture of Violence" in *The Subculture of Violence* (London: Tavistock, 1967); and Robert Merton, *Social Theory and Social Structure*, 185–214.

11. Joan Moore, *Going Down to the Barrio* (Philadelphia: Temple University Press, 1991); F. M. Podilla, *The Gang as an American Enterprise* (New Brunswick: Rutgers University Press, 1992); Ko-lin Chin, *Chinese Subculture and Criminality* (Westport, CT: Greenwood Press, 1990); Mercer L. Sullivan, *Getting Paid*; Ko-lin Chin, Jeffrey Fagan, and Robert J. Kelly, "Patterns of Chinese Gang Extortion."

12. James Q. Wilson and Richard J. Herrnstein, *Crime and Human Nature* (New York: Simon & Schuster, 1985).

13. Jack Katz, *The Seductions of Crime* (New York: Basic Books, 1990).

14. Kody Scott, *Monster: The Autobiography of an L.A. Gang Member* and numerous social–scientific ethnographic studies.

15. Cesare Lombroso, *Crime: Its Causes and Remedies* (Boston: Little, Brown, 1911).

16. Edward Banfield, *The Unheavenly City* (Boston: Little, Brown, 1970); Kate Friedlander, *The Psychoanalytic Approach to Juvenile Delinquency* (New York: International Universities Press, 1947); Seymour Halleck, *Psychiatry and the Dilemmas of Crime: A Study of Causes, Punishment and Treatment* (New York: Harper & Row, 1967).

17. Clifford R. Shaw and Henry D. McKay, *Social Factors in Juvenile Delinquency* (Washington, DC: The Wickersham Commission, vol. 13, chap. 4, U.S. Government Printing Office, 1931), 81–96.

18. Albert Cohen, *Delinquent Boys;* Edwin Sutherland and Donald Cressey, *Principles of Criminology,* 5th ed., (Chicago: J.J. Lippincott & Co., 1955).

19. David Matza, *Delinquency and Drift* (New York: Wiley & Sons, 1964); Ruth R. Kornhauser, *Social Sources of Delinquency: An Appraisal of Analytic Models* (Chicago: University of Chicago Press, 1978).

20. Gary Becker, "Crime and Punishment: An Economic Approach," *Journal of Political Economy* 76 (1968): 169–217.

21. Michael K. Block and J.M. Heinke, "A Labor Theoretic Analysis of Criminal Choice," *American Economic Review* 65, (1975): 314–325; Michelle Sviridoff and Jerome E. McElroy, *Employment and Crime: A Summary Report* (New York: Vera Institute of Justice, 1984).

22. Ronald Akers, *Criminological Theories: Introduction and Evaluation* (Los Angeles: Roxbury, 1994); H. N. Pontell, ed., *Social Deviance: Readings in Theory and Research* (Englewood Cliffs, NJ: Prentice-Hall, 1993); R. Martin, R. Mutchnick, and W. T. Austin, *Criminological Thought: Pioneers, Past and Present* (New York: Macmillan, 1990).

23. William F. Whyte, *Street Corner Society.*

24. Albert J. Reiss, "Why Are Communities Important in Studying Crime?" in Albert J. Reiss and Michael Tonry, eds. *Crime and Justice: A Review of Research: Vol. 8, Communities and Crime* (Chicago: University of Chicago Press, 1986).

25. Robert J. Kelly, Ko-lin Chin, and Jeffrey Fagan, "The Dragon Breathes Fire," 245–269.

26. Gerald R. Patterson and Thomas Dishion, "Contributions of Families and Peers to Delinquency," *Criminology* 23, (1985): 63–80.

27. Marion W. Edelman, *Families in Peril* (Cambridge, MA: Harvard University Press, 1987).

28. Sullivan, *Getting Paid.*

29. Andrew Billingsley, *Climbing Jacob's Ladder.*

30. Robert J. Sampson, "Urban Black Violence: The Effect of Male Joblessness and Family Disruption," *American Journal of Sociology* 93, no. 2, (1987): 348–382.

31. Cohen, *Delinquent Boys,* 24–32.

32. Ron Stallworth, "Gangster Rap Music: An Informal Study of Its Message and Correlation to the Gang Environment" (Part II), *Criminal Organization* 8 no. 2 (Winter, 1993): 3–21.

Index

About the Authors

Robert J. Kelly, Ph.D., is Broeklundian Professor of Social Science at Brooklyn College and professor of Criminal Justice at the Graduate School, City University of New York. He has conducted research on organized criminal activities, terrorism, violence in maximum security correctional facilities, and minority students in higher education. His publications include: *Deviance, Dominance and Denigration; Organized Crime: A Global Perspective;* and *Handbook on Organized Crime in the United States* (co-edited with Rufus Schatzberg). He has also written numerous essays and journal articles.

Rufus Schatzberg, Ph.D., retired from the New York City Police Department as a detective first grade. His publications include: *Black Organized Crime in Harlem: 1920–1930* and *Handbook on Organized Crime in the United States* (co-edited with Robert J. Kelly). He has written numerous articles on terrorism, organized crime, and crime in schools, one of which was recently published in Germany.